Haunted
BRITAIN

AA

Editor: Donna Wood

Designer: Andrew Milne

Picture Researcher: Lesley Grayson

Image retouching and internal repro: Sarah Montgomery

Cartography provided by the Mapping Services Department
of AA Publishing

Production: Rachel Davis

Produced by AA Publishing

© Copyright AA Media Limited 2010

Relief map images supplied by Mountain High Maps ®
Copyright © 1993 Digital Wisdom Inc.

ISBN: 978-0-7495-6650-0 and 978-0-7495-6661-6 (SS)

Published by AA Publishing (a trading name of AA Media
Limited, whose registered office is Fanum House, Basing View,
Basingstoke RG21 4EA; registered number 06112600).

A03632

The contents of this book are believed correct at the time of
printing. Nevertheless, the publishers cannot be held responsible
for any errors or omissions or for changes in the details given
in this book or for the consequences of any reliance on the
information provided by the same. This does not affect your
statutory rights.

Printed in China by C & C Offset Printing Co. Ltd

theAA.com/shop

Haunted BRITAIN

RICHARD JONES

Foreword by
Tom Baker

Foreword by *Tom Baker*

Ghosts have played quite a big part in my real life and an equally big part in the world of my imagination. It happened like this: I was offered the part of a ghost in a series for television called *Randall and Hopkirk (Deceased)*. In fact, I was part of a double act; Vic Reeves was my ghostly partner. I did the best I could with my character. My efforts to be convincing were based on guesswork, like most of my efforts. Judging by the fan mail I received, a lot of people believed in my ghost and many wanted to meet me.

Certain feisty ladies invited me to come and haunt them personally and offered telephone numbers and taxi expenses too. They didn't offer me dinner, on the grounds I suppose that ghosts are usually very abstemious. One lady explained that she was fed up with men who were alive and unreliable, and that her mother had advised her to try a ghost for a change. She also promised not to produce a camera as she had heard that ghosts are very camera-shy. She is right. Several other ladies wanted to know if there was anything I missed from my old life and did I ever feel tempted to spy on old flames still living? I answered these and other questions as tactfully as I could and sent charming autographed pictures of me kissing Vic Reeves full on the lips. I think this four-lips-together shot killed her appetite to meet me. Perhaps full-on French kissing was not what she had in mind. Perhaps she wanted the cooling pleasure of caresses from a dry, dead hand and the whispers and quiet murmurs of sweet nothings, smelling of primroses. Who knows?

I also had to be convincing in the ghost scene in *Macbeth*. I have to admit that the audience and the other actors were convulsed with laughter at my double-take as Banquo entered. And so from Shakespeare to Oscar Wilde I have pursued my affection for ghosts in literature and films. But in my real life I kept on hoping that some kind spirit would visit me one night soon. I longed to wake up to the plaintive sobbing of the ghost of some long-abandoned and long-dead girl seeking comfort from the man from *Randall and Hopkirk (Deceased)*.

And then, and then... what happens? A beautiful book called *Haunted Britain* happens, that's what. Yes. And suddenly my hopes are raised. Here is the very book I have been waiting for all my life. It is my guide to the world of ghosts. Where? Everywhere. The whole country is teeming with spirits all looking for sympathy and a few crumbs of comfort.

I have devoured it and I urge you to devour it too, and without delay, so that you can shiver at and enjoy the pleasures of the forlorn Senorita and the headless monk. Yes, he is headless! So what's in it for her? Sshhh, I won't spoil it for you, but she's in the book and Torre Abbey in Devon is her address. I don't know her phone number but her email address is there. There are nearly a hundred other places too, full of possibilities. Nearly a hundred! Doesn't that just make you tingle all over? Gosh, I've come over all goose pimply as I think about it. Goose pimples, tingles and frisson! What more could one want over a lovely weekend in Britain?

Noises to look forward to include sobbing, whimpering and moaning. You may also hear clankings and fearful groans. Laughter is not unknown, but it will often be chilling and will always produce the tingle we all love as it races up and down the spine; the tingle I mean, not the laughter.

There is a way to encourage ghosts to come close or even show themselves. As soon as you suspect a presence, express sympathy; after all you do not want to frighten it away, and do not raise your voice suddenly; some ghosts are very nervous. Always call the ghost by name if you know it, and always introduce your partner by name. If your partner is a man, urge him to bow. If your partner is not a man, urge her to try a little curtsey, but not too deep or the clicking of knee joints might startle the presence and that could be fatal. Keep your hands a little away from your body; sometimes it might pay to raise your arm and wave; this shows goodwill and also that you have nothing up your sleeve. But whatever you do, never show a camera, never. Ghosts are notoriously camera-shy, even ghosts of old long-dead actors. It would be an excellent idea to play soft, soothing music. I do recommend the 'Moonlight' Sonata, which has often done the trick, or perhaps a slightly more modern piece like 'Love Never Dies' (most ghosts should enjoy that); or an old 1930s' number, such as 'I'm Nobody's Baby Now'. Judy Garland used to sing that song and I still feel a frisson just thinking about it. But above all, be patient. Never give up the ghost without a sincere effort. You must make it quite clear that you have come with sympathy and even, dare I suggest it, with love.

There! Happy hunting.

Tom Baker

I shall tell you tales of heroes
and gods who walked as men.
On mountains where the wild wind blows
or across the darkling fen.
I shall tell you tales that minstrels told
of vengeful queens and warriors bold.
Of kings who sleep and ne'er grow old
in caves their dreams residing.

I shall tell you tales of outlaws
and hounds that roam the night.
Of hidden realms through secret doors
where saints and giants fight.
I shall tell you tales of long lost lands
buried now 'neath shifting sands.
Where dancing maids have long held hands
in stone their spirits writhing.

So come gather by the fire
let the moonlight be our stage.
The stars shall be our choir
and the darkness be our page.
Bring forth the souls of days gone by
with a thousand tales they'll fill the sky.
Till the glowing embers fade and die
and the night's cloak wraps around us.

Night Tales by Richard Jones

Introduction

On 8 March 1954, Dr Margaret Murray gave her presidential address to the Folklore Society. 'Belief in ghosts, like belief in the devil, is dying out,' she said. She attributed this to '… our better methods of illumination', adding that 'Ghosts are notoriously fond of darkness, but now every town and most villages have street lamps, houses are lighted by electricity, vehicles have head lamps which illuminate the dark lane, and pedestrians no longer carry a lantern with a flickering rush light, but can flash the ray of an electric torch on any uncanny-looking object they see – or fancy they see.' After the meeting she told an *Evening News* reporter that 'If you think there is something in the room, all you have to do is to put on the bedside light. Either it was all imagination, in which case the light ends one's fears, or else the ghost disappears – because no ghost is seen in the light!'

Similar sentiments were expressed almost 300 years previously by the philosopher Thomas Hobbes. He believed that ghosts were nothing more than 'the imaginary inhabitants of man's brain', and went on to opine that the superstitious 'possessed with fearful tales, and alone in the dark… believe they see spirits and dead men's ghosts walking in churchyards…' Incidentally, by a delightful twist of supernatural irony, the sceptic Thomas Hobbes now haunts Hardwick Old Hall in Derbyshire and is one of the ghosts you will find within the pages of this book!

To paraphrase Mark Twain's reaction to the publication of his obituary in a newspaper when he was still very much alive, reports of the demise of the belief in ghosts have been greatly exaggerated. Today, more than 50 years after Dr Murray confidently told the Folklore Society that people were starting not to believe in ghosts, they are probably more popular than ever, and ghost stories continue to enthral, chill and terrify the old and the young alike. At the time of Dr Murray's address – or, for that matter, as recently as 15 years ago – stately homes and ancient castles would have frowned upon and haughtily dismissed suggestions that they might have a resident ghost or two. Now they positively embrace the possibility. They offer members of the public the opportunity to explore their old rooms, creaking corridors and darker recesses on night-time ghost tours or even on overnight ghost hunts. Such is the popularity of these paranormal nights that they often sell out months in advance.

One of the most popular programmes on television allow viewers to watch as a team of presenters spends a night in the dark at a haunted location, with their investigations filmed on night-vision cameras. These programmes have, in turn, spawned a plethora of local paranormal groups that locate and investigate haunted locations and then write detailed reports of their experiences on their websites. The great thing is that, as a result, local folklore (and I truly believe that ghost stories, both ancient and modern, are an important part of our folklore) has moved away from the musty, hallowed corridors of academia and into the mainstream, where it can be enjoyed and retold by all.

Assembled within the pages of this book you will find a selection of haunted locations dotted across the spectral landscape of England, Wales and Scotland. I must confess that the conditions in which I researched and wrote the book were challenging, to say the least. I had to battle through the blizzards and treacherous conditions that saw the winter of 2009–10 declared the coldest in 30 years, and there were occasions when I thought I might end up as an entry in my own book! The advantage of visiting the locations in such conditions was that I was often on my own, and I really was able to absorb their atmosphere in a way that probably wouldn't have been possible on a bright summer's day with lots of other people present. Inevitably, with so many paranormally active places to choose from, a book such as this becomes a very personal collection, and I have chosen locations that appealed to me either for their atmosphere or for their story or, in many cases, for both. I was anxious to avoid an endless stream of green, pink, blue, white or other hue of ladies parading across the pages of the book, and have tried to include hauntings that are varied as well as spine-tingling. I have also endeavoured to present, wherever possible, the history behind each haunting. For some, this was easy to do, as many historic properties helpfully flesh out their ghostly apparitions with names and even dates. For others, this proved a little more challenging – either hard facts were difficult to come by or there were contradictory accounts. Wherever I could, I have attempted to trace the source of each story and establish precise dates and facts. Inevitably, this wasn't always possible so on those occasions I have used the most common version of a story.

One of the questions I'm frequently asked as I travel around collecting ghost stories is 'Do you believe in ghosts?' The answer has to be an emphatic 'yes'. I've listened to too many accounts from reliable, honest people who have had a supernatural experience or encounter not to believe in them. In all honesty, I don't believe that ghosts are the spirits of the dead that come back to haunt the living. My own belief is that the fabric of a building or location can, somehow, become imbued with the emotions, energies or personalities of those who have lived there over the centuries. Ghosts are simply the replaying of these sensations.

This book is intended very much as a hands-on guide, with all the locations either open to or accessible to the public. Some have an admission charge, others are free. I really would urge readers to visit them. To that end, I have included websites, where available, as well as postcodes to make finding them via sat-nav easy. In addition, I have used a suitably ghostly symbol to grade each location on either how active its ghosts are or how atmospheric I found the location to be. Five ghosts mean a place is extremely active and atmospheric, while one ghost means the location is still atmospheric but that its ghosts are perhaps not as active as those elsewhere. I should point out that the number of ghost symbols awarded to a location is in relation to other locations in the book. Since all those included are well worth visiting, the grading should not detract from a location's potential as somewhere to visit.

I hope you will enjoy reading this book as much as I have enjoyed researching and writing it, and I truly hope that you will go out and experience for yourselves the wonderful diversity of haunted places that Britain has to offer. And, should it happen that, as you explore a particular location, the temperature suddenly drops, you feel the ice-cold breath of an unseen entity on the back of your neck, or the forlorn phantom of a blue lady, a headless monk or a weeping child in old-fashioned attire just happens to cross your path, please do contact me and let me know the story of the day *you* saw a ghost.

Richard Jones, London
www.haunted-britain.com

LOCATOR MAP

CONTENTS

FOREWORD BY TOM BAKER
PAGE 4

INTRODUCTION
PAGE 7

① SOUTHWEST ENGLAND
Cornwall, Devon, Dorset, Somerset,
Wiltshire, Gloucestershire

PAGE 12

② SOUTHEAST ENGLAND
London, Kent, East Sussex, Surrey, Hertfordshire,
Bedfordshire, Berkshire, Buckinghamshire,
Hampshire

PAGE 46

③ EASTERN ENGLAND
Essex, Cambridgeshire, Suffolk, Norfolk,
Lincolnshire, East Yorkshire

PAGE 80

④ THE MIDLANDS
Oxfordshire, Warwickshire, Northamptonshire,
Leicestershire, Staffordshire, Nottinghamshire,
Derbyshire, Cheshire

PAGE 114

⑤ WALES AND THE WEST
Worcestershire, Herefordshire, Glamorgan, Powys,
Isle of Anglesey, Gwynedd, Denbighshire, Shropshire

PAGE 148

⑥ NORTHERN ENGLAND
Lancashire, Cumbria, North Yorkshire,
Tyne & Wear, Northumberland

PAGE 180

⑦ SCOTLAND
Scottish Borders, Glasgow, Edinburgh,
Clackmannanshire, Argyll & Bute, Dundee,
Aberdeenshire, Angus, Highlands

PAGE 214

INDEX AND ACKNOWLEDGEMENTS
PAGE 248

SOUTHWEST ENGLAND

1

On the lone bleak moor,
At the midnight hour,
Beneath the Gallows Tree,
Hand in hand
The Murderers stand,
By one, by two, or three!
And the Moon that night
With a grey, cold light
Each baleful object tips;
One half of her form
Is seen through the storm,
The other half's hid in Eclipse!
And the cold wind howls,
And the Thunder growls,
And the Lightning is broad and bright;
And altogether
It's very bad weather,
And an unpleasant sort of a night!

From *The Hand of Glory* by R.H. Barham (1788–1845)

SOUTHWEST ENGLAND

1	POLDARK MINE – CORNWALL	16
2	BODMIN JAIL – CORNWALL	18
3	TORRE ABBEY – DEVON	20
4	KENTS CAVERN – DEVON	22
5	KNOWLTON CHURCH AND EARTHWORKS – DORSET	26
6	STANTON DREW STONE CIRCLE – SOMERSET	28
7	WALFORD'S GIBBET – SOMERSET	30
8	SS *GREAT BRITAIN* – BRISTOL	32
9	LYDIARD HOUSE AND PARK – WILTSHIRE	34
10	TEWKESBURY BATTLEFIELD – GLOUCESTERSHIRE	36
11	ST BRIAVELS CASTLE – GLOUCESTERSHIRE	40
12	LITTLEDEAN JAIL – GLOUCESTERSHIRE	42
FEATURE – PASTIES AND KNOCKERS		**44**

INTRODUCTION

The southwest of England is a region steeped in history and mystery, and it exerts a powerful spell over those who roam its lanes and byways in search of secret, sacred and haunted places.

Our journey begins in Cornwall. Historically, the county's most precious resource was tin, so it is apt that our first visit takes us down into the chilling depths of a Cornish tin mine. Even more chilling is the time spent lingering in Bodmin Jail, which looms over the eerily bleak Bodmin Moor.

Crossing the border into Devon we encounter the wraith of a Spanish señorita that haunts a truly magnificent medieval abbey. Our next location takes us underground again to admire nature's art in the enchanting Kents Cavern, where England's oldest ghost may have been caught on film in 2009.

Two of England's most mystical sites follow as we head into Dorset to visit the forlorn ruin of Knowlton Church standing on its ancient earthworks, and then into Somerset, where we soak in the mystery surrounding the stone circle at Stanton Drew – although not as well known as Stonehenge, it is far more atmospheric.

Having lingered for as long as we dare at the site of a long-ago murder committed at a place now aptly called Dead Woman's Ditch, we head to Bristol to hop on board *SS Great Britain*, a proud testimony to Victorian ingenuity. It also happens to be the most haunted ship in the country.

Then follows a visit to a lovely country house in Wiltshire, haunted by the ghost of a 17th-century owner who lost three of his sons to the royalist cause of Charles I.

Finally, we end our exploration of the southwest in Gloucestershire. In addition to the battlefield where one of the bloodiest skirmishes of the Wars of the Roses occurred, we pay a visit to a haunted castle where a decent night's unrest can be had. Our final stop is 18th-century Littledean Jail, to explore its dark corners and enter its creepy cells.

POLDARK MINE

CORNWALL

Spectral Happenings in Britain's Deepest Mine

To descend into this chillingly atmospheric mine, and pick your way through its dark labyrinth of twisting tunnels, is to walk in the footsteps of generations of miners who once laboured in arduous conditions to pluck Cornwall's most precious resource – tin – from its eerie depths.

Indeed, as you shuffle along the low-roofed passages that have been hacked through the jagged rock, you can almost sense the spirits of these miners watching you from every nook and crevice of this subterranean world of flickering shadows.

Although there has probably been activity on the site as far back as prehistoric times, the mine's heyday was between 1720 and 1780. Then it was known as the Wheal Roots Mine and employed around 900 men and boys. However, by the 20th century the mine had been abandoned and lay largely forgotten.

In 1972, a steam engine museum opened on the site. While cutting into the hillside to position the compressor, the then owner stumbled upon the remnants of the ancient mine, and the race to restore it to its former glory was under way. A few years later its name was changed to the Poldark Mine to capitalize on the success of the *Poldark* books, written by Winston Graham, and the subsequent BBC series.

Given that this is said to be Britain's deepest mine, you can't help but admire the stoicism of those long-ago miners who, having entered it via shafts, would then inch their way down precariously balanced ladders through the pitch darkness, the only light coming from the dull glow of a tallow candle. To get at the tin they would hold a bar with a chisel-shaped end against the solid rock and strike it with a hammer, at the same time twisting the bar to ensure that it didn't jam in the fissure. That done, a fuse made of birds' quills stuffed with gunpowder would be inserted into the hole, which would then be sealed with clay.

Subterranean Perils

To ensure there was enough time to light the fuse and retire to a safe distance, the miners were meant to use four quills, each about 7.5cm (3in) long and slotted together. But, since they had to provide their own quills from their paltry wages, they were anxious to economize and often made do with three.

Having lit the fuse, the miners had to make a frantic dash to safety before the charge exploded. Inevitably, some of them didn't make it, and you can only imagine the agonizing horror they endured in their final moments. Even if they managed to survive the perils of the gunpowder, lung disease – brought on by the ever-present dust, coupled with the fumes of the gunpowder and the tallow candles – would carry the majority of them to the grave before they reached their mid-thirties.

Needless to say, with such a long history, tinged with so much tragedy, several spectres are known to lurk in the mine. Strange noises have been heard echoing from its deepest depths and darkest corners. Mysterious swirling mists have appeared on photographs taken in the tunnels, while a figure dressed in brown once appeared before a witness and then suddenly disappeared.

However, by far the most unfriendly revenant to roam the tunnels is that of a long-dead miner who, although never seen, has most certainly been heard. Indeed, following an investigation at the mine by the ghost-hunting team Mostghosts, a recording of the event was played back and the group was astonished to hear a gruff voice subjecting them to a foul-mouthed barrage of spectral abuse.

Poldark Mine

Trenear Wendron,
Helston, Cornwall
TR13 0ER

www.poldark-mine.co.uk

Haunted Rating 🁢🁢🁢🁢🁢

LEFT: *A miner being lowered into the depths of a mineshaft by a winch*

BELOW: *Men working above ground at a Cornish tin mine, circa 1860*

BODMIN JAIL

CORNWALL

Bodmin Jail

Bodmin, Cornwall
PL31 2NR

www.bodminjail.org

Haunted Rating

Infamy and Infanticide

An aura of distinct unease radiates from the crumbling walls and through the echoing corridors of Bodmin Jail. Having first driven across the bleak expanse of Bodmin Moor, you catch your first glimpse of the sinister, grey bulk of the jail looming over the surrounding houses. A feeling of utter desolation takes hold, its intensity increasing as the gloomy walls draw nearer. Once across the threshold you find yourself pitched into a twilight world where vestiges of a gruesome past still linger, and where the lost souls of long-ago prisoners still wander in turmoil.

The jail was begun in the 1770s, constructed by Napoleonic prisoners of war using 20,000 tonnes of granite quarried on Bodmin Moor. Chronic overcrowding led to the jail being extended several times in the 19th century, before it was finally closed in 1927.

Between 1785 and 1909, 55 people were executed at the prison. All but four of the hangings were carried out in public, providing a grisly source of entertainment for thousands of spectators who would congregate in adjoining fields to witness some poor wretch take his or her plunge into eternity.

Among those executed was Matthew Weeks, a crippled farmhand who was arrested for the murder of his lover, Charlotte Dymond – her body was found on Rough Tor, one of Bodmin Moor's most striking landmarks, on Sunday, 14 April 1844. Found guilty of the crime, he was hanged at the jail five months later, with 20,000 people witnessing his final moments, but in recent years considerable doubt has been cast on whether his conviction was just. Charlotte's ghost, clad in a gown and silk bonnet, is still said to appear at the site of her murder on the anniversary of her death.

The terror and misery that condemned felons, such as Matthew Weeks, must have experienced as they sat in the grim cells awaiting death can only be guessed at. But vestiges of their trepidation appear to have permeated the very walls of the prison, and many visitors are overcome by feelings of desolation and despondency as they explore the dank maze of dark corridors and claustrophobic cells.

Another former prisoner whose spirit has remained earthbound is that of Selina Wadge, who was arrested in 1878 for the murder of her youngest son, Harry. She told a constable that she had been urged to murder him by her lover James Westwood, who had promised to marry her if the boy was out of the way. Westwood denied this, claiming he had nothing against the boy.

At her subsequent trial, the jury found Selina guilty, although they recommended leniency on the grounds that she had taken good care of her children and that, in their opinion, the murder had not been premeditated. But the judge, Mr Justice Denman, disagreed and sentenced her to death.

Sobbing Selina

On Thursday, 15 August 1878, a sobbing Selina was led from her cell clutching a white handkerchief. Mounting the scaffold, she uttered her last words, 'Lord deliver me from this miserable world', and, at precisely 8am, the executioner pulled the lever of the trap and sent her plummeting to her death. Her body, still with the handkerchief in her hand, was left dangling for an hour before being cut down and buried within the prison grounds.

Her ghost, though, still wanders the prison, where she tries to reach out to small children who often enquire about the crying lady in the long dress. On the jail's third and fourth floors, pregnant women tend to become very emotional, supposedly as a result of Selina's spirit projecting her feelings of guilt and remorse onto them.

An eerie internal view of Bodmin Jail

TORRE ABBEY

DEVON

The Forlorn Señorita and the Headless Monk

Torre Abbey in Devon has the distinction of not only being Torquay's oldest building but also the best-surviving medieval monastery in Devon and Cornwall. Founded in 1196 by six canons of the Premonstratensian order – or White Canons, if you wish to avoid becoming totally tongue-tied – it grew and prospered until, by the 15th century, it had become the order's richest abbey in the country.

Following its surrender during the Dissolution of the Monasteries in the 1530s, the abbey became a private home. In 1662, it was acquired by the Cary family, who owned it for almost three centuries. They tacked a grand Georgian house onto the medieval fabric, creating in the process a truly grand and impressive dwelling.

In 1930, the property was purchased by the local authority and turned into an art gallery and museum. But, as the 21st century

ABOVE: *After the failed Armada in 1588, the so-called Spanish Barn was used to hold 300 Spanish prisoners*

approached, surveyors discovered that the building was falling down, and expensive repairs on a colossal scale were required. In 2005, a renovation project, which saw the property closed for three years, was begun. In the process, more of the medieval monastery came to light. This resulted in many of the older sections of the abbey being on public view for the first time since its reopening, enabling visitors to explore the very roots of this magnificent foundation.

Any building with over 800 years of history crackling away within its ancient fabric has had ample time to acquire a resident ghost or two, although Torre Abbey goes one better and boasts three! Chronologically speaking, its earliest ghost dates back to the 1300s when, for reasons that are difficult to ascertain, one of its abbots beheaded a young canon and then attempted to cover up his dastardly deed. Unable to find rest, the headless ghost of the murdered cleric is said to gallop around the grounds on his ghostly mount.

The Spanish Barn

The abbey's most famous haunting, though, centres on its magnificent, medieval Tithe Barn, now known as the 'Spanish Barn'. This was originally built to store the taxes, or tithes, paid to the abbey by the locals in the form of crops and other farm produce.

In 1588, the year of the attempted invasion of England by the Spanish Armada, Sir Francis Drake captured the Spanish flagship *Nuestra Señora del Rosario* and took 397 crew members prisoner. Among them was the fiancée of one of the ship's lieutenants, who, realizing that capture was imminent and not wishing to be separated from her lover, had disguised herself as a sailor. Along with the other prisoners she was put ashore and incarcerated for two weeks in the barn. In the cramped and miserable conditions, the young señorita caught a chill and died. Ever since, the ghost of the 'Spanish Lady' has roamed the barn and the surrounding grounds, quietly sobbing to herself as she searches everywhere for her lost love.

The third phantom is the smiling apparition of Lady Cary, a former mistress of the house. Resplendent in a magnificent ball gown, she is said to be driven through the grounds of her old home by an equally spectral driver in a brilliantly illuminated coach.

To explore the elegant interior of Torre Abbey is to walk back through history. Should a headless cleric go galloping by on his mare, or a smiling lady race past you in a brightly lit coach, or the wailing sobs of a forlorn señorita drift towards you on the night breezes, there's no cause for alarm. For, as the ghostly Spanish Lady can no doubt testify, worse things happen at sea.

Torre Abbey

Torquay, Devon
TQ2 5JE

www.torre-abbey.org.uk

Haunted Rating

The best surviving medieval monastery in the area, Torre Abbey's architecture reveals a fascinating history spanning 800 years

KENTS CAVERN

DEVON

England's Oldest Ghost

Kents Cavern is one of the most important Palaeolithic cave systems in Europe, where archaeologists have been making impressive discoveries for almost 200 years. This is hardly surprising given that there is evidence of human occupation at the site dating back half a million years, which makes it one of the oldest recognizable places of human habitation in the entire country. Archaeological gems unearthed here include a 37,000-year-old human jawbone, 400,000-year-old stone tools, plus the fossilized remains of some of Kents Cavern's long-ago wildlife, such as scimitar cat, bear, hyena and lion.

The cavern is both an enchanting and a beautiful place where, among other wonders, visitors can marvel at nature's art in the form of the spectacular array of stalactites and stalagmites that decorate the section known as the Rocky Chamber.

Between 1865 and 1880, self-taught archaeologist and geologist William Pengally carried out exhaustive excavations in the chambers and uncovered over 80,000 artefacts. One of these, a human arm bone, which carbon-dating has since suggested is around 9,000 years old, gave rise to great speculation in 2009 when a curator at Torquay Museum spotted seven cut marks on it. Further investigation revealed that the cuts appear to have been made deliberately around the time of death. This led scientists to hypothesize that the damaged bone could be evidence of Mesolithic Britons indulging in complex burial rituals and possibly even cannibalism.

On a more mysterious level, considerable excitement was generated in June 2009 when it appeared that Simon Howard, a visitor to the caves, had managed to catch a ghostly image of one of the oldest inhabitants with his camera.

Kents Cavern

Torquay, Devon
TQI 2JF

www.kents-cavern.co.uk

Haunted Rating 🕯️🕯️🕯️🕯️🕯️

A strange mist swirls around the rock formations at Kents Cavern

Caught on Camera

'We were on a tour round the caves,' Simon Howard recalled, 'and I happened to snap a picture inside the Bear's Den chamber while waiting for the other members of the tour to arrive. Later on when I took a look at the photo I saw this mist which was not visible at the time.'

At the centre of the mist was, what appeared to be, the bearded profile of a man's face with a large eye, a long nose and a small mouth, and wearing what seemed to be a helmet with a nose guard.

'There have been some strange and unexplained happenings in the caves down the years,' commented James Hull of Kents Cavern, '... but this is the first photograph taken that we're aware of which shows what looks like a ghost... Visitors... sometimes send us photographs taken in the caves showing strange bright orbs but these can be explained away as a camera's flash reflecting off water droplets around the caves. But I find this photograph... a lot more difficult to explain away.'

In addition to archaeological excavations, paranormal investigations have been carried out at the caves. In the course of one investigation, two of the team reported having their safety helmets lifted from their heads by an unseen hand, while others complained of an unnerving sensation that they were being constantly watched.

All in all, Kents Cavern is a special place imbued with an aura of ancient enchantment. It provided refuge for our distant ancestors, and several of them seem loath to leave its safety. Instead they remain earthbound in this underground haven that is strangely mysterious but also slightly chilling.

KNOWLTON CHURCH AND EARTHWORKS

DORSET

Spirits of Days Gone By

Surrounded by a Neolithic earthwork, the hollow shell of Knowlton Church is one of the most atmospheric places in Dorset and, it's said, also one of the most haunted. The ruins are imbued with a mystical, almost enchanting, aura, and the church's location at the centre of a pagan circle is testimony to an ancient clash of religious creeds.

The church was built in the 12th century and added to over the years. Although Christianity was well established in England by the 12th century, vestiges of paganism still clung to remote areas. Those charged with converting the local populace knew that the best way to do so was by assimilating places of pagan worship into their religion and siting the church right in the middle of it. Standing stones, held sacred for thousands of years, were broken up and used in the construction of the church, or else they were toppled and buried in the ground. In 2005, students on a dowsing course at the site unearthed one such stone. They believed that it formed part of the stone circle that the builders of the church had buried in order to demonstrate the superiority of the new faith over the old.

Although the site today is somewhat lonely and isolated, in the Middle Ages there was a thriving community in the village of Knowlton. However, by the late 15th century, the population had been decimated by the plague, and its few surviving inhabitants migrated elsewhere. The houses gradually fell into decay and were eventually ploughed into the earth, where vague traces of their foundations can still be seen a few hundred yards to the west of Knowlton Church. Nevertheless, the church continued to attract a congregation until its roof collapsed in the 18th century – its days as a place of worship were numbered. Today, despite the picturesque surroundings, an aura of melancholy hangs

over the place, and the spirits of some who have passed this way in the last 4,000 years are still said to linger. A phantom horse and rider are reported to gallop across the site in the dead of night, passing through the derelict church as though it weren't there. A ghostly face has been witnessed peering from the top window of the tower. Then there is the shade of a weeping woman, described in some accounts as a nun, seen kneeling outside the church.

A lady and her two children who were visiting the site one day were startled by a tall figure dressed in black that appeared from nowhere. It walked right across their path, then promptly vanished. Others have reported seeing the same figure in the dead of night and have commented on a truly menacing aura emanating from it. Paranormal groups investigating the site have found themselves enveloped in swirling white mists and have heard ethereal voices chattering around them, but no source of the voices can ever be traced.

Ghosts aside, there is a spiritual paradox about this ancient place. Although those long-ago holy men tried to stamp Christianity over the earlier beliefs of their pagan forerunners, their efforts eventually came to naught – for most of the past two centuries, their church has lain in ruins with only the spirit of the older faith for company.

**Knowlton Church
and Earthworks**

Near Cranborne, Dorset

www.english-heritage.org.uk

Haunted Rating

LEFT: A frosty morning view of derelict Knowlton Church, which is situated in the middle of a pagan earth circle (more clearly seen in the picture above)

STANTON DREW STONE CIRCLE

BATH & NE SOMERSET

Stanton Drew Stone Circle

Stanton Drew,
Bath & NE Somerset

Haunted Rating 👤👤👤👥👥

The Fiddler and the Bride

The Stanton Drew Stone Circle or, to be more precise, three stone circles, dates from around 3000 BC and enjoys a relatively isolated location well off the beaten track. The stones themselves stand sullen and silent – brooding guardians of ancient mysteries around which all manner of legends and ghostly tales have been woven. Although twice the size of its more famous cousins, Stonehenge and Avebury, it is a lot less well known and has managed to retain a distinctive aura of detachment and solitude.

Although archaeological excavation at the site has been minimal, there is evidence to suggest that a huge structure once stood inside the Great Circle. Consisting of 27 stones, most of which lie recumbent, the circle measures 112m (367ft) across. This prompts the theory that the megalithic remains were once part of a much more complex and important site. There are, however, no immediate plans for further excavation and, consequently, the historical facts remain sparse and the stones will be allowed to keep their secrets, at least for the foreseeable future.

Where history remains mute, however, folklore and legend have been more than happy to step into the void, providing their own intriguing explanation as to the origin of the stones. Tradition holds that they are the petrified remains of a long-ago wedding party, turned to stone by the Devil!

The story goes that a great wedding feast was held in the vicinity on a Saturday, and everyone was enjoying themselves immensely. The bride, a little intoxicated by the flowing drink and lively carousing, urged the fiddler to play on, even though the Sabbath was rapidly approaching. The fiddler refused, whereupon the bride exclaimed that the dancing would continue even if she had to go to Hell to find a fiddler.

It was an unwise outburst, for no sooner had the words left her mouth than a tall stranger appeared in their midst and struck up a merry jig. Faster and faster the guests twirled, swirled and spun, each of them unable to stop, as the dance went on and on through the night. Come the dawn they had all been turned to stone, and the fiddler, who was, of course, the Devil himself, had seized their souls and spirited them away to the fires of Hell.

So it is that the sullen stones are said to be the petrified bodies of the guests, while a grouping of two standing stones and one recumbent stone located in the garden of the village pub – the Druid's Arms – are said to be the mortal remains of the bride, bridegroom and parson.

There is also a belief that confusion, even death, awaits anyone who attempts to count the stones. Some say that this can never be done accurately because attempts to do so will always yield a different total. Others say that you will drop dead before completing the task.

WALFORD'S GIBBET

SOMERSET

Walford's Gibbet
near Nether Stowey, Somerset
Haunted Rating ◉◉◉◉◉
see www.haunted-britain.com/walford

Pen, ink and watercolour drawing of onlookers at the gibbet by Thomas Rowlandson (1756–1827)

Chilling Encounters on Woodland Paths

The Quantock Hills rise majestically from the sea, commanding magnificent views over the Bristol Channel to South Wales. Towards their eastern edge, on the summit of a high hill, there stands an Iron Age fort called Dowsborough Camp.

Legend holds that the fort was once commandeered by a group of marauding Danish pirates and used as a base from which to rob and pillage nearby villages. They would bring their spoils, together with any womenfolk they had kidnapped, back to this easily defendable fortress. But the kidnapped women turned the tables on their captors one night by encouraging them to let down their hair and enjoy a drunken feast. With the Danes incapacitated by drink, the local men were able to steal up the hillside and massacre all but one of the marauders.

The survivor was a young minstrel who had fallen in love with a local girl, to whose house he had fled as the skirmish began. She hid him for a few days but then the locals discovered him and he, too, was killed. His spirit now roams the hillside, singing softly to itself. Occasionally, on wild autumn nights, the sound of ghostly revelry, followed by the clash of swords, is also heard echoing across the slopes of the hill.

Dead Woman's Ditch

Located on the hill is an ancient earthwork that labours under the chilling name of Dead Woman's Ditch. The woman in question is reputedly Jane Walford, whose body was found here in July 1789.

Jane was the wife of John Walford, whom she had married in June 1789 after becoming pregnant by him. The fact that John had previously been betrothed to the local miller's daughter, Ann Rice, meant that his marriage to Jane was not exactly one made in heaven. From the outset, Jane, described by a contemporary as 'a poor stupid creature, almost an idiot; yet possessing a little kind of craftiness… an ordinary squat person, disgustingly dirty, and slovenly in her dress', is said to have taunted John about his lost love, Ann.

Less than a month into their marriage the couple went drinking one night at a local inn and, as they walked home, they began arguing. John, somewhat the worse for drink, suddenly seized his wife and slit her throat. He hastily buried her body in a shallow grave at the site now called Dead Woman's Ditch.

The body was soon discovered and John was arrested for murder. At his trial he was found guilty and sentenced to be hanged close to the scene of his crime. The judge also instructed that, once dead, his body was to remain hanging in chains for a year and a day as a deterrent to others.

On 20 August 1789, a huge crowd turned out on the hill to watch John Walford pay the price for the murder of his wife. As per the judge's instructions, his body was left hanging at the site for a year and a day. When the allotted time had expired, his remains were cut down and buried 3m (10ft) beneath the ground at the site of his execution, which ever since has been known as Walford's Gibbet. The site, carpeted by bracken and covered with trees, has a melancholic aura, and the knowledge of what occurred here all those years ago keeps you looking warily over your shoulder. This sense of trepidation isn't helped by reports of visitors to Walford's Gibbet hearing the eerie clank of invisible chains or being overcome by the repulsive smell of rotting flesh. If you add to this the fact that John Walford's ghost, a handsome figure wearing the rough clothes of a charcoal burner, has been encountered on the road and pathways hereabouts, you begin to understand why there are those who steer well clear of this place at all times of the day and night.

Gibbets & Hanging Chains

For those who had committed particularly heinous crimes, 18th-century judges could impose the punishment of gibbeting or hanging in chains in addition to the death penalty. These gruesome, cage-like structures were placed on hills and near public highways to make them as visible as possible, and the corpse left in them, often until it rotted away. The hope was that these grim reminders of the iron will of the law would act as a deterrent to those of a criminal disposition.

SS GREAT BRITAIN

BRISTOL

The plush interior of the main dining room aboard SS Great Britain

Life and Death on the Ocean Waves

Built in Bristol and designed by the pioneering Victorian engineer Isambard Kingdom Brunel (1806–1859), SS Great Britain was launched in 1843. At that time, she was the largest ship in the world, a state-of-the-art luxury vessel, designed to carry 252 passengers across the Atlantic.

However, her first voyages were blighted by a series of mishaps and she attracted far fewer passengers than anticipated, plunging her owner, the Great Western Shipping Company, into financial crisis. During her second season, in 1846, she ran aground on the sands of Dundrum Bay on the north coast of Ireland, where she remained for almost a year. The cost of refloating her exhausted the owner's depleted finances and she was sold.

In the early 1850s, her then owners, deciding to capitalize on increasing emigration to Australia, commissioned a complete refit, after which she was able to carry over 700 passengers. When she made her first voyage to Melbourne in 1852, she caused such a sensation among the locals that 4,000 people paid a shilling each to go on board and admire her. For the next 24 years, and over the course of 32 voyages, she carried 16,000 emigrants to Australia, gaining such a reputation for speed that she was known as 'The Greyhound of the Seas'.

By the 1880s, her age had started to show and she was converted again, this time to carry Welsh coal to San Francisco, via Cape Horn. On her third voyage in 1886, she ran into trouble rounding the Horn and was severely damaged. Forced to put in to Port Stanley in the Falkland Islands, she was deemed too costly to repair and was given over as a hulk for storing bales of wool. Finally, in 1937, she was towed out to sea, holed and left to settle on the ocean bed.

Then, in the 1960s, discussions were held about bringing her back to Bristol. Raised from the water, she was patched up and her final journey began. On 5 July 1970, thousands lined the banks of the River Avon to welcome the SS *Great Britain* home. On 19 July – the 127th anniversary of her launch – she was eased into the dry dock at Great Western, the place where she had been built. She has now been lovingly restored and, although she will never sail again, visitors can step aboard this monument to Victorian ingenuity and experience for themselves its gripping history.

In the process they might also make the acquaintance of one of the ghosts that roam what has been dubbed 'the most haunted ship in Britain'. A seafaring mystery lies at the root of one haunting. John Gray was the ship's longest-serving captain. He took charge of the vessel in 1854 and remained at the helm for 18 eventful years. But, in the 1870s, he began suffering from kidney disease, which, in turn, led to depression. On a return journey from Australia, in November 1872, he disappeared. A search of the ship revealed an open porthole in his cabin, but of the captain there was no sign. It was assumed that he had committed suicide, although some say that he accidently fell overboard, while others maintain that he was murdered for the gold that he kept in his cabin.

Nevertheless, the spirit of Captain Gray remains with his ship, and the ghostly sound of his hobnail boots striding across decks or ascending stairs has chilled the blood of several witnesses. It may also have been his spectral legs that one lady saw walk through a door into the Captain's State Room and vanish.

Elsewhere, the shades of a Victorian woman and her child have been seen in the family cabin on the promenade deck. Those who like a little light accompaniment to their ghostly experiences should listen out for spectral piano music that has been known to drift across the saloon.

SS *Great Britain*

Great Western Dockyard, Bristol BS1 6TY

www.ssgreatbritain.org

Haunted Rating 👤👤👤👤👤

Flags flying on SS Great Britain, known as the most haunted ship in Britain

LYDIARD HOUSE AND PARK

WILTSHIRE

Lydiard House and Park

Lydiard Tregoze, Swindon,
Wiltshire SN5 3PA

www.lydiardpark.org.uk

Haunted Rating 👤👤👤👤👤

St Mary's Church, Lydiard Tregoze

Sir John St John and the Golden Cavalier

In 1420, Oliver St John acquired Lydiard House, and successive generations of his family rebuilt and remodelled it until, in 1937, the by then dilapidated house and grounds were purchased by Swindon Corporation. In addition to the usual fixtures and fittings, the council also acquired the spirits of several members of the St John family whose home this was for over 500 years.

Predominant among these is the ghost of Sir John St John (1585–1648), a man whose life was beset by tragedy. During the English Civil War, Sir John supported the royalist cause, and three of his sons were killed in the conflict. He is buried in the local church of St Mary's, which nestles behind the house. Prior to his death, he erected some of the finest family monuments in England in this church. One of the most spectacular commemorates his son Edward, who was killed at the second Battle of Newbury in 1645. Often referred to as 'The Golden Cavalier', this full-size gilded effigy is of Edward emerging from his campaign tent, dressed in cavalry armour and holding a shield that bears the family coat of arms.

The church is haunted by several ghosts, although whether they are members of the St John family is difficult to ascertain, since nobody knows for certain whose ghosts they are. The most chilling of these is a hooded figure dressed in grey, from which, witnesses say, a feeling of utter malevolence emanates. The sound of an invisible, sobbing woman has been known to chill the blood of visitors, while solemn organ music has been heard echoing from inside the church at times when it is known to be empty.

Civil War Spirits

Meanwhile, Sir John St John's ghost is a frequent visitor to Lydiard House, where he favours the morning room and the adjoining library, in which he has been seen leaning against the fireplace. His appearances are often preceded by an alarming drop in temperature, followed by the strong aroma of sweet tobacco. He has a melancholic air about him, and witnesses often comment that he appears as a very solid figure who, were it not for his 17th-century dress, could easily be mistaken for a living person.

Following Sir John's death, the estate passed to his youngest son, Walter, who, despite having supported the Parliamentarians during the Civil War, was able to ingratiate himself with Charles II when the monarchy was restored in 1660.

In 1743, the house was rebuilt and the surroundings were re-landscaped to create the stunning grounds that visitors still admire today. It is in these grounds that Lydiard's other ghosts are known to wander. The apparition of Sir John St John has been seen strolling around them, and the shade of a little drummer boy, who may date from the Civil War when royalist soldiers are said to have been garrisoned in the park, has also been spotted tapping on his drum, although no beat is ever heard. A white lady has been observed drifting around the grounds, while a phantom coach and horses is said to appear on the avenue that leads up to the house.

In its heyday, Lydiard House ranked as one of Wiltshire's loveliest stately homes. Today, thanks to the dedicated efforts of Swindon Borough Council, it has been restored to its former glory, providing visitors with an insight into how the other half lived in days gone by.

Recent History

In the early part of the 20th century, the Lydiard Estate was broken up in a series of land sales beginning in 1920. By the start of World War II the house had fallen into a state of disrepair.

Lydiard Park was requisitioned in 1941 and an American Forces hospital was established in the grounds, near where the sports pitches are currently situated. The hospital served the 101st American Airborne Division and treated casualties from the D-Day landings before becoming a German prisoner of war camp for a time.

After the war, the house and 147 acres of surrounding parkland were bought by Swindon Corporation and a restoration project began. The house was opened to the public in 1955.

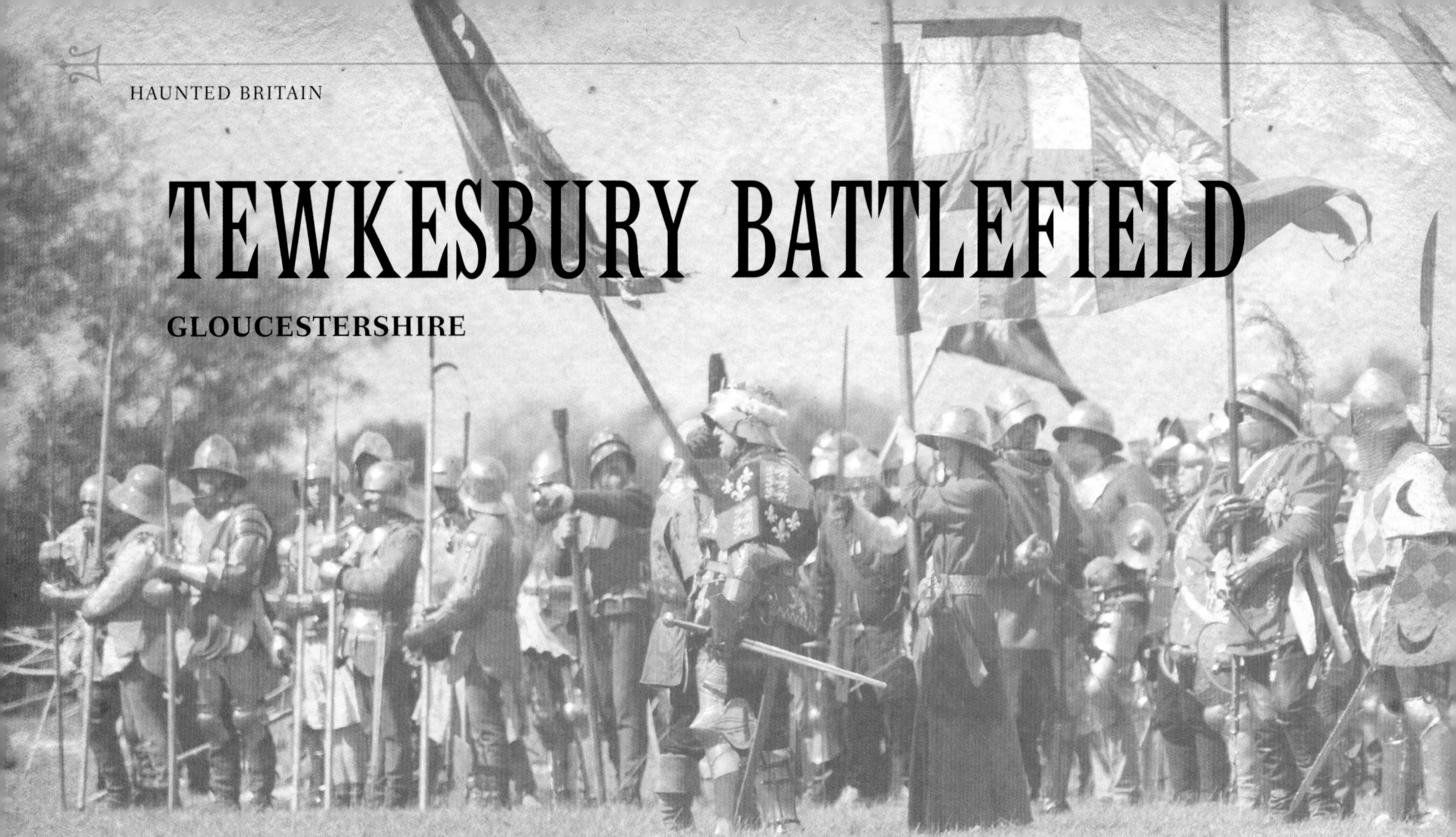

TEWKESBURY BATTLEFIELD

GLOUCESTERSHIRE

Tewkesbury Battlefield

Tewkesbury, Gloucestershire

Haunted Rating 👤👤👤👤👤👤

The Battle Continues

On 14 April 1471, Queen Margaret of Anjou, wife of the Lancastrian king Henry VI, landed on the southwest coast of England with her son Edward, Prince of Wales, and 1,000 mercenaries. Her husband had been imprisoned in the Tower of London by the Yorkist monarch Edward IV, and it was Margaret's intention to wrest the crown of England back from Edward. She joined forces with the Earl of Devon and the Duke of Somerset in a campaign that formed part of the series of civil wars fought in England from 1455 to 1487, known as the Wars of the Roses – the red rose was the emblem for the House of Lancaster, the white rose for the House of York.

Hearing of their landing, Edward IV gathered 6,000 troops and headed to Windsor to await further news. There he learned that the Lancastrians, with Somerset in command, were on their way to Wales, where they hoped to rendezvous with the forces of the Earl of Pembroke. Edward sent orders that the gates of Gloucester were to be

locked to prevent the Lancastrians from crossing the River Severn into Wales at that point, and set off to intercept the enemy.

Unable to cross the River Severn at Gloucester, the Lancastrians headed for the next crossing point at Tewkesbury, with Edward IV hot on their heels. Unwilling to attempt the dangerous crossing with the enemy so close, Somerset decided instead to turn and fight. The stage was set for one of the bloodiest and most decisive encounters of the Wars of the Roses.

On the morning of 4 May 1471, the Duke of Somerset deployed his numerically superior, but by this time physically exhausted and militarily inferior, army in fields to the south of the town, and the two sides prepared for battle.

The Yorkists found themselves hampered by a number of ditches and hedges that lay between them and their adversaries. But, having launched a bombardment of the Lancastrian lines, Edward IV gave the order to advance. At this point, Somerset came upon the Yorkist left and attacked, but the rest of the Lancastrians failed to lend their support, and Edward's cavalry soon routed Somerset's force.

This setback drained the Lancastrians' morale and, as they found themselves being pushed back towards the town and the River Severn

The Wars of the Roses

The Wars of the Roses were a series of civil wars fought in medieval England from 1455 to 1487 between the House of Lancaster and the House of York. The name comes from the emblems used by the two sides, the red rose for the Lancastrians and the white rose for the Yorkists. Both sides were direct descendents of Edward III.

The 19th-century illustration (right) depicts the brutal murder of the young Prince Edward at Tewkesbury in 1471, where echoes of the skirmish are said to resonate to this day.

by the advancing Yorkists, they began to flee. Edward's soldiers gave chase, slaughtering a huge number of the enemy on what is still known as 'The Bloody Meadow'. To this day, those of a psychic persuasion still pick up on the feelings of terror that are said to resonate at the spot.

Somerset, along with his fellow commanders, took shelter in Tewkesbury Abbey, but the Yorkists dragged them from this safe haven, tried them and executed them. The greatest loss for the Lancastrians was that of Edward, Prince of Wales, who was found near a forest by the Duke of Clarence and summarily executed. He remains the only Prince of Wales ever to have been killed in battle.

Although the Yorkists were the victors at the Battle of Tewkesbury, 14 years later Henry Tudor would defeat Richard III (who, as the Duke of York, had fought at Tewkesbury) at the Battle of Bosworth. Henry then married Elizabeth of York, the daughter of Edward IV, thus uniting the houses of Lancaster and York and so ending the Wars of the Roses.

Paranormal groups investigating what remains of the battlefield continue to detect and experience echoes of the skirmish. There are reports of hands suddenly becoming very cold, and a member of one group even saw a soldier in medieval armour on horseback galloping across the site.

ST BRIAVELS CASTLE

GLOUCESTERSHIRE

St Briavels Castle

St Briavels, Lydney,
Gloucestershire GL15 6RG

Haunted Rating ⊗⊗⊗⊗⊗

View by appointment only

The picnic tables in the gatehouse courtyard look innocent enough, but this could be Britain's spookiest youth hostel!

England's Most Haunted Castle?

St Briavels Castle is a magnet for ghost hunters, and few who cross its threshold in search of paranormal encounters leave disappointed. Indeed, such is its reputation for otherworldly happenings that it has often been dubbed the most haunted castle in England.

The castle was begun in 1131 by Milo Fitz Walter, Earl of Hereford, to 'curb the incursions of the Welsh'. It was Milo who established one of the castle's oldest traditions, that of the 'St Briavels Bread and Cheese Dole'. Today, on each Whit Sunday, locals dressed in medieval costume gather outside the castle to catch bread and cheese that is tossed from its walls. Originally a 'Dole Claimer' was someone who had paid a penny to the Earl of Hereford for the right to gather firewood from nearby Hudnalls Wood. Some believed that the titbits thrown from the castle were imbued with magical properties – local miners, for example, thought they would protect them against accidents – and so they preserved them for good luck.

On Christmas Day 1143, Milo was killed by a stray arrow while out hunting and the castle passed to his son. Over succeeding centuries, the castle became the administrative centre for the Royal Forest of Dean and the residence of the Royal Constable. It was visited by several kings, most notably King John (1167–1216) who used it as a hunting lodge. Today, the solar in which he stayed is known as King John's Bedroom in his honour. This room was later used as a courtroom, and notches on the stone of its huge fireplace are reputedly the result of it being struck with a sword whenever someone was sentenced to death.

Those awaiting sentence, and those who had been sentenced, would be kept in the Prison Room situated in the gatehouse. Many who enter this room today comment on its decidedly 'strange' atmosphere, their feelings of unease no doubt compounded by its walls being adorned with graffiti carved by prisoners long ago. 'Robin Belcher. The Day will come that thou shalt answer for it for thou hast sworn against me, 1671', reads one intriguing example.

Since 1947, the castle has been one of Britain's most unique Youth Hostels, where seekers of rural solitude can bed down for a restful night. Meanwhile, those who come in search of more ethereal pursuits can most certainly look forward to a decent night's unrest.

King John's Bedroom is home to one of the castle's most persistent ghosts, an unseen baby whose pitiful cries frequently disturb the slumbers of those sleeping in it. In the Hanging Room, so called because it was where prisoners who had been sentenced to death were brought to await their fate, the psychically inclined often experience the terrifying sensation of being gripped by the throat.

In the Oubliette Room, a rug conceals one of the castle's most chilling secrets. If you pull it back and lift the wooden trap door underneath, you will find yourself looking down into a sinister oubliette, or small dungeon – the name is derived from the French *oublier* meaning 'to forget' – into which unfortunate captives would be cast and left to die. Visitors to the room have felt their clothes being tugged at by unseen hands, while guests sleeping here have been known to depart suddenly in the middle of the night unable to stand the oppressive atmosphere any longer.

Other spirits that lurk at the castle include a black dog that trots around the rooms, a grey lady who glides along the top corridor, and a knight in burnished armour who appears in the grounds.

History has most certainly left its mark on the time-wearied walls of St Briavels Castle, and tales of its ghostly goings-on help illuminate dark corners of its brutal and eventful past. It is a place of creaking floorboards where the past and present co-exist and occasionally merge with truly alarming results.

Gargoyle on a carved wooden seat outside the castle

LITTLEDEAN JAIL

GLOUCESTERSHIRE

At Home Among the Revenants

If you were searching for a cosy family house in which to live, a haunted former jail might not, at first glance, seem the ideal location. But, for Andy Jones and his wife Nicola, 18th-century Littledean Jail is very much home, sweet home. Since 2005, they have been opening their doors to visitors who can explore its 24 very creepy cells, while enjoying Andy's 'Crime Through Time' museum – a private collection of items associated with crime, punishment, sleaze and scandal over the centuries.

Dubbed the 'Alcatraz of the Forest', Littledean Jail was designed and built by pioneering prison reformer Sir George Onesiphorous Paul and leading prison architect William Blackburn. Originally a House of Correction, intended to reform as well as punish criminals, it was considered the most up-to-date prison of the age when it opened in 1791. The first prisoner to sample its state-of-the-art hospitality was Joseph Marshall, a 19-year-old labourer convicted of stealing a spade, who arrived on 18 November 1791. Subsequent prisoners were committed here for crimes such as desertion, fraud, embezzlement, assault and battery, and murder. Women were locked up for lewd acts or for petty theft, and, since there was no segregation of the prisoners, three babies, of whom only one survived, were conceived and born here between 1837 and 1838. Children as young as eight were also incarcerated, and punished for transgressions by being birched or whipped.

In 1854, Littledean was converted to a remand prison, and a few years later it became a courthouse and a police station. Police Sergeant Samuel Beard, the first Gloucestershire policeman to be killed in the line of duty, was stationed at Littledean. He was on plain-clothes operations on the night of 17 August 1861, watching for nighttime poachers in the Forest of Dean, when he confronted four suspects who bludgeoned and kicked him so viciously that he died of his injuries.

The police station closed in 1972, and the last sitting of the court was held on 24 October 1985, after which the jail was bought by an insurance company, which sold it to Andy and Nicola in 2003.

Ghosts of Former Inmates

Having witnessed so much history and infamy, it comes as no real surprise to learn that Littledean Jail is haunted. Indeed, it would be more of a surprise to find that it wasn't. Among the apparitions that lurk behind its forbidding sandstone facade is a woman in a white shirt and ragged black trousers seen in the upstairs cells. Meanwhile, the ground floor is haunted by something or someone that quite unnerves the family dog – it will stare along the corridor whimpering at something it can apparently see but which remains invisible to humans.

Museum exhibits have been known to shake of their own volition, while lights have flickered, then suddenly gone out, plunging visitors into darkness. Inexplicable bangs have sounded from the depths of the jail at all times of the day or night, while heart-rending sobs have been heard echoing from the cells.

In spite of all this, the Jones's are not in the least bit afraid of their ghostly residents and are perfectly happy to share their home with the spirits of former inmates. 'This place has all the serenity and splendour of a baronial family home,' comments Andy. 'It's more like living in a castle than in a jail. It's wonderful having an 18ft-high sandstone wall around your property. It's like living on your own little island.'

The entrance to Littledean Jail, now a museum of crime and punishment

Littledean Jail

Littledean, near Cinderford, Forest of Dean, Gloucestershire GL14 3NL

www.littledeanjail.com

Haunted Rating

View by appointment only

Pasties and Knockers

Today Cornwall's best-known export is probably the ubiquitous Cornish pasty. Sold all over Britain, it can contain fillings as diverse as beef with stilton, or even chicken tikka.

However, long before it became synonymous with Cornwall, the pasty had been a staple of the wealthy upper classes since at least the 13th century, and it wasn't until the 17th and 18th centuries that it became popular with Cornish tin miners. Wives would bake pasties in the morning to sustain their husbands during their long and arduous shifts in the mines, since the depths at which they worked meant resurfacing for lunch wasn't viable. In order that their menfolk could recognize whose pasty was whose, each wife would carve his initials into the pasty's crust as a means of identification.

Traditionally, a pasty contained beef, onion and swede, all of which was then sealed in its own crust, providing a self-contained meal. However, Cornish women would, in fact, put anything and everything into their pasties – according to an old legend, the reason that the Devil never crossed the River Tamar into Cornwall was because he feared that he might end up as the contents of a Cornish pasty.

If made correctly, the crust of a pasty should be able to survive the impact of being dropped down a mine shaft, an important consideration given the precarious conditions under which the tin miners worked. In the mines, arsenic was commonly found alongside the tin, so the crust, which the miners didn't eat, would prevent the grime on their hands contaminating the meal within.

Wheal Coates Tin Mine, St Agnes, Cornwall

The slang word for pasty in Cornish was *ogee*, derived from *hoggan*, which was a type of bread. Some of the tin mines used to provide stoves for raw pasties to be cooked on site. When they were ready, the bal maidens – the women who dressed the ore on the surface, but who also did cooking and laundry – would shout down the mine 'Oggy Oggy Oggy', to which the hungry miners would reply 'Oi! Oi! Oi!' This is said to be where the well-known chant often heard at football matches comes from.

As well as sustaining the miners during their gruelling day, the pasty could also be employed supernaturally to placate the knockers who lurked in the deepest, darkest corners of the mines. Knockers were said to be pixie-like creatures, about 60cm (2ft) tall with thin arms and legs and large hooked noses. Often dressed in miniature versions of a miner's garb, they generally kept to themselves, working the rich lodes deep underground, from where their picks could be heard chipping away at the ore. They were generally thought of as benevolent beings, who would, for example, lead favoured miners to the richest lodes. They would also warn of an impending shaft collapse by knocking to raise the alarm, hence their name. But the knockers also had a mischievous side and would sometimes steal miners' tools or pinch their ears. However, rudeness on the part of the miners, such as swearing, whistling or shouting at them, would send the knockers into a rage, and this was when they became dangerous. They would deliberately lead miners who had offended them into the most dangerous parts of the mine and leave them lost in the darkness. Even worse, they would cause a mine shaft to collapse with dire consequences for their unfortunate victims. It was, therefore, imperative to keep the knockers affable, and to thank them for their warnings of impending disaster. Miners would always leave a small segment from the crust of their pasties in the mine to placate them. Some would even leave the section of crust that bore their initials on it so there would be no confusion about who had left the offering.

By the late 19th century, the knockers were said to be the ghosts of miners who had been killed in previous mining accidents and who now lingered behind to protect the virtuous and punish wrongdoers (see pages 16–17). Another popular belief was that the arrival of the knockers was an ill omen, presaging the closing of the mine. But once the mine was closed, the knockers would remain to guard it. Indeed, there are some who believe that in the abandoned tin mines littering the Cornish landscape, the knockers still keep watch, awaiting the day when they can once more guide miners to the richest lodes, tweak their ears and steal their tools, or warn them when danger approaches.

Cornwall's last working tin mine closed in 1998 and with its demise four millennia of mining came to an end. The hollow shells of their brick engine houses and their soaring chimney stacks now dot the landscape, eerie reminders of days gone by. But those who live near them say that, from time to time, faint knocking can be heard echoing from deep underground. When they hear it, they know it's time to reach for another Cornish pasty and ensure that a morsel of the crust is broken off – just in case.

SOUTHEAST ENGLAND

Next died the Lady who yon Hall possessed;
And here they brought her noble bones to rest.
In Town she dwelt:- forsaken stood the Hall:
Worms ate the floors, the tapestry fled the wall:
No fire the kitchens cheerless grate displayed;
No cheerful light the long-closed sash conveyed;
The crawling worm, that turns a summer-fly,
Here spun his shroud and laid him up to die
The winter-death:- upon the bed of sate,
The bat shrill-shrieking wooed his flickering mate;
To empty rooms the curious came no more,
From empty cellars turned the angry poor,
And surly beggars cursed the ever-bolted door.

From *The Lady of the Manor* by George Crabbe (1754–1832)

SOUTHEAST ENGLAND

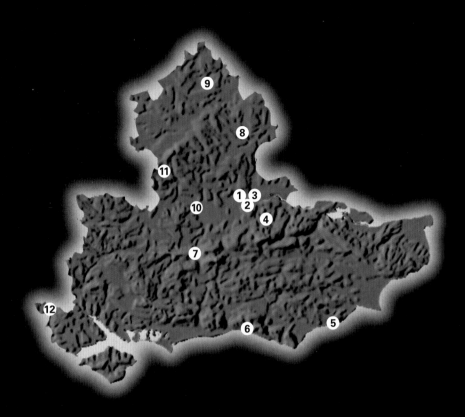

1	50 BERKELEY SQUARE – LONDON	50
2	CHURCHILL MUSEUM AND CABINET WAR ROOMS – LONDON	52
3	THEATRE ROYAL – LONDON	56
4	CHISLEHURST CAVES – KENT	58
5	HASTINGS CASTLE – EAST SUSSEX	60
6	PRESTON MANOR – EAST SUSSEX	62

	FEATURE – SPRING-HEELED JACK	64
7	GUILDFORD CASTLE – SURREY	68
8	CLIBBON'S POST – HERTFORDSHIRE	70
9	CARDINGTON HANGARS – BEDFORDSHIRE	72
10	THE OSTRICH – BERKSHIRE	74
11	HELL FIRE CAVES – BUCKINGHAMSHIRE	76
12	BREAMORE HOUSE – HAMPSHIRE	78

INTRODUCTION

The southeast of England is an area of contrasts, and our journey through it takes us from the bustling, traffic-clogged streets of London to a sequence of locations that are both historic and mysterious, with some downright terrifying!

We begin in Berkeley Square, with a graceful 18th-century house that once had a reputation so chilling that it was known as the most haunted house in London. A short distance away we descend underground to explore the labyrinth of the Cabinet War Rooms. During the dark days of World War II, they provided a safe haven for Winston Churchill and his fellow ministers from the frequent bombing raids to which London was subjected. Several of the wartime workers seem unwilling, or unable, to move on, and they still linger there as spirits. Our final London site is the Theatre Royal, Haymarket, where the ghost of a Victorian actor-manager has been seen on many occasions, most recently in 2009 by Sir Patrick Stewart.

Heading south from the capital, we journey underground again to explore Chislehurst Caves and their haunted pool. Via the ragged remnants of Hastings Castle, we find ourselves crossing the threshold of one of Brighton's most haunted houses, Preston Manor, where the wraiths of long-ago residents linger on. Our next destination is the once-mighty Guildford Castle, before forging north and pausing at a roadside memorial to an infamous Hertfordshire criminal.

Having marvelled at two huge hangars and discovered the airfield from which the R101 airship began its ill-fated maiden voyage in 1930, we hear how her captain returned from the dead to recount the final moments of his vessel. After pausing at a delightful old inn to learn of the murderous exploits of a landlord long ago, we forge west in search of the forlorn phantom bride who haunts the notorious Hell Fire Caves. Our southeastern journey ends at Breamore House, where a series of tragic events occurred in the 17th century, leaving an indelible stain on the fabric of this beautiful Elizabethan mansion.

50 BERKELEY SQUARE

LONDON

ABOVE: *Berkeley Square is one of London's most sought-after addresses, but it is also the home of the city's most haunted house*

The Most Haunted House in London

When you catch your first glimpse of the plain Georgian exterior of No. 50 Berkeley Square, there is little to suggest that the very mention of the house once evoked feelings of fear and fascination in equal measure.

The building is now home to Maggs Bros, the antiquarian booksellers. Once inside, you find yourself almost cocooned in a time warp, with sweeping stairs, high plaster ceilings, overmantel mirrors, marble floors and fireplaces imbuing the interior with an aura of times long gone. As you absorb the atmosphere that the house undoubtedly possesses, it seems impossible to conceive that it was once plagued by happenings so sinister that, for much of the late 19th and early 20th centuries, No. 50 Berkeley Square was universally known as the most haunted house in London.

Indeed, such was the house's sinister reputation that no one could be found to take on the lease, and so for many years in the late 19th century, it stood empty. In 1879, the magazine *Mayfair* published an article about the house, commenting that its windows were 'caked and blackened by dust' and telling how it was 'full of silence and emptiness… with no notice about it anywhere that it may be had for renting…' The article goes on to tell of several terrifying incidents that reputedly occurred at the property. One concerned a man who moved into the house with his two teenage daughters, the eldest of whom immediately complained of a strange musty smell, rather like that of animal cages at a zoo. Shortly after their arrival, the elder girl's fiancé was due to visit and a maidservant was sent to prepare his room. No sooner had she gone upstairs to do so than the household heard frantic screams. The maid was found collapsed on the floor of the room, crying softly in a trembling, terrified voice, 'Don't let it touch me'. No one was able to ascertain exactly what 'it' was, however, as the unfortunate girl died in hospital the following day.

Charles Harper in *Haunted Houses*, published in 1907, told of a 'sceptical and practical' man who, before retiring to bed in the haunted room, gave instructions to the rest of the household that if, in the dead of night, he were to ring the bell once, they were to take no notice, as he might simply be a little nervous without due cause. But, if he were to ring twice, they must rush to his assistance immediately. So saying, he retired to bed. All was quiet at first, but when the clock chimed midnight, there was a single ring on the bell. As per the man's instructions, the household ignored it, but suddenly the bell began to jangle furiously. Racing to his room, they found the man in convulsions of terror. Like the maidservant before him, he was unable to say what he had seen and died shortly after.

Certainly something has been lurking in the ether at 50 Berkeley Square for many years and, although the ghosts are no longer as threatening as they appear to have been in the past, they are certainly still present. The apparition of a girl in a plaid dress has been glimpsed on the stairs, a column of brown mist has been seen in a room on the very top floor, while cleaners at the building often complain of a sensation of being watched by unseen eyes.

50 Berkeley Square	
London W1 5BA	
Haunted Rating	

BELOW: *The house is now home to the antiquarian booksellers Maggs Bros Ltd*

CHURCHILL MUSEUM AND CABINET WAR ROOMS

LONDON

ABOVE: *Up-to-the-minute office equipment in the Administration Room of the Cabinet War Rooms, where time stands still at 4.58pm*
RIGHT: *The Cabinet War Room*

The Bunker where it's always 4.58pm

Beneath the streets of Westminster in London, there is a vast labyrinth of rooms and passages, whose origins go back to 1938, when war with Germany was becoming very likely. Realizing that war would include prolonged attacks from the air, military strategists set about planning an underground refuge from which the War Cabinet and the Chiefs of Staff could direct operations.

A set of storerooms under a government building in Whitehall was made fit for purpose, and on Sunday, 27 August 1939, one week before the outbreak of World War II, the Cabinet War Rooms became fully operational. For the next six years, protected from falling bombs by concrete 1.5m (5ft) thick, an army of civil servants, government ministers, military strategists and even the Prime Minister, Winston Churchill, lived a troglodyte existence, waging a round-the-clock war on Germany.

One of the first rooms to greet visitors today is the Cabinet War Room. 'This is the room from which I will lead the war,' Winston Churchill declared when he visited it for the first time in May 1940. At first, however, he wasn't particularly keen on skulking underground, preferring instead to lead from the thick of the action above ground.

Churchill Museum and Cabinet War Rooms

King Charles Street, London
SW1A 2AQ

www.cwr.iwm.org.uk

Haunted Rating

Chemical Toilets and Chamber Pots

On 14 October 1940, a huge bomb damaged 10 Downing Street and fell uncomfortably close to the underground War Rooms. 'Pity it wasn't a bit nearer so that we might have tested our defences,' Churchill observed nonchalantly. The next day, though, the War Cabinet met in the underground War Room, and over the next five years held no fewer than 115 further meetings there. However, Churchill continued to insist on being in the thick of the action and, when the bombs started falling, he would exasperate those charged with his protection by hurrying to the roof of the building above to observe the destruction first hand.

For the ordinary men and women who worked here, conditions were cramped and facilities minimal. There was no sewage system, so occupants had to make do with chemical toilets and chamber pots, while washing facilities consisted of buckets and bowls. Vermin, such as rats and mice, were an ever-present nuisance, and the fact that the smoking ban in the workplace lay some 60 years in the future meant that people went about their duties immersed in a fug of cigarette and cigar smoke.

In August 1945, with the war over, the lights in the War Rooms were switched off for the first time in six years, the doors were locked and the huge bunker fell silent.

RIGHT: Churchill's bedroom

ABOVE: *The hub of underground operations was the Map Room*

Since the 1980s, the warren of corridors and cramped rooms has been open to the public. As they have been preserved more or less exactly as they were during the war, you get the eerie sense that the uniformed men and women of the war years have merely nipped out for a tea break and will be back at any moment.

It is a place where time literally stands still – all the clocks are frozen at 4.58pm, the time at which the War Cabinet met here for the first time on 15 October 1940. Yet the hands of one of the clocks have been known to move mysteriously to a different time, and no one has ever discovered why. Many employees at the War Rooms today complain of feelings of unease, while phantom cigarette smoke has been smelt. Spectral footfall is sometimes heard echoing along the corridors, and the imprint of a military-style boot has occasionally appeared on the freshly waxed floors.

For some of those dedicated men and women who faced the might of Nazi Germany from deep beneath the streets of Westminster, it would seem that the war still goes on.

THEATRE ROYAL

LONDON

Sir Patrick Stewart

Waiting for Buckstone

During a performance of Waiting for Godot *at London's Theatre Royal, Haymarket in 2009, Sir Patrick Stewart came offstage during the interval and told his co-star, Sir Ian McKellen, 'I just saw a ghost, on stage, during Act One.' Nigel Everett, a director of the theatre, later commented that 'Patrick… was stunned. I would not say frightened, but I would say impressed.'*

According to Stewart the apparition was that of a man who was standing in the wings wearing what looked like a beige coat and twill trousers. The consensus among stage hands was that Sir Patrick had seen the ghost of John Baldwin Buckstone (1802–1879), who had a long association with the Theatre Royal in the 19th century, first as a comic actor, then as a playwright and finally as its actor–manager from 1853 to 1877, during which time he staged some 200 productions, pioneered the concept of the afternoon matinée, and transformed the house into the leading comic theatre of the day.

Buckstone was a great friend of Charles Dickens (1812–1870), who once confessed that, as a boy, he had been so moved by Buckstone's performances that he went home to 'dream of his comicalities.' In 1857, Ellen Ternan, the young actress who was said to have been Dickens' mistress, appeared at the theatre in Buckstone's burlesque *Atalanta*. Dickens appears to have been instrumental in obtaining this and other roles for her since he wrote to Buckstone, 'I shall always regard your remembering her as an act of personal friendship ... on the termination of the present engagement, I hope you will tell me, before you tell her, what you see for her coming in the future.'

Although Buckstone didn't die in the building (he died at home in Kent), his ghost made the first of its returns to the Theatre Royal, Haymarket within a year of his death. Since then, several illustrious theatrical figures have seen his spectral form in parts of the building, where he seems to appear whenever comedies are being staged.

Sir Donald Sinden saw him while playing in *The Heiress* with Ralph Richardson in 1949. As Sir Donald and the actress Gill Cadell were coming down the stairs from their dressing rooms *en route* to the stage, they passed the solid figure of a man dressed in an old-fashioned dark suit looking out of the window into Suffolk Street, which is located at the back of the theatre. Since this was the floor where Ralph Richardson's dressing room was located, they presumed it was him, bade him 'Good evening Ralph,' and, on receiving no reply, continued on their way towards the stage. But, having descended one flight, they suddenly realized that Richardson should be on stage at that moment. Hurrying back up to see why he wasn't, they were surprised to find the figure had gone. Indeed, there was no sign of the man anywhere.

Buckstone's ghost was also seen by the actress Fiona Fullerton while she was performing in an Oscar Wilde play. People passing what was once the Number One Dressing Room, which had been Buckstone's room, but which is now the manager's office, have heard someone rehearsing their lines within. But when they open the door the room is always found to be empty.

Theatre Royal

Haymarket, London
SW1Y 4HT

www.trh.co.uk

Haunted Rating 👤👤👤👤👤

Sir Donald Sinden

CHISLEHURST CAVES

KENT

The Ghostly Challenge

Chislehurst Caves are, in fact, a series of mines consisting of over 20 miles (32km) of interconnecting passages from which people have been extracting chalk and flint for over 5,000 years. They can be explored only on guided tours and, to illuminate their way, visitors are provided with oil lamps, the flickering flames of which cast strange shadows across the walls, contributing enormously to the overall creepiness of the place.

The caves are divided into three parts – Saxon, Druid and Roman – each section named for the reputed ages of the workings. There is a metal drum in the Druid section, which, when struck, sends a thunderous boom echoing through the caves for a full 39 seconds, causing many an unsuspecting visitor to jump out of their skin.

During World War II, the caves provided an ideal air-raid shelter and, over the course of the war, thousands of people sought safety in their depths. To make their stay more comfortable, amenities such as a church (which is still consecrated) and a hospital were installed. Following the war, the caves were used to grow mushrooms, then, in the 1960s and '70s, they became a concert and dance venue. They have long been a popular tourist attraction and, more recently, provided the location where many of the subterranean scenes in the popular television drama *Merlin* were filmed.

The Haunted Pool

Needless to say, with such a long history the caves have had plenty of time to acquire some spectral residents in its labyrinth of dark and creepy tunnels. One of these is the ghost of a girl who was, reputedly, killed in 1939 when she and her brother were attempting to dig their own entrance into the caves, only to have it collapse onto them. Her spirit now makes occasional returns in the early morning, and guides sometimes hear her childish giggles reverberating from the depths of the caves before they open for the day. Some visitors return from their tours to enquire about the crying child, whose sobs they have heard echoing from the darkness.

The Haunted Pool is one part of the caves that visitors have little need to enquire as to whether or not it is haunted. A ghostly white lady, who was supposedly murdered here a long time ago, has been known to emerge through a mist from the bottom of the pool to frighten many an observer witless. Several visitors have found this a truly troubling spot and have asked to be led away from it within seconds of arriving.

The chamber in which the pool is located was once the location for the infamous Chislehurst Challenge – a reward was offered to anyone brave enough to spend a night alone there. Tradition maintains that the last person to accept the challenge was terrified when the ghostly white lady suddenly emerged from the pool and all his candles were blown out. Gripped by panic, he ran for the entrance, only to knock himself out on the roof of a low passage. He was still unconscious when he was found the next morning. Since then the challenge has been withdrawn.

All in all, Chislehurst Caves are interesting, mysterious and most certainly very creepy. There is something about the atmosphere that sets your nerves on edge, and you really do feel the need to stay close to the tour group as you explore the subterranean maze. It is a place to enjoy but not to linger in alone.

Chislehurst Caves

Chislehurst, Kent
BR7 5NL

www.chislehurstcaves.co.uk

Haunted Rating 🎃🎃🎃🎃🎃

The start of the Druid Maze at Chislehurst Caves

HASTINGS CASTLE

EAST SUSSEX

Hastings Castle
Hastings, East Sussex
Haunted Rating 👤👤👤👤👤

Revenants on the Ramparts

Hastings Castle was the first Norman castle to be constructed in England by William of Normandy after his victory at the Battle of Hastings in 1066. The original structure was a wooden fort but, in 1070, William granted the town of Hastings to Robert, Count of Eu, who replaced it with a substantial stone castle. Inside the castle, he established the Collegiate Church of St Mary. The Counts of Eu held the castle for most of the Norman period, and it became a place of great strategic importance, guarding the port of Hastings, which was the point of embarkation and disembarkation for those travelling between England and Normandy.

There was always the danger that the castle might fall into the hands of the French, and it was this fear that led King John to order its dismantling in 1216. John died that same year, and his son, Henry III, recognizing its importance, ordered it to be rebuilt in 1220.

However, the French and the weather combined saw to it that the days of glory of this impressive fortress were short-lived – just how impressive Hastings Castle must have been can be gleaned from the

Sunset over Hastings Castle and pier

ragged vestiges that still survive. In 1287, violent storms that had been battering the south coast of England for several months finally caused parts of the sandstone cliffs on which the castle stood to collapse into the sea, taking the tower and large sections of the walls with them. Furthermore, the silting up of the harbour led to its decline in strategic importance, and Hastings became a fishing village instead of a port.

During the Hundred Years' War (1337–1453) between England and France, the town was twice attacked by the French, while the erosion of the cliffs continued and more of the castle was lost to the sea. The final blow was dealt by Henry VIII during the Dissolution of the Monasteries, when the Collegiate Church of St Mary inside the castle was dissolved. The castle was abandoned and the site sold to the Pelham family, who used it as farmland. Gradually, the once-mighty walls disappeared beneath a dense carpet of bracken, weed and other vegetation. By the early 1800s, it was little more than a distant memory.

In 1824, the fragmented remains were excavated, then repaired and rebuilt, and the site became a popular tourist attraction. Following bomb damage during World War II, the castle was sold to Hastings Council, and today visitors from all over the world come to absorb its atmosphere and admire what remains.

Inevitably, with a building of this age, the spirits of those who lived here long ago have been known to cross the paths of modern-day visitors. Occasionally, the apparition of a woman in a brown-hooded cloak has been seen on West Hill below the castle. According to some accounts, she carries a baby in her arms. She makes her way towards the south wall of the castle and, on reaching it, she and the baby simply melt into the stonework. Some hold that she is the ghost of a Victorian girl who had an affair with a fisherman, who then abandoned her. Unable to bear the shame, she killed herself and the baby, since when their ghosts have made periodic returns to relive the tragic event.

PRESTON MANOR

EAST SUSSEX

The Restless Bones

At first glance, Preston Manor might not strike you as the typical haunted house of tradition. In fact, far from giving off an aura of sinister foreboding, the house seems to bask in the splendour of Edwardian opulence. But as you delve deeper into the atmospheric interior, the mood begins to change. So much so that, by the time you've explored the house fully, you come away with the distinct impression that the ghosts of former residents have possibly been watching your every step. It then comes as no surprise to learn that Preston Manor is one of Brighton's most haunted houses.

Preston Manor experienced its heyday in the early 20th century. It still retains an aura of formal Edwardian grandeur

The present building dates from 1738, although it stands on the site of a much older property, which was originally owned by the Bishops of Chichester. The present-day appearance of the house came about in 1905. The then owner, Ellen Thomas-Stanford, commissioned the architect Charles Stanley Peach to turn the house into a grand Edwardian villa, where she could entertain eminent guests such as Queen Victoria's daughters, the Princesses Beatrice and Helena, and the author Rudyard Kipling.

Ellen married twice, and was constantly at odds with her son John from her first marriage. He made no secret of his intention to turn the house into a girls' school or sell it for re-development when he finally inherited it. Horrified at what might become of their beloved home, Ellen and her second husband Charles bequeathed the house to Brighton Borough Council. The council took it over following their deaths in 1932 and opened it as a museum. Today, Preston Manor remains frozen in time – its rooms have changed little since the days when the great, the good and the obscenely rich of Edwardian society came to enjoy the lavish hospitality of the Thomas-Stanfords.

The White Lady

Over the years, a great number of paranormal phenomena have been recorded at Preston Manor. Guests sleeping in the Southwest Room would awake to find a disembodied hand moving up and down one of the bed posts. A new silk dress left hanging in this same room was found to have diamond-shaped tears slashed into its fabric. In addition, strange noises and muffled footsteps have been heard shuffling along corridors in the dead of night.

Preston Manor's most famous ghost was that of the white lady, whose appearances, reputedly, go back to at least the 16th century. Her heyday was the 1890s, when she was apparently seen at least once a month. In 1896, Ellen Thomas-Stanford's half-sister, Lily Macdonald, was fitting a shade onto a lamp in the drawing room when she turned to find a lady in a white dress, with long flowing hair and a deathly pallor, walking towards her. Silently the apparition drifted past, continued through the billiard room, then paused at the foot of the stairs. At this point, the fearless Lily attempted to put her arm around the lady, only to have the apparition pass straight through her.

Determined to learn more about their ghostly house guest, on 11 November 1896, the family held a seance and made contact with the spirit of a nun called Sister Agnes. She claimed to have suffered the indignity of being excommunicated by the church for a transgression she had not committed. As a result, she had been buried in unconsecrated ground outside the house, a fact that meant she was unable to find eternal rest.

On 29 January 1897, workmen carrying out repairs on a drain close to the south terrace of the manor uncovered the skeleton of a woman. A doctor who examined it pronounced that it was several hundred years old. The bones were reburied in the churchyard, which still sits in the grounds of Preston Manor. A year to the day after the discovery of the bones, another seance was held. Sister Agnes came through to say that she was now happy to be lying in consecrated ground and she would trouble the family no more.

Nevertheless, her ghost appears to have been replaced by that of a grey lady who has been seen descending the great staircase. This, coupled with other phenomena such as lights turning off of their own volition, ensures that Preston Manor's reputation as one of Brighton's most haunted buildings is safe for at least the near future.

Preston Manor

Preston Drove,
Preston Park, Brighton
BN1 6SD

Haunted Rating 👻👻👻👻👻

The spirit of a nun was said to haunt the house, unable to rest because she had been buried in unconsecrated ground

Spring-heeled Jack

In September 1837, a businessman heading home late one night across the wilder reaches of Barnes Common, just outside London, was suddenly startled by a hideous-looking figure. Bounding over some high railings, it landed with a thud right in front of him. Although the creature did him no harm, one look at its pointed ears, glowing eyes and prominent nose was enough to send the businessman fleeing from the scene in terror.

A month after the initial attack, a servant girl by the name of Mary Stevens was returning to the house where she worked in Lavender Hill, on the outskirts of south London, after visiting her parents in Battersea. As she walked over Clapham Common, a hideous creature leapt out at her from a dark alley. Grabbing hold of the terrified girl, the creature started kissing her face, while ripping her clothes and touching her flesh with its claws, which according to a statement that she made later, were 'cold and clammy as those of a corpse'. The girl's terrified screams caused the creature to flee into the night and brought local residents racing to the scene. But, despite a thorough search, no sign of the hideous entity could be found.

The next day the creature launched another assault near the Mary Stevens house in Lavender Hill. Leaping out in front of a carriage, it caused the coachman to lose control of his horses, which bolted in terror. The carriage then crashed, seriously injuring the coachman. Witnesses claimed that the monster had escaped by leaping over a 2.7-m (9-ft) high wall while emitting an ear-piercing, high-pitched peal of laughter.

As the attacks grew more frequent and word of them reached a wider audience via newspaper reports, the public at large nicknamed the creature Spring-heeled Jack, and a Victorian legend was well and truly born.

LEFT: *Spring-heeled Jack, a devil-like character of English urban legend, makes an appearance to a terrified chimneysweep*

A Victorian Legend

On 9 January 1838, the Lord Mayor of London, Sir John Cowan, made public a letter he had received a few days before from an anonymous complainant. The letter told how a group of noblemen had dared a 'mischievous and foolhardy companion' to appear in villages near London in three different disguises – a ghost, a bear and a Devil. Having accepted the wager, this individual had 'deprived seven ladies of their senses, two of whom are not likely to recover'.

At first, the Lord Mayor was inclined to scepticism, but a member of the audience announced that maidservants in Kensington, Hammersmith and Ealing were telling 'dreadful stories of this ghost or devil'. More letters were received, telling of attacks by the mysterious fiend, and the search began for whomever was responsible.

One night in February 1838, Jane Alsop answered the door of her father's house in Bearhind Lane, Bow in East London, to a man claiming to be a police officer. Breathlessly, the man, who was wearing a large cloak, told her to fetch a light and follow him, 'for we have caught Spring-heeled Jack'. Fetching a candle, she handed it to the man and followed him away from the house. They had gone only a short distance when the man suddenly threw off his cloak, and Jane found herself confronted by a hideous creature with eyes like 'red balls of fire', who proceeded to belch blue and white flames at her. Grabbing hold of her, he then started tearing at her clothes with his claws, which, as she later reported, were 'of some metallic substance'. Wriggling free of his clutches, she ran screaming back towards the house, only for the creature to catch her on the doorstep and scratch her neck and arms. Fortunately, her sister came running to her rescue and the creature fled.

Not long afterwards, 18-year-old Lucy Scales and her sister Margaret were walking home along Narrow Street, in Limehouse, East London, when the same creature leapt out at them from a dark alley and spat blue flames into Lucy's eyes, blinding her. Witnesses later claimed that Spring-heeled Jack had then leapt from the ground onto the roof of a nearby house and escaped over the rooftops.

The cases of Jane Alsop and Lucy Scales caused a sensation when reported in the press, and panic-stricken Londoners began to form vigilance committees in an attempt to catch the attacker.

Over the next few years, Spring-heeled Jack became one of the most popular characters of his age. Stories about his exploits appeared in the so-called 'Penny Dreadful' pamphlets and magazines, and plays about him were performed at low-class theatres.

As his fame increased, so the attacks decreased and the panic began to subside. A series of sightings across the country in 1843 caused a resurgence of the scare, and throughout the 19th century and on into the early 20th century appearances were reported in locations as far apart as Devon, Lincolnshire, Birmingham and Liverpool. However, by that time the public's fear of the demonic creature had waned.

Although no one was ever brought to justice for the crimes, a plausible suspect for the original attacks was thought to be Henry Beresford, 3rd Marquess of Waterford. He was renowned for his drunken antics, sadistic practical jokes and pathological dislike of women. Physically he most certainly resembled witness descriptions of Spring-heeled Jack, even down to having large protruding eyes, one of the creature's most prominent characteristics, according to his victims. Although his death in 1859 would exclude him from being responsible for the later attacks, he is certainly a likely contender for having created the leaping, fire-breathing devil that brought terror and panic to the citizens of 19th-century London.

Penny Dreadful Magazines

The 'Penny Dreadfuls' were 19th-century magazines specializing in shocking serial stories. They were printed on poor-quality paper and aimed primarily at the expanding urban working classes from the 1830s onwards; hence each edition cost just one penny. Some editions were based on reworkings of classic tales, while others introduced contemporary characters such as Varney the Vampire and the London folk demon Spring-heeled Jack.

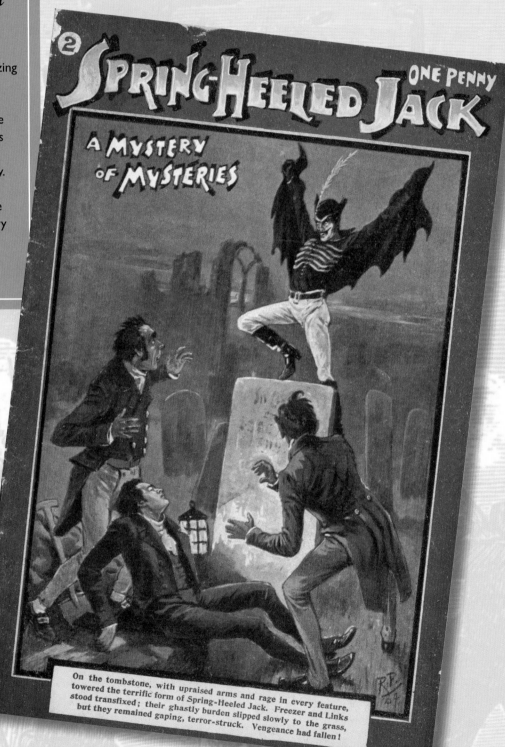

On the tombstone, with upraised arms and rage in every feature, towered the terrific form of Spring-Heeled Jack. Freezer and Links stood transfixed; their ghastly burden slipped slowly to the grass, but they remained gaping, terror-struck. Vengeance had fallen!

GUILDFORD CASTLE

SURREY

A Ghostly Keepsake

Although a castle was probably built in Guildford shortly after the Norman Conquest of 1066, all that remains of the earlier fortress is the motte on which the current castle keep was built, probably in the early 12th century. Initially, the keep would have been a valued stronghold intended to protect the strategically important route between London and the south coast as the Normans tightened their grip on their newly conquered dominion.

In the late 12th century, the keep became the sheriff's headquarters and was pressed into service as the jail for Surrey and Sussex. Many of those incarcerated here were accused of serious crimes, such as murder, and were held within the mighty castle walls pending the arrival of the courts to hear their cases. Those found guilty were returned to the keep to await execution.

The keep remained a jail until the early 1600s, when prisoners were locked away elsewhere. Thereafter, the castle fell into disrepair. In the late 19th century, the then owner, Lord Grantley of Wonersh, sold it to Guildford Corporation, which opened the grounds as a pleasure park in 1888. During a massive restoration project between 2003 and 2004, the floors and a roof were added to the building for the first time in over 400 years. During this work, the original battlements and other features were rediscovered.

Emaciated Figure

The renovation work appears to have also disturbed the slumbers of some of the castle's earlier reluctant residents. Families entering the ground-floor area have come running out, carrying their children who are almost hysterical. The children, it transpires, have been frightened by an emaciated figure that they have seen chained to the walls. Philip Hutchinson, the castle's custodian, who also operates the popular Guildford Ghost Walk, explains that the children, who had no previous knowledge of the history of the keep, have seen the figure in the area where the prisoners were most certainly kept. 'On many occasions,' he continues, 'fetters were ordered so that prisoners could be chained to the walls.'

Philip, too, has experienced inexplicable phenomena at the castle. In February 2008, while getting the inside of the keep ready for the upcoming summer season, he left the keep to take his lunch break. Leaving all the lights and heaters on to warm the interior after the long winter closure, he shut the door behind him, locking it with a heavy padlock. When he returned, the padlock was still locked but all the lights and heaters inside had been switched off. No one, as far as he could ascertain, had entered the room while he had been away.

The keep at Guildford Castle is a special place, with the mark of history most certainly daubed across its time-scarred walls. The fact that the spirits of some of those associated with its rich and diverse past apparently still linger here makes a visit essential by all those who wish to experience a location that is both haunted and haunting.

RIGHT: Guildford Castle, floodlit by night

Guildford Castle

Guildford, Surrey
GU1 3SX

Haunted Rating 🔑🔑🔑🔑🔑

CLIBBON'S POST

HERTFORDSHIRE

The Never-Ending Journey

As you drive along the delightful country road that runs between Datchworth and Bramfield, having passed through the tiny settlement of Bull's Green, you come across a solitary wooden post by the side of the road, surrounded by encroaching woodland. Should you pause to inspect the post, you will see the words 'Clibbon's Post' carved into it, along with the date 28.12.1782. It marks the site where Walter Clibbon, one of 18th-century Hertfordshire's most notorious villains, was killed and, reputedly, lies buried.

Walter Clibbon and his three sons were piemen, who sold their wares at markets and fairs throughout the county. But, as well as filling the bellies of hungry market- and fair-goers, they operated a lucrative sideline. Eavesdropping on customers' conversations, they would ascertain which tradesmen and farmers had made money that day and would therefore be carrying substantial sums on their journey home. Having identified their targets, the Clibbons would change into the garb of highwaymen and ambush them as they made their way along the lonely roads of Hertfordshire. Any victims who resisted were subjected to a vicious beating.

The Clibbon brood finally got their comeuppance on 28 December 1782, when they accosted a young Datchworth man by the name of William Whittenbury as he made his way through the woods close to the spot where the post now stands. Whittenbury handed over his cash without resistance but then hurried to the home of his uncle, Benjamin Whittenbury, at nearby Queen Hoo Hall to raise the alarm.

Uncle and nephew, together with a servant named Shock North, armed themselves with a gun and headed back to the woods, where they found the Clibbons awaiting another victim. A fight ensued, during the course of which the Whittenburys and their servant proved no match for these seasoned veterans of villainy. As the skirmish turned against them, Benjamin Whittenbury was felled by a blow and, with Walter

Clibbon moving in for the kill, he shouted to his servant to fire. North pulled the trigger and Walter Clibbon fell to the ground. One of his sons then fled the scene but the other was overpowered, taken prisoner and later executed.

One version of the story maintains that Walter Clibbon was killed instantly, another that he survived and was tied behind a horse and dragged to nearby Bull's Green, where the locals meted out their own rough justice by clubbing him to death.

What both versions agree on, however, is that his body was then taken to the spot where he fell, and he was buried with the wooden post driven through his heart to prevent his spirit from wandering. Since then the post has been replaced several times, and it must be said that the current one looks a little the worse for wear and age. It hasn't proved particularly successful either at preventing the restless wraith of Walter Clibbon from roaming the area. Indeed, those who are brave – or foolish – enough to walk along this lonely stretch of country road, when darkness has fallen, have from time to time heard a horse's hooves. Some even claim to have witnessed a spectral horse dragging a body along the lane, as the infamous pieman is condemned to relive his last journey over and over again.

Clibbon's Post

Bramfield Road,
near Datchworth,
Hertfordshire

Haunted Rating 👻👻👻👻👻

LEFT: An old illustration showing a man being robbed, having his hands tied behind his back and being forced to sit backwards on his horse

CARDINGTON HANGARS

BEDFORDSHIRE

Cardington Hangars
Cardington, Bedfordshire
Haunted Rating

The Tragic Captain and the Medium

What do the film Batman, *the entertainers Paul McCartney and Rod Stewart and the R101 airship disaster of 1930 have in common? The answer is the Cardington Hangars. Built in 1917, these two massive structures dominate the surrounding countryside. Now a decrepit, rusting hulk, Hangar 1 is most certainly showing its age, but Hangar 2 was recently restored for use as a theatrical set by Warner Bros. You can gauge its enormity by the fact that Gotham City was constructed inside it for the films* Batman Begins *and* The Dark Knight! *What's more, Paul McCartney and Rod Stewart have both used its vast interior for concert rehearsals.*

However, Cardington is indelibly linked with one of British aviation's greatest disasters. It was inside the immense interior of Hangar 1 that the R101 airship was constructed in the late 1920s, and from the airfield outside that she set off on her maiden voyage in 1930 – a journey that was destined to end in disaster.

At the time of its completion, the R101 was the largest man-made object ever to fly and was intended as a symbol of Britain's engineering prowess. For her maiden voyage, which was scheduled for 28 September 1930, it was decided that she should fly the then Secretary for Air, Lord Thomson, and several other dignitaries to Karachi and back. On his return, Thomson would then be able to trumpet the superiority of British technology to Commonwealth heads of state at the Imperial Conference, due to take place in London

Cardington Airship Hangars

on 20 October 1930. He, therefore, wasn't best pleased when technical setbacks, coupled with adverse weather conditions, meant that her maiden flight had to be delayed. With the conference date rapidly approaching, Thomson grew ever more impatient, and official pressure was brought to bear on the crew and technical staff. Despite the fact that several of them had grave reservations about her worthiness for such a long flight, at 6.24pm on 4 October 1930, the R101 set out on her maiden voyage under the command of Flight Lieutenant H. Carmichael Irwin. On board were 54 crew and passengers, including Lord Thomson and Sir Sefton Brankner, the Director of Civil Aviation.

In the early hours of 5 October, after flying over Beauvais, northwest of Paris, the R101 suddenly dived twice, then crashed in flames, killing 48 of the people on board. They now lie buried in a communal grave in Cardington Cemetery, across the field from the giant hangar where the R101 was constructed and from where they left on the ill-fated voyage.

The hangars and the airfield have long been reputed to be haunted by crew members of the R101. Security guards patrolling the site at night have encountered all manner of inexplicable phenomena, while their dogs often behave very strangely around the giant hangars. Even in daylight, the hangars can give off an oppressive and eerie aura.

The disaster is renowned in spiritualist circles for another reason. Several days after the disaster, a group of people gathered at the National Laboratory of Psychical Research in London to attend a seance with the medium Eileen Garrett. Their intention was to contact Sir Arthur Conan Doyle, who had died three months before. However, instead of the spirit of Conan Doyle, Garrett reached the dead captain of the R101, who went into a great deal of technical detail about the ship and the cause of the crash. When news of the seance appeared in the press, it caused a sensation. Several military officials took an interest, among them Major Oliver Villiers, who attended several further seances with Garrett. At these meetings, Irwin and other passengers and crew came through to provide details of the final moments of the R101. Villiers was so convinced that he had communicated with Irwin that he presented the evidence he had gathered at the seances to Sir John Simon, who was heading the investigation into the disaster. Simon, however, rejected it on the grounds that testimony from the dead was inadmissible in a court of law.

Perhaps the last word, though, should go to Major G.H. Scott, another crewman who perished in the disaster. In the course of one seance, he announced, 'Villiers, it's all too ghastly for words. It's awful. Think of all the lives, experience, money, material. All thrown away. What for? Nothing.'

THE OSTRICH

BERKSHIRE

Mein Murderous Host

The Ostrich claims to be the UK's third oldest inn, an assertion that's far less likely to provoke a challenge than if it declared itself the oldest. Originally called The Hospice, the inn was founded in 1106 by Milo Crispin 'for the good of travellers in this world and the salvation of their souls in the next'. Its name was later changed to The Crane, then to The Ostrich. As The Ostrich, it has the distinction of being the first pub in England to feature in a novel: Thomas of Reading, written in 1597 by Thomas Deloney. The book immortalized the exploits of a former landlord of the inn called Jarman. He was so determined to fulfil Crispin's founding sentiments concerning the salvation of the souls of 'good travellers' in the next world that he speeded their progress into it when they availed themselves of his unique brand of hospitality.

Jarman's crimes are said to have taken place around the 1300s, at a time when wealthy travellers would stop off at his inn to change from their mud-spattered clothes into the finery expected for appearances at nearby Windsor Castle. In those days, travellers carried their cash with them, a fact that led Jarman and his wife to devise a cunningly profitable method of relieving his guests of their money and their lives.

Whenever an affluent guest arrived, Jarman would ply them with strong drink and, once they had retired to bed, allow time for them to fall asleep. What the guests didn't realize was that their bed was situated over a trap door and that the familiar sensation of falling usually experienced just before dropping off to sleep was, on this occasion, actually happening – Jarman had undone the bolts of the trap, causing the foot of the bed to drop suddenly, pitching the guest through the opening into the kitchen below. Here, Mrs Jarman kept a large cauldron of water constantly on the boil so that the unfortunate guest had no time even to cry out before being dunked, scalded and drowned.

Their murderous career came to an end when the Jarmans befriended a well-known clothier by the name of Thomas Cole, who entrusted them to look after a rather large sum of money. According to one account, they asked him to write a will in their favour one night before he retired to bed – a request that would, doubtless, have caused him to smell a very large rat. However, all accounts agree that, once Cole was sound asleep, the Jarmans employed their usual method of despatching him.

Unfortunately for them, Cole's horse was found wandering the streets, and a search was launched for its owner. Cole's body was found in a nearby brook. Since he had last been seen entering The Ostrich, Jarman and his wife were questioned and they confessed all. On the gallows, Jarman is said to have boasted of murdering more than 60 people, although the actual total was probably no more than 15.

Today, several ghosts that roam the premises may or may not be linked to Jarman's murderous exploits. A woman in a grey dress appears on an upstairs corridor, sometimes accompanied by sundry shadowy figures. Staff are often troubled by the sinister atmosphere that seems to hang over certain sections of the inn, while several landlords have complained of being woken at night by the eerie sound of creaking boards, ghostly sighs and spectral bumps.

The Ostrich

Colnbrook, Berkshire
SL3 0JZ

www.theostrichcolnbrook.co.uk

Haunted Rating

LEFT: *The main turret of nearby Windsor Castle seen over trees in the Great Park*
ABOVE: *The ghost of a man, murdered for his money, haunts the house where he was buried by his murderers*

HELL FIRE CAVES

Hell Fire Caves

West Wycombe,
Buckinghamshire
HP14 4EQ

www.hellfirecaves.co.uk

Haunted Rating 👻👻👻👻👻

The Bride Wore White to Her Death

In the 18th century, Sir Francis Dashwood set out to alleviate the poverty of the villagers living in the area around his family seat at West Wycombe Park. By employing local men to excavate a series of tunnels into the hill opposite his house, he earned the villagers' undying gratitude. They were then only too willing to turn a blind eye to the completed caves and passages being used by him and his fellow aristocrats for meeting like-minded ladies, specially brought in to participate in the rites, rituals and general drunken cavorting of what became known as the Hell Fire Club.

Today, you can still explore these caves and, although drunken cavorting is generally frowned upon, there is a chance you might encounter the phantoms of those who frolicked here in the past.

The best known of the Hell Fire Caves ghosts is that of Sukie, a girl in a white dress, whose appearances are so prolific that the title of 'resident ghost' has long been bestowed upon her. Tradition holds that Sukie was a servant girl who worked at The George and Dragon in the

BELOW: The Banqueting Hall, Hell Fire Caves

nearby village of West Wycombe in the 18th century. Three local boys were much taken with the pretty maid and vied with each other for her attention. But Suki had set her sights on becoming the mistress of an aristocrat and told these would-be suitors in no uncertain terms that she had no intention wasting herself on the likes of them.

One day an obviously wealthy young man arrived at the inn and seemed quite taken with Sukie. Spotting her chance to escape a life of drudgery, she promptly set about ensnaring him. Soon the handsome young buck was besotted with her and began paying daily visits to the inn. This so irked the three rejected suitors that they decided to teach Sukie a lesson. They composed a letter, which purported to come from her noble suitor, informing her that he wished to elope with her. She was, he instructed, to don a white dress and meet him that night in the West Wycombe Caves. Elated, the unsuspecting Suki dressed accordingly and set off for her rendezvous.

Arriving at the mouth of the caves, she lit a flaming torch and set off into the labyrinth. Hidden behind a large rock, the spurned local men watched her approach and, as she passed them, they grabbed the torch and dashed it to the ground, extinguishing the flame. The terrified girl fled into the darkness of the caves, with her whooping tormentors in hot pursuit. It was then that the prank turned to tragedy. As the frightened girl rounded a corner, she tripped over a rock and hit her head against the cave wall, knocking herself unconscious. Her tormentors summoned help, and the villagers arrived to carry the comatose girl back to her room at The George and Dragon, where she died in the early hours of the next morning.

Sukie's ghost has haunted the caves ever since. Visitors often enquire what time the wedding will take place in the Banqueting Hall of the caves, where they have seen a bride in a white dress.

BREAMORE HOUSE

HAMPSHIRE

Breamore House

Near Fordingbridge,
Hampshire SP6 2DF

www.breamorehouse.com

Haunted Rating 👤👤👤👤👤

The Cursed Portrait and the Ghostly Lady

In January 1600, William Dodington, the then owner of Breamore House, flung himself to his death from the tower of St Sepulchre's church in London. He had become depressed when a legal dispute with his neighbours, the Bulkeleys, went against him. His suicide sent shock waves reverberating through the corridors of power, since, in addition to being a powerful Hampshire landowner, he was also the auditor of the Royal Mint at the Tower of London. His suicide note read, 'John Bulkeley and his fellows by perjury have brought me to this. Surely after they had thus slandered me, everyday that I lived was to me an hundred deaths, which caused me to choose to die with Infamy, than to live with Infamy and Torment.'

His grieving widow, Christian, commissioned a portrait of herself in mourning clothes and had it hung inside the house in the magnificent Great Hall. After she died, a story circulated that as she lay on her death bed, she cursed anyone who dared to move the portrait. Although there is no evidence to support this, no one has dared to test the curse by having it removed from that day to this.

William Dodington's estate eventually passed to his son, also called William, and things seemed to improve for the family when King James I bestowed a knighthood on him when he was crowned in 1603. However, fate was lurking in the wings to heap further ignominy upon the family. William's son, Henry, incensed by his mother scolding him for his dissolute lifestyle, 'drew his sword and ran her twice through, and afterwards, she being dead, gave her many wounds'. Henry was hanged for the crime. His father, Sir William, began to wonder whether his father's suicide, his wife's brutal murder and his son's execution might be punishment from God for the family having built

Breamore House on what had, until the Dissolution of the Monasteries, been monastic land. He, therefore, set about trying to atone for this transgression by doing good works for the church and devoting himself to his public duties. However, his attempts to redeem his family did little good since only one of his sons, John, survived him, but only by six years. The family line died out when John's daughter, Anne, inherited the estate and married Robert Greville, Lord Brooke.

In 1748, the house and estate were purchased by Sir William Hulse, on express condition that the portrait of Christian Dodington was not removed. Sir William passed the house to his son Sir Edward Hulse, 'Physician in Ordinary' to Queen Anne, George I and George II. Sir Edward took up residence in 1760, and successive generations of his family have lived there ever since, with a brief absence during World War II, during which time the house was requisitioned by the US military. Furniture and art treasures were moved out during the American occupation, but even then the portrait of Christian Dodington remained untouched.

The portrait still looks down on visitors from the position high up on a wall that it has occupied since she allegedly placed her curse upon those who would dare disturb her likeness. If the portrait is not sufficient reason for those in search of haunted Britain to pay a visit to Breamore House, there is always the chance of an encounter with the tragic wife of Sir William Dodington. Having been murdered by her deranged son, she still returns in ghostly form to haunt the Blue Room.

ABOVE: *The portrait of Christian Dodington dressed in full mourning clothes, which she commissioned to commemorate the death by suicide of her husband William*

EASTERN ENGLAND

Tread lightly, she is near
Under the snow,
Speak gently, she can hear
The daisies grow.

All her bright golden hair
Tarnished with rust,
She that was young and fair
Fallen to dust.

Lily-like, white as snow,
She hardly knew
She was a woman, so
Sweetly she grew.

Coffin-board, heavy stone,
Lie on her breast;
I vex my heart alone,
She is at rest.

Peace, peace, she cannot hear
Lyre or sonnet,
All my life's buried here,
Heap earth upon it.

Requiescat by Oscar Wilde
(1854–1900)

EASTERN ENGLAND

3

①	COALHOUSE FORT – ESSEX	84
②	ST NICHOLAS CHURCH – ESSEX	86
③	OLIVER CROMWELL'S HOUSE – CAMBRIDGESHIRE	88
④	PETERBOROUGH MUSEUM – CAMBRIDGESHIRE	90
⑤	LANDGUARD FORT – SUFFOLK	92
⑥	CHRISTCHURCH MANSION – SUFFOLK	94
⑦	FELBRIGG HALL, GARDEN AND PARK – NORFOLK	96
⑧	THE MUCKLEBURGH COLLECTION – NORFOLK	98
⑨	THE VINE HOTEL – LINCOLNSHIRE	100
	FEATURE – BLACK SHUCK	102
⑩	GUNBY HALL – LINCOLNSHIRE	106
⑪	YE OLDE WHITE HARTE – HULL	108
⑫	RAF HOLMPTON – EAST YORKSHIRE	112

INTRODUCTION

Much of our eastern journey takes us through the counties that once formed the ancient kingdom of East Anglia. For centuries, this was a remote and mysterious region, its people hardy and resourceful, although prone to superstition. Numerous invaders arrived in England at its shoreline, with Romans, Angles, Saxons and Danes all leaving their mark on the landscape. During World Wars I and II, many of the nation's defences, from airfields to military bases, were located here. It is perhaps inevitable that many of the haunted sites featured in this chapter are connected with these abandoned bases, where people who passed through them in life still linger there in death.

Our journey begins in Essex, where we explore the creepy passageways and subterranean tunnels of Coalhouse Fort, an abandoned 19th-century complex that is home to numerous ghostly goings-on. Moving on through the Essex countryside, we pause at the village of Canewdon, once a renowned centre of witchcraft, where we learn of the legends that swirl around its ancient church. Crossing into Cambridgeshire, we visit Ely to discover the former home of England's Lord Protector, Oliver Cromwell, to which his spirit may still return. To Peterborough next, to encounter the wraiths that roam its truly creepy museum. As we progress through Suffolk, we take in Landguard Fort, where the sad shade of a long-ago lady still mourns her executed husband. Still in Suffolk, our journey takes us to Christchurch Mansion in Ipswich, a lovely old haunted building furnished in the style of several ages. From here, we make our way through Norfolk and Lincolnshire, tracking down ghosts as diverse as an 18th-century bibliophile, a moaning figure heard in the back of a former military ambulance, the 19th-century poet laureate Alfred, Lord Tennyson, and the lovelorn spectres of a girl and a groom. Having stopped off to soak up the spooky atmosphere in one of Hull's oldest pubs, we end our journey in East Yorkshire in a vast underground bunker, where a desk-bound pilot often chills the blood of visitors.

COALHOUSE FORT

ESSEX

Coalhouse Fort

East Tilbury,
Essex RM18 8PB

www.coalhousefort.co.uk

Haunted Rating ☠☠☠☠☠

Terror by the Thames

Opened in 1874 and built on the site of earlier defences, Coalhouse Fort was intended to guard against foreign invasion by way of the River Thames. It was constructed following a recommendation by the 1860 Royal Commission on the Defence of the United Kingdom, which had expressed concerns about a possible French invasion. The chief exponent of the fort-building programme designed to strengthen the country's defences was the then Prime Minister, Lord Palmerston.

This led to the forts being known collectively as Palmerston's Forts. They would become Britain's costliest and most extensive system of fixed defences ever constructed in peacetime. However, by the time Coalhouse was finished in 1874, the forts had been nicknamed Palmerston's Follies, as the threat of a French invasion had waned considerably, largely as a result of the Franco-Prussian War of 1870.

Over the years, a large proportion of these forts has either been demolished or drastically altered, but Coalhouse, although modified and updated, remains largely as it was when it first opened. It is, therefore, one of the finest examples of its kind in Britain.

Creepy Passageways

The fort saw service in both World Wars and remained operational until 1962. It was then closed down and acquired by Thurrock District Council, which surrounded it with a public park and allowed the fort itself to fall into decay. It wasn't until 1983 that a dedicated band of volunteers, concerned at the sorry state of this local landmark, formed the Coalhouse Fort Project and set about restoring it to its former glory. In so doing, they began to wake the spirits of several of those who had passed through it over the years.

A maze of dark, creepy passageways and tunnels snakes their way beneath the fort, and these seem particularly prone to paranormal activity, with all manner of strange occurrences reported. The ghosts of soldiers have been witnessed, white mists have been known to rise and then dissipate in front of astonished onlookers, while phantom footsteps have been heard echoing from the darkness. A huge, dark figure has appeared and sent observers fleeing in terror, while another entity takes a ghoulish delight in grabbing hold of people in the pitch-black and throwing them to the ground. When members of the Ghost Club, the world's oldest organization for psychical research, conducted an overnight investigation at the fort, several members commented on an overpowering smell of garlic that appeared to follow them through the tunnels. Add to all this the alarming drops in temperature that often occur all over the fort, the sound of heavy objects being dragged around rooms that are known to be empty and the chatter of disembodied voices, and you can appreciate why so many who visit this historic landmark agree that it is one of the creepiest places imaginable.

LEFT: Coalhouse Fort is a large casemated fort in East Tilbury. The inset shows its austere exterior, with windows with metal bars set in granite walls

ST NICHOLAS CHURCH

ESSEX

Witches, Ghosts and a Cunning Man

Before the advent of motorized vehicles and public transport, the tiny Essex village of Canewdon was an isolated community, renowned for its associations with witchcraft. In 1580, a local spinster by the name of Rose Pye was accused of bewitching a child to death. She was subsequently acquitted of the crime at the Chelmsford Assizes, but Canewdon's reputation as a haven of witchcraft, demons and ghosts continued to grow.

By the 19th century, legends abounded concerning the village's supernatural connections. Many of those legends centred upon the village church of St Nicholas, a 14th-century building, the tower of which was reputedly added by Henry V, to celebrate his victory at the Battle of Agincourt in 1415. The church stands on a hill, its tower rising majestically over the bleak expanse of wide open Essex countryside that surrounds the village. Notable legends concerning the church state that as long as the tower stands, there will always be six witches in Canewdon, and that whenever a stone falls from the tower, one of those witches will die to be replaced by another. It's also said that if you walk seven times around the church in an anticlockwise direction on Hallowe'en, you will see a witch. If you are brave enough to walk around it 13 times, the Devil will appear. Canewdon has, needless to say, become a popular magnet for thrill-seekers on Hallowe'en, so much so that on 31 October each year the police now close off approaches to the village to all non-residents.

Tradition maintains that, during the 19th century, Canewdon was terrorized by witches. They inflicted locals with ailments and illnesses, released plagues of lice upon them and caused the wheels of their carts not to turn. The 'Master of the Witches' in the late 19th and early 20th centuries was believed to be George Pickingill, a farm labourer and noted local eccentric, supposedly descended from a long line of witches. Pickingill was known as a 'cunning man' who possessed the ability to charm warts away and locate lost property by divining. He died in 1909, apparently at the ripe old age of 105, and was buried in the churchyard. On the day of his funeral, as the hearse drew up outside the church gate, it is said that the horse cantered out of the shafts and trotted off up the lane.

The churchyard of St Nicholas, with its scattered, leaning gravestones and dense vegetation, possesses a strangely subdued air, and it comes as little surprise to learn that it is haunted. Strange lights have been seen flickering over the gravestones when darkness has fallen. The sound of someone chopping wood has been heard echoing from the churchyard in the dead of night. There are also reports of a ghostly lady (in some accounts she is headless; in others she is merely faceless) who has been seen in both the churchyard and hovering over the nearby road.

The churchyard is most certainly an eerie location and well worth a visit by seekers of the supernatural. Just avoid doing so at Hallowe'en. Should you attempt to make the journey along the lonely Essex byways on 31 October, you are likely to encounter a tall living figure in a blue uniform, who will ensure that you don't get close enough to walk around the church tower.

St Nicholas Church

High Street, Canewdon,
Essex SS4 3QA

Haunted Rating 🕯🕯🕯🕯🕯

OLIVER CROMWELL'S HOUSE

CAMBRIDGESHIRE

Echoes of the Past

In 1636, Oliver Cromwell inherited this striking black-and-white timbered building from a maternal uncle, and for the next ten years it was his family home. The family then moved to London where, following the execution of Charles I in January 1649, Cromwell, as Lord Protector, would live in palatial splendour. This was far removed from the cramped living conditions at the Ely house, which he and his wife shared with their six children, Cromwell's two unmarried sisters and his mother.

Since 1990, Cromwell's House has been home to the Ely Tourist Information Centre, which contains a museum telling the story of Cromwell's life and times. One of the rooms is called the 'Haunted Room', so-called because several people have encountered unexplained phenomena in it. The psychically inclined sometimes find it a little overwhelming and have to leave, overcome by a feeling of nausea. Two newspaper reporters who decided to see if they could spend a night in the house found the experience so terrifying that they left before the night was over.

In their book *Haunted Ely*, Vivienne Doughty and Margaret Haynes tell of a disturbing occurrence experienced by a female guest who was staying at the house in April 1979. At the time, the building was a vicarage, and the room above what is now the Tithe Office was used as a guest bedroom. In the early hours, the woman, who was sleeping in the room with her husband, awoke to find herself standing in a corner of the room. Her arms felt like they were being held very tightly in front of her by an invisible male presence. She later recalled that he possessed an indomitable and authoritative personality, yet she didn't feel in the least threatened by him. On the contrary, she felt a distinct bond. Suddenly the man released his grip, and the woman returned to bed where she slept until morning. When she awoke, her arms felt very sore and, on pulling back the bedclothes, she discovered that red finger marks were clearly visible on both her arms. Since the Tithe Office was

RIGHT: It could be that the ghost of Oliver Cromwell himself haunts this timber-framed building that now houses the tourist information centre in Ely, Cambridgeshire

once Oliver Cromwell's office, it has been suggested that the lady may well have encountered the invisible entity of Cromwell himself.

The ghostly activity has continued into the house's latest incarnation as a Tourist Information Centre and Museum. A former member of staff was standing inside one of the dimly lit rooms when he looked down to find that his shoelaces were being untied by an unseen hand. After bending down to retie them, he stood up only to have them untied again. This happened several more times before he decided enough was enough and fled the room.

Other reported supernatural activity includes a female figure disappearing through a wall, footsteps plodding along corridors, strange lights dancing around the rooms, and cold spots. The dark rooms and creaky floorboards at Cromwell's House can be very unnerving, and there is most certainly a sense that those who have lived here in the past are lurking close by as you make your way around its rooms.

Oliver Cromwell's House

29 St Mary's Street,
Ely, Cambridgeshire
CB7 4HF

Haunted Rating ☗☗☗☗

PETERBOROUGH MUSEUM

CAMBRIDGESHIRE

BELOW: Australian soldiers fought on the French front in Vendelles during the Great War. Some, like Thomas Hunter, died far from home in the Peterborough Museum which was, at that time, a hospital

Ghosts on Show

Peterborough Museum occupies a Georgian building, which was built in 1816 and was originally the town house of Thomas and Charlotte Coke. They sold it to the 3rd Earl Fitzwilliam in 1856. A year later, it became the city's first hospital, serving the community until 1928. It was then converted into a museum and opened to the public in 1931.

The museum's only full-time member of staff in those early days was a caretaker by the name of Mr Yarrow. He, his wife and their two sons lived on the premises, occupying a first-floor flat in what is today part of the museum's geology gallery. Not long after the museum opened, Yarrow took the children out one afternoon, leaving his wife to lock up the museum after the last few visitors had left. Once she had done so, she went upstairs to the flat to start preparing the evening meal, and was surprised to hear footsteps coming up the main staircase. Thinking that her husband and children had returned, she went to greet them. Instead, she saw a young man aged about 30, with brown hair and wearing a grey suit, ascending the stairs. Believing that she had locked a visitor in, she stepped forward to apologize and to escort him off the premises. But, as she did so, she noticed two things about him that sent a chill racing up and down her spine. First, his footsteps were unusually loud and, second, he wasn't actually walking on the stairs but floating above them. The apparition then proceeded to glide past her and vanish into thin air.

Reports of this same apparition on the stairs and first-floor corridor have continued up to the present day, the most recent being in June 2009. He is believed to be the ghost of Thomas Hunter, an Australian soldier who was wounded in France in the Great War in 1916. He was brought back to the building, which was then the hospital, where he died of his injuries on 31 July 1916. The fact that he died so far from home is thought to be the reason for his restless wraith's appearances at the museum.

Roman Soldier

However, the lonely Anzac warrior is not the only soldier to haunt the museum. The apparition of a Roman soldier, last seen in September 2006, appears in the archaeology gallery and is reputed to be inseparable, even in death, from his sword which is displayed there. A foreboding male presence has been sensed, rather than seen, near the re-creation of a period shop on the museum's first floor. Whether he is connected to the phantom footsteps often heard in this area is uncertain.

In October 2008, two visitors to the museum were alarmed when the apparition of a white lady appeared and proceeded to follow them around the upper floor. Paranormal investigation teams have picked up the ghostly voice of a little girl on recordings made in the geology gallery. Her full-blown apparition has been known to scare the wits out of workmen there.

One of the spookiest places in the museum is, without doubt, the cellar. Indeed, this has such a reputation for regular paranormal activity that a live webcam allows people to observe it between the hours of 5pm and 8am. A group of ghost hunters conducting an investigation of the cellar in April 2009 were shocked when an invisible entity began throwing things at them. Whether the culprit was the hooded figure that regularly appears in the cellar is not known.

There is little doubt that Peterborough Museum is genuinely and consistently haunted. This, coupled with the fact that members of the public can explore its warren of haunted rooms on candlelit tours or overnight ghost hunts, has made it a justifiably popular venue with those who enjoy the thrill of searching for spectral residents.

Peterborough Museum

Priestgate, Peterborough,
Cambridgeshire
PE1 1LF

Haunted Rating 🯄🯄🯄🯄🯄

ABOVE: The ghost of a Roman soldier has also been seen at the museum

LANDGUARD FORT

SUFFOLK

Landguard Fort

Viewpoint Road, Felixstowe,
Suffolk IP11 3TW

www.landguard.com

Haunted Rating 🎭🎭🎭🎭🎭

The Mournful Shade of the Portuguese Lady

Standing defiantly at the mouth of the River Orwell, Landguard Fort was designed to guard the entrance to the port of Harwich. The first fort was constructed here during the reign of Henry VIII in 1543, but that quickly fell into decay, and by 1553 its guns had been returned to the Tower of London. In 1628, a new fort was begun and this was completed in 1666. Its defences were put to the test in 1667 when, during the second Anglo-Dutch War, 1,500 enemy marines landed nearby and attacked the fort. Captain Nathaniel Darell, the fort's commander, and his garrison put up a valiant defence, and the would-be invaders were driven away.

The fort was again rebuilt in the early 18th century and then, in 1744, a new pentagram-shaped, red-brick structure was built, the walls of which still survive. In 1871, the fort was renovated once more, this time using yellow London bricks, and it is this incarnation that greets visitors today. The fort was finally decommissioned in 1956. Sealed up and left to its own devices, the fort began to fall apart until, in the 1980s, concern was expressed about its fate. English Heritage came to the rescue, restoring it and then placing it in the care of the Landguard Fort Trust, which now opens the fort to the public. You can explore its atmospheric interior and you may perhaps encounter one or more of the many ghosts that have remained earthbound during the fort's long and eventful history.

A plethora of paranormal activity has been experienced at Landguard Fort. The shade of a melancholic musketeer, reputedly the only defender to have been killed during the Dutch attack in 1667, has been seen drifting back and forth along the ramparts. He only ever appears when Britain is in danger, and was particularly active during World

War II when he was seen by several soldiers stationed at the fort. Thankfully, it is now some years since he took a spectral stroll, but dogs still find the ramparts distinctly unnerving and become decidedly on edge when taken for a walk along them.

The shade of a Victorian artilleryman has been seen in the fort's shop. On one occasion he startled a female worker by stepping out of the wall of the shop, leering at her and then turning around and disappearing back into the wall.

By far the most famous of the fort's phantoms is the ghost of Maria, whose spectral saunterings began in the 18th century. Maria was the Portuguese wife of the fort's paymaster sergeant. The wives of the other soldiers stationed at the fort resented and mistrusted Maria, and when a silk handkerchief went missing, they were only too happy to blame the theft on her. Her husband was ordered by his superiors to deal with the matter and, convinced of his wife's innocence, he left the fort to enlist outside help in clearing her name. When he returned four days later, however, he was promptly arrested for desertion, court-martialled, found guilty and sentenced to death by firing squad. After the sentence was carried out, the inconsolable Maria raced to the ramparts and flung herself to her death. Her ghost, still mourning her husband, returns to walk along the ramparts, and visitors often hear weeping and sorrowful murmurings in a foreign tongue.

Other ghosts that linger on at the fort include that of an 18th-century soldier who, on returning from a foreign tour of duty, came down with a tropical sickness that caused his skin to erupt in pustules. Anxious to stop the disease spreading, and wishing to avoid a panic among the other soldiers, the officers chose to keep his condition a secret. They locked the young man up in solitary confinement somewhere within the depths of the fort, where he wasted away and died. Mediums visiting the fort have since made contact with his spirit, and he even told one that he was the only son of a widow and that he wanted his mother to know that he had not deserted her.

Languard Fort is a genuinely atmospheric location, which has, in recent years, become popular with ghost-hunting groups. Brushing aside the cobwebs as you explore its chilling interior, you can understand why those who come here to communicate with the spirits of former residents seldom leave without doing so. The past is very much ingrained here in the time-scarred fabric of its ragged walls.

ABOVE A plethora of paranormal activity has been experienced at Landguard Fort

CHRISTCHURCH MANSION

SUFFOLK

Christchurch Mansion

Soane Street, Ipswich,
Suffolk IP4 2BE

Haunted Rating ⛑⛑⛑⛑⛑

A Step Back in Time

There is something very magpie-like about Christchurch Mansion, a magnificent stately home on the outskirts of Ipswich which nestles amid 70 or so acres of parkland. Its rooms are crammed with an eclectic mix of furnishings, antiques, bric-a-brac and priceless works of art. However, few, if any, of the objects are original to Christchurch Mansion – most have found their way there from Ipswich's grand old houses when they were being demolished throughout the 20th century. The result is that, as you explore the rooms, you are literally wandering through the ages, from Tudor times to Victorian.

Built in 1548 by Edmund Withypoll on the site of the Augustinian Priory of the Holy Trinity, Christchurch Mansion achieved a major coup in 1579 when Queen Elizabeth I visited and stayed for six days. Over the next 300 years, other Royals would partake of the hospitality of subsequent owners of the house. Charles II paid a visit in 1662 and enjoyed a game of bowls in Christchurch Park. Much later, Prince Albert, the Consort of Queen Victoria, visited in 1851.

In 1894, the house was acquired by a syndicate, which announced plans to demolish it and replace it with terraced houses. Fortunately for Ipswich, wealthy banker and philanthropist Felix Cobbold came to the rescue. He bought the house and surrounding land and then gifted it to the people of Ipswich, with the proviso that the house be preserved. He also bequeathed £20,000 for the purchase of works of art. Today, Christchurch Mansion is home to a splendid art collection, including the largest number of paintings by John Constable and Thomas Gainsborough outside London.

In 1897, as part of the celebrations for Queen Victoria's Golden Jubilee, Cobbold paid for a six-hour party in Christchurch Park at which 10,650 local youngsters were entertained, their enjoyment only slightly diminished by a fierce thunderstorm that broke out in the afternoon.

Today, Christchurch Mansion is a truly stunning and fascinating property. Inside, you really can soak up the atmosphere of bygone days and perhaps make the acquaintance of the ghosts that are known to reside there. However, the fact that so many of the furnishings are not original to the house can present those in search of supernatural residents with something of a spectral conundrum. Are the ghosts that roam its rooms and corridors those of former residents indigenous to the house, or have they come into the property with items that Christchurch Mansion has acquired, a little like spectral woodworm?

Wherever they came from, the mansion's ghosts are an active, though harmless, bunch. They include a Victorian lady who has been seen walking straight through a glass door without opening or breaking it. The apparitions of a lady and two children have been seen dancing hand in hand along a first-floor corridor. Poltergeist activity has also been known to take place in the house. Books have been thrown across rooms by unseen hands; paintings have been found mysteriously turned to face walls; and a lady who visited the mansion in 2008 caught the voice of a woman whispering 'Freda' on her camcorder, even though there was no one near at the time.

FELBRIGG HALL, GARDEN AND PARK

NORFOLK

Books and Spooks in the Library

In November 1972, David Muffon was working alone in the magnificent Gothic library of Felbrigg Hall, the 17th-century former home of the Windham family. Looking up from his work, he found that he had been joined by a man in 18th-century dress, sitting in an armchair by the fireplace reading a book. David, who had been charged with the task of putting the estate in order following its acquisition by the National Trust in 1969, was not particularly perturbed. As he later put it, 'It was so natural I thought nothing about it.' However, he was slightly bemused when, after about 15 seconds, the man set down his book on the table and simply melted away into thin air.

When Muffon later asked the former family butler if the house was haunted, he was told, 'Oh, yes, there's the ghost of William Windham who sits in the armchair on the far side of the fireplace.' The butler then went on to reveal how, for many years, one of his jobs had been to lay a specific set of books out on the table in the library in a particular order for Windham's ghost to read.

William Windham was an 18th-century statesman. His pride and joy at Felbrigg Hall was the magnificent Gothic library, which includes books that once belonged to the great lexicographer Dr Samuel Johnson and at whose funeral Windham had acted as a pallbearer. It was Windham's love of books that led to his own death.

On 8 July 1809, he was heading along Conduit Street in London when he noticed a house on fire. His friend, Frederick North, lived just a few doors away from the inferno and, mindful that he had a valuable

library, Windham set about moving North's books to safety before the fire reached his house. Unfortunately, while carrying a batch of heavy books, he tripped and bruised his hip. The injury caused a tumour, which his physician, Dr Lynn, operated on to remove. Although the operation was a success, the shock proved too much for Windham's constitution. On the night of 3 June 1810, as Dr Lynn moved him into a more comfortable position, Windham whispered, 'I thank you; this is the last trouble I shall give you. You fight the battle well, but it will not do.' So saying, he fell asleep and never woke up. On 8 June 1810, his body was laid to rest in the family vault at Felbrigg church.

After his death, the estate passed to his half-brother's son, William Lukin, who changed his name to William Windham on moving into the house. His grandson, William Frederic, known as 'Mad Windham' on account of his numerous eccentricities such as patrolling the estate dressed as a London policeman, squandered the family fortune. As a consequence, Felbrigg Hall was sold to wealthy Norwich grocer John Kitton in 1863.

It wasn't long before the Kitton family realized that, in addition to the usual fixtures and fittings, they had also acquired an otherworldly house guest. When the writer Augustus Hare visited Felbrigg Hall in 1885, he was told by one of the 'Miss Kittons' that 'Mr Windham comes every night to look after his favourite books in the library. He goes straight to the shelves where they are: we hear him moving the tables and chairs about. We never disturb him, though, for we intend to be ghosts ourselves some day, and to come about the place just as he does.'

Felbrigg Hall, Garden and Park

Felbrigg, Norwich, Norfolk NR11 8PR

www.nationaltrust.org.uk

Haunted Rating

ABOVE: *Brick and stone Felbrigg Hall was built in 1620 for Thomas Windham*

THE MUCKLEBURGH COLLECTION

NORFOLK

The Ghosts of Warriors Past

During World War II, the site now occupied by the Muckleburgh Collection was Weybourne Military Camp, which had been established in 1935. However, the coast hereabouts had been strategically important for many centuries before that and its defence had long been a priority. Would-be invaders from the Spanish Armada of 1588, through to Napoleon in the late 18th and early 19th centuries, had been only too aware of the advantages afforded by the deep natural harbour at Weybourne. It was the perfect landing place for an invasion force, as illustrated by a 16th-century couplet:

> He who old England would hope to win,
> Must at Weybourne Hope begin.

With the outbreak of World War II, the camp become an important centre for the training of anti-aircraft troops, and many experiments with anti-aircraft guns were carried out here. Tragedy struck in the course of one session when an anti-aircraft gun exploded during a training exercise and six women lost their lives.

In the wake of the Dunkirk evacuation in 1940, and fearing a German invasion, Winston Churchill visited the camp to ensure its defences were fit for purpose. A demonstration of projectile firing given during his first visit left him particularly unimpressed. Churchill gave the camp's commander seven days to improve the standard of the defences. A second demonstration was arranged, which proved equally disappointing. Tradition holds that all the senior officers were replaced the following day.

The last guns were fired at the camp in October 1958 and it was closed down the following year. The site then went into decline as different ideas for its development were mooted back and forth. Holiday camp pioneer Billy Butlin even came to inspect the site with a view to opening a centre on it.

In the 1980s, the site was acquired by Berry Savory and his son Michael. They began a restoration project, which included knocking down 200 buildings and clearing away 45,000 tonnes of rubble. The work was completed in 1988 and the site opened as the Muckleburgh Collection of military artefacts, named after Muckleburgh Hill at the foot of which the camp had been situated.

Originally the collection consisted of around 30 exhibits but it has now grown to over 120 tanks, anti-aircraft guns, military vehicles, as well as thousands of other related items. The exhibits have been amassed from all over the world, and the vehicles have been restored to full working order.

In recent years, the Muckleburgh Collection has achieved a fair amount of recognition for its ghostly activity. There is little doubt that certain parts of the museum and several of the exhibits are, to say the least, somewhat eerie. Visitors and staff alike have experienced cold rushes of air brushing across them, as though someone has walked by in a hurry. The vehicles on display at the museum have all seen action of some sort or another, and you can imagine the gamut of emotions experienced inside them. So it is perhaps inevitable that paranormal activity has been experienced around several of them. Ghostly voices have been heard chattering from inside one of the tanks. More disturbingly, cries and screams of anguish and pain are regularly heard from the back of a military ambulance. For some of the crews that once manned these vehicles or the casualties that were carried inside, it would appear that their battles have extended into the afterlife.

The Muckleburgh Collection

Weybourne, Norfolk
NR25 7EH

www.muckleburgh.co.uk

Haunted Rating 👤👤👤👤👤

BELOW: *The cluttered interior of an armoured car at the Muckleburgh Collection*

THE VINE HOTEL

LINCOLNSHIRE

The Vine Hotel

Vine Road, Seacroft,
Skegness, Lincolnshire PE25 3DB

www.thevinehotel.com

Haunted Rating ●●●◐◯

BELOW AND FAR RIGHT: Alfred, Lord Tennyson found inspiration at the Vine Hotel and his ghost is rumoured to linger there today

Smugglers, the Excise Man and a Poet Laureate

Alfred, Lord Tennyson was exceptionally fond of the Vine Hotel, particularly its exquisite grounds, which positively inspired him. In the ornamental garden at the rear of The Vine, you will find the 'Tennyson Tree' or, to be more precise, the Tennyson stump, since the tree itself fell victim to Dutch elm disease and very little of it now survives. Tennyson spent a great deal of time at the Vine in the mid-19th century. According to the plaque that now adorns the surviving fragment of the tree '… he could often be found leant against this tree reflecting and composing his work'. It is said that it was the peace and tranquillity of the Vine's garden that provided the muse for his poem 'Come into the Garden, Maude.' Although Tennyson died in 1892, his ghost has, apparently, been a little reluctant to bid the old hotel farewell. His bearded figure has been seen both in the garden and inside the building itself.

Originally known as the Skegness Hotel, the Vine Hotel was built in the mid-18th century. In the early 19th century, it became a favoured haunt of smugglers, who met here to discuss when and where their next cargo of contraband would be landed and how they would then dispose of it. These nefarious villains were constantly forced to pit their wits against the customs men, whose job it was to ensure that the tax revenue due to the crown from cargoes such as brandy and tobacco was collected and that those who traded in illicit imports were duly and suitably punished.

It was always rumoured locally that, in the early 19th century, a lone customs officer had attempted singlehandedly to catch a group of smugglers in possession of their illegal spoils but, having entered the Vine to arrest them, he was never seen again. In the early 20th

century – according to most accounts it was in 1902 – some credence was apparently given to the tale. During renovation work at the Vine, builders knocked down part of a wall to fit a display cabinet and came across a hidden recess. Inside, they found the skeletal remains of a man dressed in the rotting uniform of a customs officer.

The shade of the unfortunate man now haunts the hotel, where he appears wearing what witnesses describe as a centuries-old uniform. He is a harmless ghost that bothers no one. Indeed, he appears to be more afraid of the living than the living of him – the moment anyone notices him, he simply melts away into thin air.

The Vine Hotel is a delightful and special place, a cosy haven with log fires and beamed ceilings. Add to that the possibility of making the acquaintance of the restless wraith of a murdered customs officer, or enjoying a poetical encounter with the roaming revenant of Alfred, Lord Tennyson, and you have the perfect location in which to rest your head till the 'black bat, night, has flown'.

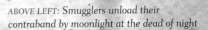

ABOVE LEFT: Smugglers unload their contraband by moonlight at the dead of night

Black Shuck

On 4 August 1577, a 'Straunge and terrible Waunder' occurred at the church of St Mary, Bungay, in Suffolk. As the morning service began, a fearsome tempest suddenly blew up outside the building. Lightning streaked across the heavens, and great rolls of thunder shook the church to its foundations. Moments later, the doors burst open and a hideous black dog bounded in upon the alarmed parishioners. It padded along the aisle with 'greate swiftnesse and incredible haste' and, as it moved between two members of the congregation, the others watched in horror as the demon 'wrung the necks of them bothe'. The hound brushed against another onlooker, rendering him 'as shrunken as a piece of leather left in a hot fire'. Not long after, the creature paid a visit to nearby Blythburgh church, where he killed three parishioners and left deep claw marks on the north door, which are still visible today.

Witnesses to these terrible happenings knew that they had seen Black Shuck, the demon hound. Although this fearsome spectre haunts the darker recesses of the local consciousness in many parts of Britain, it is to the bleak expanse of the East Anglian coastline and the untamed stretches of its wild fens that its legend clings most vigorously. The hound arrived here with the Viking invaders, who brought with them tales of Odin's hounds. The Anglo-Saxons singularized them, creating the legend of Black Shuck – the name is derived from the Anglo-Saxon *succa*, meaning demon, the moniker by which the dreaded creature has been known in these parts for over a thousand years. At some stage, long ago, it managed to spring from the realm of fantasy and come bounding onto the East Anglian byways – a hound of hell, able to strike terror into those who, like the parishioners of Bungay and Blythburgh, were unfortunate enough to cross its fearsome path.

Black Shuck's favourite haunts were said to be the old straight roads, which it trotted along in the dead of night in search of lone wayfarers. The first its victims knew of its presence was the padding sound made by its heavy paws as it approached. From the corner of their eye, they would catch a glimpse of a swirling mass of darkness, which, the nearer it got, would take on the outline of a huge hound. As they then quickened their pace, the ghost hound would track their footsteps, following a little distance behind. It was well known that anyone who turned around and looked into the hound's fiery eyes would die within 12 months. As Black Shuck was usually content to scare people witless as opposed to doing them any physical harm, the best course of action for anyone being pursued was to keep their head down and hurry on their way.

Over the years, there have been many reported sightings of Black Shuck, and they have continued into relatively modern times. A young boy, rescued from the North Sea in 1890, told his rescuers that he had been chased into the water by a huge black hound that swam behind him, forcing him to swim out further and further. In the 1920s and 1930s, at Sheringham in Norfolk, fishermen claimed they heard the baying of a hound, echoing from the cliff tops on storm-tossed nights. There were also sightings of Black Shuck padding across Great Yarmouth beach in the 1980s. Perhaps the phantom hound is not some ancient superstition with no place in the modern age.

From Suffolk to Dartmoor

Whatever Black Shuck's origins, one thing is certain – his legend has long been used to shock, chill and inspire generations of visitors and locals alike. In 1901, Sir Arthur Conan Doyle, the creator of Sherlock Holmes, took a golfing holiday in Cromer on the Norfolk coast with his friend, the journalist Fletcher North. Hearing local tales of Black Shuck's exploits, North, who hailed from Devonshire, told Conan Doyle about similar phantom hounds that were said to roam Dartmoor. Conan Doyle subsequently wrote to his publishers at the *Strand* magazine in London, informing them that 'I have an idea of a real creeper...'

Later, Conan Doyle visited North in Devon, and together they spent days exploring the bleak expanse of Dartmoor. North kept Conan Doyle entranced with his tales of the black dogs that were known to roam the moor, where they were known as Wish Hounds. The pair were driven around on these adventures by a coachman called Harry Baskerville. Ever after, he claimed that he was part inspiration for Sherlock Holmes's most famous and chilling adventure *The Hound of the Baskervilles*.

Although Conan Doyle set his tale on Dartmoor, it was in Norfolk that the seeds for the story were sown, his imagination fired by the tale of the huge and fearsome night-time hound, Black Shuck.

LEFT: *A scene from* The Hound of the Baskervilles *showing Holmes and Watson watching the sinister hound*
RIGHT: *The confrontation: 'Holmes emptied five barrels of his revolver into the creature's flank'...*

GUNBY HALL

LINCOLNSHIRE

ABOVE AND RIGHT: The elegant red brick house is surrounded by stunning gardens, where the Ghost Walk is situated

Death Does Them Part

The present Gunby Hall dates from the early 1700s. Sir William Massingberd, whose family had risen from the ranks of sturdy Saxon yeomanry to baronetcy, decided to replace the draughty, old-fashioned medieval manor house with a splendid family home of plum-red brick. A range of coach houses was added in 1735 and, in the 19th century, a two-storey extension was tacked onto the north wing of the house itself. Gunby Hall may not be the most spectacular of country houses, but it certainly possesses an elegant, though compact, simplicity, which has led to it being described as a 'living doll's house'.

Although the last Massingberd baronet died some 20 years after the hall was built, both the name and the house itself stayed with the family, passing down through the female line. Calamity almost befell the estate in the 1840s, when it was inherited by the teenage Algernon Massingberd, a true wild-child, who proceeded to drink and gamble away the family fortune. He sold many irreplaceable treasures to pay off his debts, and then disappeared on an expedition up the Amazon never to be seen again.

Disaster nearly struck again almost 100 years later. With the outbreak of World War II, the Air Ministry put a huge amount of pressure on the then owner Sir Archibald Montgomery-Massingberd to allow his house to be pulled down to make way for an airfield. To prevent this, Sir Archibald presented the house to the National Trust in 1944, and it remains in their care to this day.

Locating the haunted part of Gunby Hall is not particularly difficult: there is a section of the lovely gardens surrounding the house called the Ghost Walk. Along it, there is a canal-shaped pond, bounded by a thick hedge of yew. The hedge, which is overhung by brilliant white roses, has a decidedly Gothic air and can elicit cold shivers even on the warmest of summer days.

According to tradition, a long-ago Miss Masingberd fell madly in love with a groom and agreed to elope with him – as with so many country-house ghostly tales, no one has attempted to ruin this story by adding dates or solid facts. Unfortunately, her father found out about the plan, shot the couple dead and disposed of their bodies in the pond. The two lovers have since been bound in spirit to the place where their love affair reached its violent climax – however many years ago it was. The shade of the young lady has been seen floating serenely over the surface of the water, while her ghostly beau walks the path beside the pond. Their differing social statuses keep the two forlorn phantoms apart in death, much as they would have been in life.

Gunby Hall

Gunby, near Spilsby,
Lincolnshire PE23 5SS

Haunted Rating

YE OLDE WHITE HARTE

HULL

Freda and the Skull

Ye Olde White Harte, tucked away down a narrow alley, is everything an historic pub should be. Its timeless interior is resplendent with huge fire-scarred oak beams, large open fireplaces, an ancient, creaking, dark-wood staircase, two copper-topped bars and even stained glass windows. If that isn't enough to set you racing to stake your claim to a seat by one of its blazing fires, there's the added attraction of making the acquaintance of Freda, the resident ghost.

Freda's skull leers at you from inside a glass case behind the smaller of the two bars. Nobody knows for certain exactly how old it is, nor whose shoulders it sat upon in life, nor, for that matter, whether it is male or female, or even exactly when or where it was discovered.

There are several tales to account for its presence in the pub. One maintains that it is the skull of a servant boy and that a slight fracture mark visible on it came about when a sea captain long ago, drunk on French brandy, lashed out at the boy with the butt of his pistol, killing him. His body was then secreted under the pub's staircase until a fire in the 19th century brought his remains to light.

Another story holds that the skull belonged to a poor servant girl. She had become involved in an illicit liaison with a landlord of the pub and he murdered her to stop their affair from becoming known. He then sealed her body in a dark recess in the attic, where it remained hidden until the fire in the 19th century.

Whatever the origins of the gruesome artefact, those of a psychic persuasion have sensed a female presence in the vicinity of the bar behind which the skull is kept. Some have even seen the full-blown manifestation of a girl.

Ye Olde White Harte

25 Silver Street,
Hull HU1 1JG

www.yeoldewhiteharte.co.uk

Haunted Rating 🗝️🗝️🗝️🗝️🗝️

The Plotting Parlour

Other paranormal activity has been experienced in a lovely old upstairs room known as the Plotting Parlour, and several paranormal investigation groups that have spent time in the room have picked up on various energies that seem to reside there.

The pub was, reputedly, the home of Sir John Hotham, Governor of Hull and a prominent Parliamentarian. In January 1642, with the English Civil War brewing, King Charles I made known his intention to seize the massive arsenal of weapons and ammunition that was at that time being stored in Hull. Ordered by Parliament to retain this arsenal at all costs, Hotham called a meeting in this parlour (hence the name Plotting Parlour) at which the dignitaries of Hull voted in favour of denying Charles I access to the town.

On 23 April 1642, when the king arrived at the town's Beverley Gate, he found it locked against him. Charles demanded admittance but Hotham refused. The furious king called Hotham a traitor, and a three-week siege of Hull by the royalists later ensued. Although unsuccessful, the siege proved a major factor on the road to Civil War, the first major battle of which took place at Edgehill the following October. Sir John Hotham was ultimately beheaded in January 1645.

Ye Olde White Harte is not only one of Hull's most historic and atmospheric pubs but also one of the most haunted. The moment you enter the narrow little alleyway leading to its door, you can sense the energies of some of the thousands of people who must have crossed its threshold over the centuries.

The Significance of the Skull

Images of the skull act as powerful reminders of our own mortality, and have been used for this purpose by artists throughout the ages. Early artists such as Hans Holbein the Younger often incorporated them into their work to signify some hidden message. The most famous example of this is perhaps Holbein's acclaimed painting *The Ambassadors* (1533), in which an elongated skull has been incorporated into the painting but is visible only from certain angles. The skull could be a warning of impending doom, or just a timely reminder that death is never far away. Shakespeare's Hamlet, who is obsessed with thoughts of suicide, death and murder, famously picks up the skull of his one-time friend Yorrick in a graveyard and meditates on the fragility of life. In a complex speech, which is one of the best known of Shakespeare's works, he compares the skull to the faces of living people who, no matter how young and beautiful, must all come to this state.

RAF HOLMPTON

EAST YORKSHIRE

Chained to His Desk Deep Underground

RAF Patrington, as RAF Holmpton was originally called, came into being as an early warning radar station in World War II. Later, during the Cold War, it was changed to a master control radar station and, by the end of the 1950s, it had expanded to encompass a site of some 36 acres and been renamed RAF Holmpton.

However, the station's most important facilities lay deep underground. Their existence was such a closely guarded secret that, for nigh on 50 years, many of those who lived close by knew nothing about them. A vast subterranean Command Bunker covering some 3,252sq m (35,000sq ft), had been constructed. Set on two floors, this colossal 'world beneath the surface' comprised computer rooms and communication centres, as well as three Operations Rooms, a Situation Room, Command Pit, a canteen, dormitories, an Officers' Mess, kitchens and offices, all connected by dark tunnels. At any one time, this immense complex was home to some 350 military personnel, and some 17,000 of them passed through it during its operational years between 1953 and 1974.

From 1974 to 1986, it was used as a training facility for radar engineers. Following a multi-million pound refit, it became the National Wartime (Emergency) Command Centre of RAF Support Command. Had World War III broken out, the supply chain for the RAF throughout the British Isles would have been managed from here.

Although it is now open to the public, the site remains fully functional and could be pressed into service at

RAF Holmpton

Withernsea, East Yorkshire
HU19 2QR

www.rafholmpton.com

Haunted Rating

very short notice in the event of a national emergency. In addition to the daytime tours, RAF Holmpton also operates overnight ghost hunts. It is a delightfully different location in which to search for paranormal activity – if you dare!

Over the years, there have been numerous reports of uniformed figures appearing at various locations around the site, then suddenly vanishing into thin air. The shade of a man has been seen on a regular basis in one of the Operations Rooms and by many people at the same time. Visitors to the site have spoken of an uncomfortable feeling of being watched, and some have even complained of being pushed to the floor by unseen hands. There is also the ghost of a former pilot to contend with. Following an accident, this unfortunate man was reduced to doing a desk job, a form of employment he didn't take to after the excitement of flying. He became depressed and started drinking heavily. Since his death, when you'd think it couldn't get any worse for the poor chap, his spirit has been condemned to remain at the desk, where many mediums have picked up on his energy.

Recently, Sara Woodward of Deadhauntednights. com was conducting an overnight investigation at RAF Holmpton when an officer in uniform appeared in front of her in one of the rooms. Keeping her composure, Sara raised her camera, saw the figure in the view finder and took a photograph. But when she looked at the camera screen there was no sign of the officer.

RAF Holmpton is most definitely a haunted site and makes a change from creaky old manor houses, ruined castles or historic inns. The fact that its ghostly residents are from the last 50 or so years, as opposed to a dim and distant past, makes it an even more chilling and exciting place to explore.

THE MIDLANDS

4

And as the moon from some dark gate of cloud
Throws o'er the sea a floating bridge of light
Across whose trembling planks our fancies crowd,
Into the realm of mystery and night, –

So from the world of spirits there descends
A bridge of light, connecting it with this,
O'er whose unsteady floor, that sways and bends,
Wander our thoughts across the dark abyss.

From *Haunted Houses*
by Henry Wadsworth Longfellow (1807–1882)

THE MIDLANDS

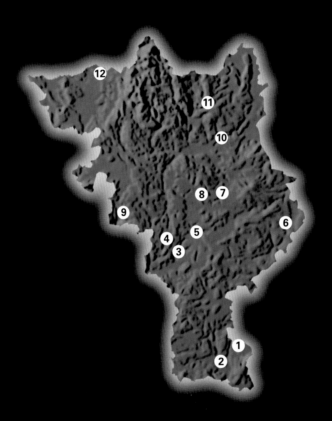

1 RYCOTE CHAPEL – OXFORDSHIRE 118

2 DORCHESTER ABBEY – OXFORDSHIRE 120

3 GUY'S CLIFFE HOUSE – WARWICKSHIRE 122

4 BADDESLEY CLINTON – WARWICKSHIRE 126

5 COOMBE ABBEY HOTEL – COVENTRY 128

6 LYVEDEN NEW BIELD
– NORTHAMPTONSHIRE 130

7 LEICESTER GUILDHALL – LEICESTERSHIRE 132

8 BOSWORTH BATTLEFIELD HERITAGE CENTRE
AND COUNTRY PARK – LEICESTERSHIRE 134

9 THE CROOKED HOUSE – STAFFORDSHIRE 136

10 GALLERIES OF JUSTICE MUSEUM
– NOTTINGHAM 138

11 HARDWICK OLD HALL – DERBYSHIRE 140

12 TATTON OLD HALL – CHESHIRE 142

FEATURE – MARY, QUEEN OF SCOTS
BRITAIN'S BUSIEST GHOST 144

INTRODUCTION

Our journey around the Midlands begins in Oxfordshire with a visit to a delightful little chapel. Visited by kings and queens in the past, it offers those in search of spectral activity the opportunity of making the acquaintance of at least two ghosts. From here we move on to the lovely Dorchester Abbey, where a poignant inscription on a tombstone is a reminder of a tragedy long ago that resulted in one of Oxfordshire's more persistent hauntings. Crossing the border into Warwickshire, we encounter the forlorn shell of a once grand house that is indelibly linked with the ghost and the legend of Guy of Warwick. Our next destination is the beautiful moated manor house of Baddesley Clinton, where ghostly footsteps and eerie sensations are very much the norm. There then comes the chance to unwind at a truly luxurious hotel that began life as a Cistercian abbey and to which at least two former residents are still attached in spirit. Next, another atmospheric shell of a building at Northamptonshire's Lyveden New Bield, which has links to the 1605 Gunpowder Plot and is haunted by a ghost that manages to stand on thin air. We then head for Leicestershire to discover the spirits that haunt Leicester's ancient Guildhall before moving on to seek the illustrious shade of Richard III, who returns to Bosworth Battlefield where he was the last English king to die in battle. Having tried to partake of a drink and discover the ghosts at Staffordshire's aptly name The Crooked House pub, we cross the threshold of one of the region's most haunted places – Nottingham's Galleries of Justice. After exploring its sinister caves and psychically active rooms, we shake ourselves free of its aura and make our way to Derbyshire. Here we unearth a spectral conundrum in the form of the ghost of a man whose living self didn't actually believe in ghosts. Our journey ends in Cheshire at a true hidden gem, Tatton Old Hall. As well as learning of the numerous ghosts that haunt it, we get to bask in the glorious wooded landscape that surrounds it.

RYCOTE CHAPEL

OXFORDSHIRE

A Timeless Relic

Rycote Chapel seems to hide itself away from the outside world. Located at the end of a short drive, it is surrounded by tall trees, which look as though they are cradling it in a sylvan embrace, protecting its time-hallowed walls from the unwanted attentions of the modern age.

The immensely wealthy and influential Richard Quatremayne, a councillor to both Richard Duke of York and his son Edward IV, built this private chapel next to his mansion. Three priests, one of whom lived in the tower of the church, were retained to say daily mass for the family.

By 1535, the estate, along with its chapel, had passed into the hands of the Williams family, who rebuilt the adjacent house. Sir John Williams was employed to watch over Princess Elizabeth, the daughter of Henry VIII by Anne Boleyn, while she was held captive at Woodstock during the reign of her half-sister Mary I. He treated her with such kindness that she grew immensely fond of him and referred to him as 'my favourite uncle'. She also became great friends with Sir John's daughter, Marjorie – whom she nicknamed 'mine own crow' – and was delighted when Marjorie married Henry Norreys in 1560.

Henry's father, also called Henry, had held the unenviable position of 'Groom of the Stool' to Henry VIII, presiding over the 'Office of Royal Excretion'. However, this intimate service to the king didn't prevent his being accused of adultery with Henry's second wife, Anne Boleyn, and he was executed in 1536.

Princess Elizabeth, whose mother Anne Boleyn was also executed, became queen in 1558. She felt a great affinity with the Norreys and honoured them with a royal visit in 1566, during the course of which she bestowed a knighthood on Henry. Elizabeth would pay further visits to Rycote in 1570, 1572 and 1592, and it became very much a countryside haven for her. She was meant to visit in 1582 but had to change her plans at the last moment and sent Robert Dudley, the Earl

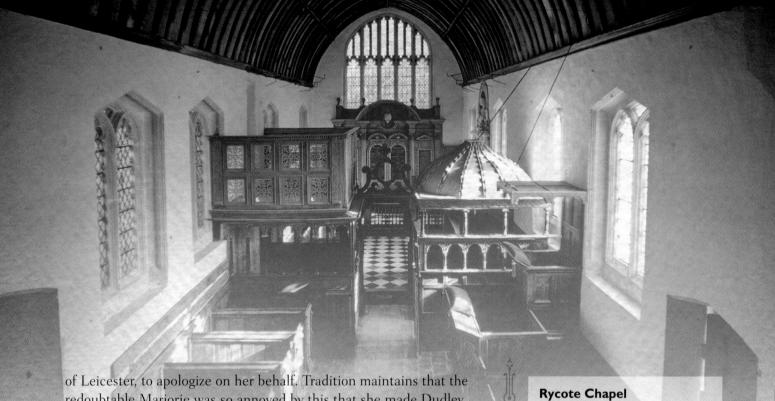

of Leicester, to apologize on her behalf. Tradition maintains that the redoubtable Marjorie was so annoyed by this that she made Dudley sleep in the stables.

The Norreys were responsible for adding the sumptuous roofed pew with a minstrels' gallery above it that adorns the north of the nave of the chapel and which dates from around 1610. A similarly grand pew, rising from the other side of the nave, was erected for a visit by Charles I in 1625. Charles returned to Rycote in 1643 and again in 1645 *en route* to Oxford as he tried to govern his troubled realm during the Civil War.

By the 1740s, the house had passed to the Bertie family, the Earls of Abingdon, during whose tenure it was destroyed by fire in October 1745. Tragically, the ten-year-old heir, James Bertie, perished in the flames. The house was rebuilt and flourished again until it was inherited by the 4th Earl of Abingdon, who proceeded to squander his legacy. His son, Montague, the 5th Earl, decided to cut his losses and had the house demolished in 1807.

The chapel, which has witnessed royal visits and served successive generations of different families, now seems strangely aloof, an aged relic alone with its memories of past glories. But, from time to time, vestiges of distant halcyon days stir within its ancient fabric, and ghosts of the past return to this place that was undoubtedly held in great affection in life. The most prominent phantom is that of a grey lady who has been witnessed both inside the chapel and in the grounds that surround it. She shares her spectral beat with the wraith of a monk in brown robes and a 17th-century milkmaid, both of whom have been seen inside, and in the vicinity of, the church.

Rycote Chapel

Near Thame,
Oxfordshire
OX9 2PE

Haunted Rating

ABOVE: *The interior of Rycote Chapel*
BELOW: *Queen Elizabeth I paid several visits to Rycote during her reign*

DORCHESTER ABBEY

OXFORDSHIRE

The entrance porch to Dorchester Abbey

A Martyr to Excessive Sensibility

On the floor in a side aisle at Dorchester Abbey you will find the tombstone of Sarah Fletcher, with a truly heart-rending inscription. 'Reader,' it implores, 'if thou has a Heart famed for Tenderness and Pity, Contemplate this Spot. In which are deposited the Remains of a Young Lady, whose artless Beauty, Innocence of Mind and gentle Manner once obtain'd her the Love and Esteem of all who knew her.' The inscription continues with the tantalizing remark, 'But when Nerves were too delicately spun to bear the rude Shakes and Jostlings which we meet in this transitory World, Nature gave way. She sunk and died a Martyr to Excessive Sensibility.' The inscription continues with a little biographical detail. Sarah was the 'Wife of Captain Fletcher' and 'departed this Life at the village of Clifton on the 7 of June 1799 in the 29 year of her age'. It ends with the wish: 'May her Soul meet that Peace in Heaven which this Earth denied her.'

The inscription is remarkable as much for what it doesn't tell you about Sarah Fletcher as for what it does. Her grave makes an excellent starting point from which to track down her ghost, which has appeared at sundry locations nearby.

Captain Fletcher, Sarah's husband, was a naval officer and frequently unfaithful to his beautiful wife. He met a wealthy young heiress and, unwilling to let a little thing like being already married stand in his way, he became betrothed to her. Sarah only learned of his bigamous plans on the day of the wedding, and she arrived at the church to prevent it taking place just as the ceremony was beginning. Her thwarted husband stormed off to his ship and set sail for the East Indies. Heartbroken, Sarah returned to their house in the nearby village of Clifton Hampden, and hanged herself from the curtain-rod of her bed using a pocket handkerchief attached to a short piece of cord.

As a suicide, Sarah could not be buried in consecrated ground. However, at the subsequent inquest into her death, the jury took pity on her and brought in a verdict that her desperate act was a result of lunacy. She was buried at Dorchester Abbey, and the poignant inscription on her tomb was composed to suggest that she died of her nerves rather than by her own hand.

It appears, though, that despite the closing plea on her tombstone, Sarah's soul has not found 'that Peace in Heaven which this Earth denied her'. Her ghost is said to haunt The George Hotel, which stands next door to Dorchester Abbey. She has also been seen in the village of Clifton Hampden, where she has a fondness for the pub car park at the Barley Mow, a lovely old thatched inn that features in Jerome K. Jerome's *Three Men in a Boat*.

In the 19th century, there were reports of Sarah's phantom footsteps being heard at her house, which, by that time, had been converted into a boys' boarding school. Despite knowing nothing of its history, pupils sleeping in the room where she committed suicide would often wake in the dead of night screaming in terror, convinced that they had seen a woman without a head. A nurse who later slept in this room, and who also knew nothing of its history, told how someone would enter in the early hours of the morning and throw themselves onto the other bed. Yet, when she struck a light, there was never anybody there. Apparently, the 'Shakes and Jostlings' of this transitory world have continued into the next for poor Sarah Fletcher.

Dorchester Abbey

High Street,
Dorchester-on-Thames,
Oxfordshire OX10 7HH

www.dorchester-abbey.org.uk

Haunted Rating

Sarah Fletcher's restless ghost is said to haunt The George Hotel, among other places in Dorchester

GUY'S CLIFFE HOUSE

WARWICKSHIRE

Guy's Cliffe House

Guy's Cliffe, Warwick,
Warwickshire
CV34 5YD

www.guyscliffehouse.co.uk

Haunted Rating 👻👻👻👻👻

A Very Haunted House

The forlorn ruin of Guy's Cliffe House perches precariously atop a sandstone ridge, almost hidden from view by the profusion of trees and bushes that surrounds it. A melancholic aura radiates from its time-scarred walls, while legions of legends come marching from its past. Chief among these is the tale of Guy of Warwick, a celebrated knight whose story, although first appearing in the 13th century, was firmly rooted in Anglo-Saxon times. Today, an impressive 2.4-m (8-ft) tall, weather-beaten carved stone effigy of this fabled figure can still be seen in Guy's Cliffe's chapel, which is now used as a masonic temple.

According to legend, Guy of Warwick was a servant at the household of the Earl of Warwick. One day, while attending to his duties, Guy set eyes upon the earl's beautiful daughter Felice, and became besotted with her. However, since Guy was socially inferior to Felice, the only way that he could hope to win her hand in marriage was by becoming a knight and accomplishing a series of chivalric challenges, such as battling dragons and giants and, in one version of the story, by proving his prowess as a warrior in foreign wars. Guy performed these tasks admirably and he was finally able to marry the woman of his dreams.

But, as is often the case when those of a heroic disposition rise from humble beginnings to acquire their heart's desire, fate intervened to ensure that Guy and Felice did not live happily ever after. For no sooner had Guy hung up his spurs and set down his sword than he began to feel extreme guilt about the violent nature of his road to wedded bliss. To make amends with his conscience, he abandoned his wife and embarked on a pilgrimage to the Holy Land. After several years' absence, he returned to England, a changed man in both mind and body. Back in Warwickshire, he became a religious hermit and took up residence in a cave in the sandstone ridge, on which the present-day Guy's Cliffe House stands, and devoted himself to a life of prayer

RIGHT: The melancholy ruin of Guy's Cliffe House is one of the spookiest places in Britain

and piety. He didn't even bother to reveal his true identity to his wife, the saintly but dim Felice, and although she kept the holy hermit well supplied with alms, she failed to recognize him as her missing husband. But many years later, as Guy lay upon his deathbed at the age of almost 70, he finally confessed his deceit to his soon-to-be widow. The fair Felice could have been forgiven if she had reacted by throwing her sanctimonious spouse off the cliff, speeding up his journey into paradise, but thoughts of vengeance never crossed her mind. Instead, she hurled herself from the top of the cliff and was drowned in the River Avon below. Since then, Guy of Warwick's ghost – a tall, handsome figure with a full beard – is said to roam the cliffs and the grounds around the house.

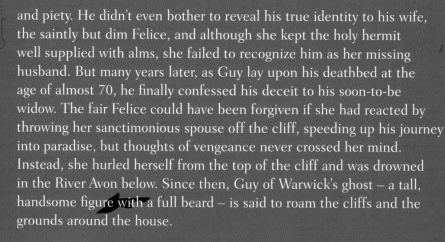

ABOVE: *The Refectory, Guy's Cliffe House*

Overnight Ghost Hunts

Although used as a hospital for injured soldiers during World War I, and as a school for boys in World War II, the passage of time has not dealt kindly with the old house. Aside from its 15th-century chapel, which has been pressed into service as a masonic lodge, the house has gradually fallen into ruin. Its decline was speeded up when, in 1992, during the filming of an episode of Granada Television's *Sherlock Holmes*, a pyrotechnical stunt simulating a large fire at the property went wrong, causing a real large fire.

However, thanks to the dedicated efforts of the Friends of Guy's Cliffe House, work has commenced to halt the decline and to preserve as much of the building as possible. As a consequence, the ruins of the house are now open to the public several times a year. There are even overnight ghost hunts for those eager to make Guy of Warwick's acquaintance. Participants may hear phantom footsteps, which have been known to follow visitors in the wine cellar, or a distressed girl crying 'help me', which has been picked up on sound recordings. Add to this the apparition of a disembodied hand caressing a wall in what is now the Butchery Room and you can see why those who look after Guy's Cliffe House describe it as 'a very haunted house'.

Will You See A Ghost?

Obviously, when visiting a haunted property, your experience would be greatly enhanced if one of its ghostly residents just happened to honour you with an appearance. All manner of ghost-hunting equipment, ranging from night-vision cameras to thermometers to Electric Magnetic Field monitors, are available to assist the dedicated investigator in locating the presence of a spirit energy. Indeed, ghost hunting can prove quite an expensive pastime.

However, it doesn't have to be. Your own senses can often be the best aid to detecting a spectral presence, and there are most certainly signs to watch out for that suggest a spirit form is close by. It must be said that a full-blown manifestation isn't all that common. People often don't see ghosts, but rather *experience* ghosts. You might hear noises that you can't explain. Commonly recorded supernatural sounds include rapping, knocking, ringing bells, footsteps and voices. Another common occurrence is when objects move of their own accord or, at least, with human intervention. Smell is another regular accompaniment to ghostly activity, inexplicable fragrances such as perfume, tobacco smoke or even incense being the most frequent. A sudden drop in temperature is another oft-reported phenomenon that suggests a ghost is around. You might even sense that you're not alone or possibly feel ghostly breath on the back of your neck.

So, by all means invest in ghost-hunting equipment, but also keep in mind that our own senses are often the best detectors of paranormal activity.

BADDESLEY CLINTON

WARWICKSHIRE

Baddesley Clinton

Rising Lane,
Baddesley Clinton,
Warwickshire
B93 0DQ

Haunted Rating

Phantom Footfall and the Indelible Stain

Baddesley Clinton is a true gem of an abode. The very embodiment of what a medieval manor house should look like, it has close on 800 years of passion and personalities crackling away within its ancient fabric. With its tall red chimneys and wisteria-clad walls reflected in the tranquil waters of the picturesque 13th-century moat, one thought grips your mind as you first gaze upon the crenellated gatehouse: this place must surely be haunted.

The house was begun by the Clinton family in the early 13th century. At the time, the estate was known simply as Baddesley, but the Clintons tacked their name onto it and lived there until 1438, when it was sold to John Brome, Under Treasurer of England under Henry VI, a position that he lost when the Lancastrian Henry was deposed by the Yorkist Edward IV in 1461. Further ignominy followed in 1468, when he was murdered by John Herthill, steward to the Earl of Warwick. However, family honour was restored by his son Nicholas Brome, who avenged his father's death by killing Herthill in 1471.

Nicholas, a man who seems to have revelled in his violent reputation, inherited Baddesley Clinton. On arriving home unexpectedly one day, he found the vicar of Baddesley Clinton Church in what is now the house's library, tickling his wife under the chin. Quickly ascertaining that the priest's motives were more temporal than spiritual, Nicholas whipped out his knife and impaled the cavorting cleric. A mark in front of the fireplace has long been pointed out as the indelible stain of the victim's blood, although scientific analysis recently ruined a perfectly good yarn by proving that it is pig's blood! Pardoned for his crime by both the Pope and the King, Nicholas was given the penance of funding the raising of the walls of Baddesley Clinton Church and building its tower. When he died in 1517, he was buried under the entrance, so that he would be walked over by everyone entering the church.

Nicholas's daughter Constance married Sir Edward Ferrers, whose descendents owned the house for the next 500 years. Their great-grandson Henry Ferrers, who inherited the property in 1564, rented Baddesley Clinton to Anne Vaux and Eleanor Brooksby, two staunchly Catholic sisters who used it to harbour priests during the religious persecutions of Elizabeth I's reign. They constructed three priest-holes which still exist inside the house. Phantom footsteps heard pacing along corridors are thought to be the echoes of those long-dead Catholic priests hurrying to their hides to evade their Protestant pursuers.

In the late 19th century, another family member, Rebecca Ferrers, wrote how she had 'heard the solemn tread' of spectral footsteps and seen a door handle being 'jerked loudly' just a few feet away, yet she had seen no one. Around the same time, there were reports of an apparition of a man wearing a scarlet jacket, with a white belt across his chest, on the house's upper landing. When Rebecca discovered a miniature of Major Thomas Ferrers, who died in France in 1817 following a fall from the ramparts of a fortress, she was struck by how much he resembled the ghostly visitor. Anxious to grant this ancestor peace in the afterlife, she had a priest say a mass for Thomas in 1887. After this, his figure was seen no more and the spectral footsteps became less frequent.

ABOVE: Portrait of Thomas Ferrers by an unknown artist
BELOW: A handsome gabled entrance at Baddesley Clinton

COOMBE ABBEY HOTEL

COVENTRY

Coombe Abbey Hotel

Brinklow Road,
Binley, Coventry
CV3 2AB

www.coombeabbey.com

Haunted Rating

The Torment of Abbot Geoffrey

If a ghost were asked to choose the perfect place in which to wander for the whole of eternity, Coombe Abbey would surely feature high on the list of most desirable haunts. It is a truly enchanting place, where you find yourself falling under the magic of its powerful spell from the first moment you cross its historic threshold.

Set amid 500 glorious acres of majestic parkland and looming over a picturesque moat, the building – now a luxurious hotel – was constructed around a 12th-century Cistercian abbey. Following the Dissolution of the Monasteries, the abbey was surrendered to Henry VIII and it remained under the ownership of the Crown until 1581. It was then purchased by Sir John Harrington, who built himself a fine new house incorporating parts of the abbey buildings. In 1622, the building was purchased by Elizabeth Craven, widow of Sir William Craven, who had been one of the richest men of his age.

The grand facade of Coombe Abbey

The Craven family remained in residence for the next 300 years before selling the estate to the Coventry builder John Gray in 1923. He leased Coombe Abbey to the General Electric Company, which used it as a residential training centre, and then sold it to Coventry City Council. In 1992, it was bought by the No Ordinary Hotel company, which restored it and turned it into a magnificent hotel. Guests can now look forward to being pampered in the lap of luxury, with the added bonus of a chance encounter with the ghosts of former residents.

Coombe Abbey's most famous spectre is that of a monk, reputedly Abbot Geoffrey, who was murdered here in 1345. His murderer, thought to have been a fellow monk, was never caught. This causes the forlorn phantom to return to the abbey where, for as long as anyone can remember, his hooded figure has chilled the blood of many a visitor as he glides past. One of the spookier aspects of his appearances is that he floats a good three feet off the ground! He also seems to be responsible for poltergeist activity, as objects are often flung around the rooms when his apparition is witnessed. Perhaps he is simply venting his frustration at the fact that his killer was never brought to justice.

However, Abbot Geoffrey is not the only figure from the past who returns to Coombe Abbey in phantom form. One of the most poignant wraiths is that of a young Romany girl. Tradition remembers her as Matilda, and her dainty footsteps are sometimes heard padding across the cobbles by the stables. From time to time, her full-blown apparition, dressed in rags and looking very sad, has also been known to materialize.

Matilda supposedly became involved with a male member of the Craven household at some stage during their years in residence. However, after finding herself with child, she was abandoned by her hard-hearted suitor. Sadly, the baby was still-born, and Matilda was so heartbroken that she spat a curse upon the Craven family, condemning the first-born of successive generations to an early death. Her curse proved particularly effective as the family was blighted by bad luck over the years, with several of them dying young.

Other ghosts seen at this lovely old property include a figure on horseback galloping through the grounds, and a spectral lady in Edwardian-style clothing riding an old-fashioned bicycle on the road outside the abbey.

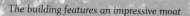
The building features an impressive moat

LYVEDEN NEW BIELD

NORTHAMPTONSHIRE

Lyveden New Bield

Near Oundle,
Northamptonshire
PE8 5AT

www.nationaltrust.org.uk

Haunted Rating 🗝️🗝️🗝️🗝️🗝️

Suspended in Time

Lyveden New Bield is the pitiful shell of what could have been an extremely grand house but which was never finished. It was designed and built between 1595 and 1605 for Sir Thomas Tresham, a fervent Catholic. During the Elizabethan religious persecutions, Sir Thomas spent a great deal of time imprisoned for his faith, and he was also repeatedly fined, which left him in considerable debt. In spite of this, he wished to make a declaration of his religious beliefs with New Bield and conceived a building that would represent the Passion of Christ in bricks and mortar – the foundations are in the shape of a cross.

Sir Thomas died on 11 February 1605, with his estates passing to his son Sir Francis Tresham. He couldn't afford to finish the grand house that his father had envisaged, and building work stalled in early 1605. It was completely abandoned when, later that year, Sir Francis found himself implicated in the Gunpowder Plot – a Catholic conspiracy to blow up James I and Parliament. Whether Sir Francis was an actual plotter is open to debate. Evidence suggests that he was merely an unfortunate Catholic nobleman caught up on the periphery of a conspiracy instigated by his younger cousin Robin Catesby. However, once the plot was uncovered, Sir Francis found himself languishing in the Tower of London. Following his lingering death from an infection on 23 December 1605, his body was decapitated and his head posted above the gates of Northampton.

With Sir Francis's arrest, the family's properties were confiscated by the authorities, although his mother was able to petition for their return. She then set about repairing the family finances, and had largely achieved this by the time of her death in 1615. Unfortunately, her son Lewis, to whom the estate passed following Francis's death, was something of a spendthrift. He set about undoing his mother's hard work, which resulted in his son being forced to sell the estate in 1643.

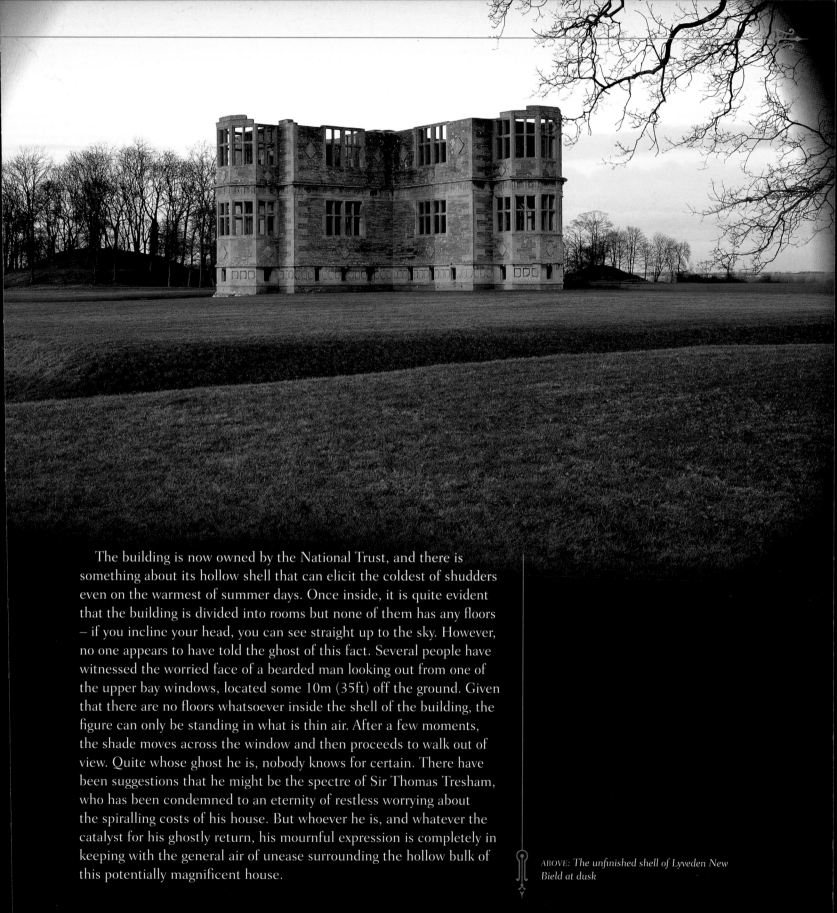

The building is now owned by the National Trust, and there is something about its hollow shell that can elicit the coldest of shudders even on the warmest of summer days. Once inside, it is quite evident that the building is divided into rooms but none of them has any floors – if you incline your head, you can see straight up to the sky. However, no one appears to have told the ghost of this fact. Several people have witnessed the worried face of a bearded man looking out from one of the upper bay windows, located some 10m (35ft) off the ground. Given that there are no floors whatsoever inside the shell of the building, the figure can only be standing in what is thin air. After a few moments, the shade moves across the window and then proceeds to walk out of view. Quite whose ghost he is, nobody knows for certain. There have been suggestions that he might be the spectre of Sir Thomas Tresham, who has been condemned to an eternity of restless worrying about the spiralling costs of his house. But whoever he is, and whatever the catalyst for his ghostly return, his mournful expression is completely in keeping with the general air of unease surrounding the hollow bulk of this potentially magnificent house.

ABOVE: *The unfinished shell of Lyveden New Bield at dusk*

LEICESTER GUILDHALL

LEICESTERSHIRE

The Page-turning Spectre

Leicester's Guildhall is one of the best-preserved timber-framed halls in England and, over its 600 years in existence, it has been put to many different uses. The Great Hall, which forms the hub of the building, was constructed in around 1390 as a meeting place for the Guild of Corpus Christi, whose members comprised some of the most powerful and influential men in Leicester.

Over the next 100 years, the building was extended with the addition of two wings at either end. Following the dissolution of the Guild in 1548, the Corporation of Leicester purchased the building and used it as a meeting place. The East Wing was used to house the town library

Leicester Guildhall

Guildhall Lane,
Leicester
LE1 5FQ

Haunted Rating 👻👻👻👻👻

in 1632, and the ground floor of the West Wing was refurbished and pressed into service as the Mayor's parlour. Trials were frequently held in the Great Hall, with an adjoining jury room added to the building above the Mayor's parlour. But the Great Hall also hosted the more sociable pursuits of the corporation and was used as a venue for theatrical performances, banquets and civic events. As the town expanded during the 19th century, the Guildhall proved too small for the needs of the rapidly growing local government departments and, in 1876, council business was transferred to a new town hall in Horse Fair.

The Guildhall was then put to several different uses, including serving as the local police headquarters and as a school. By the 1920s, it was in a very sad and sorry state, and there were calls for it to be pulled down. Fortunately, the local council intervened, restored it and, in 1926, opened it to the public as a museum. Today, visitors can step inside this symbol of bygone Leicester, absorb its atmosphere and, perhaps, encounter one of the many ghosts known to haunt it.

Predominant among the ghostly visitors known to lurk in its darker recesses is the White Lady. Rarely seen, she prefers to make her presence known by moving the heavy Tudor furniture around. She also appears to have a fondness for the large Bible that sits upon the library's main table. Staff have lost count of the number of times they have closed the Bible at the end of the day only to find it open at the same page the next morning. Other phenomena experienced in the library include heavy footsteps heard plodding across the roof space and, strangest of all, legs growing from the portrait of Henry of Huntingdon, which hangs in the Mayor's parlour.

ABOVE AND LEFT: Its heavily beamed interior and old leaded windows proclaim Leicester Guildhall's ancient origins

BOSWORTH BATTLEFIELD HERITAGE CENTRE AND COUNTRY PARK

LEICESTERSHIRE

King Richard III (1452-1485)

Richard III's Last Stand

The Battle of Bosworth was fought on 22 August 1485 between the forces of Richard III, the last Plantagenet king of England, and troops assembled under the banner of Henry Tudor, the Earl of Richmond. It was the decisive battle of the Wars of the Roses – its outcome established the Tudor dynasty on the throne of England and set the country on the road to the Renaissance.

Indeed, it could be said that modern Britain began on that day in 1485 when Richard Plantagenet became the last king of England to die in battle. Strange, then, that the Battle of Bosworth is one of the worst-documented battles in English history. No eyewitness accounts of it have survived. Even the exact location where it took place has, over the years, been the subject of intense debate. However, in February 2010 it was announced that archaeologists, who had spent five years going over the area with metal detectors, had uncovered cannon balls, sword mounts and badges, including a small silver badge in the shape of a boar – Richard III's personal emblem. This led them to conclude that they had, at last, pinpointed the site of the battle, although its exact location has been kept secret to deter treasure hunters.

Whether the battle was actually fought on the site now occupied by the Bosworth Battlefield Heritage Centre is debatable, but it is to this informative and fascinating place that visitors flock to learn about the encounter that, literally, changed the course of English history.

Despite the fact that Richard III's troops outnumbered those of Henry Tudor, he was dependent upon the support of several nobles, and their loyalty was by no means guaranteed. Chief among these were the Stanley brothers, Sir William and Thomas, the Earl of Derby. They had lined their troops up on a nearby ridge overlooking the battlefield but were showing a marked reluctance to join their king's ranks. Here

RIGHT: An engraving showing Richard III's dead body being removed from the battlefield at Bosworth

they remained as the battle began. Richard's loyal supporters, the Duke of Norfolk and Lord Ferrers, were killed early on in the fierce hand-to-hand combat. Worried that without the intervention of the Stanleys, the battle might go against him, Richard's closest surviving supporters begged him to flee the field. Proclaiming that he would live or die as King of England, Richard refused point-blank even to consider a retreat. Suddenly, a messenger pointed out a group of horsemen waving aloft the banner of the red dragon, the standard of Henry Tudor, cantering across the plain towards Sir William Stanley.

Realizing that Henry was attempting to enlist the support of the Stanley brothers, Richard leapt onto his horse and, with his household cavalry in tow, charged towards his adversary. He plunged into the enemy ranks with such force that, despite his slight stature, he managed to cut down the immensely strong Sir John Cheney and killed Henry's standard-bearer, William Brandon. But, at that moment, Sir William Stanley threw his support behind Henry and brought his troops into the fray. Now outnumbered and with his men falling around him, Richard fought bravely on. Unhorsed, he raised his sword and made a last desperate attempt to kill Henry. But the combined Tudor and Stanley forces fell upon him, beating him to the ground. 'Treason! Treason!' he screamed, as their weapons smashed through his armour and hacked him to death. Sir William Stanley, so legend claims, then retrieved Richard's crown from beneath a nearby thorn bush and, placing it on Henry Tudor's head, proclaimed him King of England.

Psychic echoes of the battle and its aftermath have reverberated around the area ever since. Visitors to the Bosworth Battlefield Heritage Centre have encountered ethereal hooded figures and heard the sound of an invisible phantom army marching past them. Mediums have detected numerous spirit energies around the heritage centre. These include a peasant woman, a wounded soldier who uses his sword as a crutch, and the headless figure of a soldier who died in the battle. But the most illustrious spirit contacted by those with psychic abilities is that of Richard III himself, who repeatedly returns to the vicinity where, on that distant August day, he became the last King of England to die in battle.

**Bosworth Battlefield
Heritage Centre and
Country Park**

Sutton Cheney, near Market
Bosworth, Leicestershire
CV13 0AD

www.bosworthbattlefield.com

Haunted Rating 👤👤👤👤👤

The dead Body of Richard the Third thrown across a Horse after the Battle of Bosworth Field.

THE CROOKED HOUSE

STAFFORDSHIRE

The Crooked House

Coppice Hill, Himley,
Staffordshire
DY3 4DA

www.thecrooked-house.co.uk

Haunted Rating

Lopsided Hospitality

To say that The Crooked House is an unusual pub is something of an understatement. It is positively bizarre! But it is also one of the most unique haunted pubs you could possibly encounter. Mind you, the fact that everything about the place is decidedly askew could lead to some intriguing results once you rise from your chair and attempt to negotiate a graceful exit.

You enter the pub via a front door that leans to the left. The inside door slopes to the right. Once over the threshold, there comes a moment of adjustment as you try to retain some measure of equilibrium. This is not as easy as you might at first imagine. The floors slope, the walls lean, the curtains hang away from the walls, while the swing of the pendulum in the grandfather clock is positively at odds with the laws of gravity. On a wall ledge in the lounge bar you can even roll a marble uphill, a trick that delights children and adults alike. The whole place is delightfully eccentric and the overall ambience is pleasingly – well – crooked.

It wasn't always so. When the pub was built in the 19th century, its site adjoined the estate of Sir Stephen Glynne. As lord of all he surveyed, both above and below the ground, he decided to extract the rich deposits of coal that lay beneath his estate. As it so happened, the mine workings halted directly under one wall of the farmhouse.

While the miners were toiling away on his behalf, the presence of underground passages didn't have much impact on the lives of those who lived above. But, once the seam of coal was exhausted, the mine was abandoned and the tunnel was flooded. The consequence was that the land at one end of the farmhouse began to subside and the walls began to lean gracefully, leaving one side wall higher than the other.

By this time, it had become impossible to find tenants willing to risk rolling out of bed in the dead of night or to pursue their peas uphill across their plates at mealtimes. The building became an alehouse which, in deference to the local estate-owners, was named the Glynne Arms, but to those who came to enjoy its decidedly lopsided hospitality, it became known quite simply as The Crooked House.

Unfortunately, those charged with the task of maintaining the principles of health and safety failed to appreciate the glories of drinking beer while leaning sideways, and the alehouse was condemned as unsafe in 1940. Luckily, the local brewery, which had acquired the property, saw the marketing opportunities afforded by its uniqueness. They re-enforced the building with steel girders and propped up the lower of the side walls with a solid buttress, ensuring that the pub would not become any more crooked. Today, people come from all over the world to sink a pint in this unconventional hostelry.

Several ghosts haunt the pub, including a servant girl and a child, while a ghostly man stands by the fireplace. Mysterious footprints have appeared on freshly mopped floors, and handprints have been found upon brass objects that have just been cleaned. The pub is also prone to poltergeist activity which, given the lopsided nature of the place, makes you feel sorry for the poor poltergeist in its bid to throw things around.

ABOVE: *The front door of The Crooked House leans to the left, while the inside door slopes to the right. It is almost impossible to leave the premises without staggering drunkenly*

GALLERIES OF JUSTICE MUSEUM

NOTTINGHAMSHIRE

The Turmoil and the Torment Continue

Nottingham's Galleries of Justice are located in the Old Shire Hall, a place that seems to droop under the weight of the infamy to which it has borne witness. As you explore its expansive interior, you find yourself almost cringing at the knowledge of the turmoil and torment that must have been experienced here over the centuries. Inmates long ago could be tried, found guilty, sentenced and executed without having to leave its confines. It is little wonder that the restless souls of many imprisoned here have been condemned to linger at the site of their anguish for as long as the gloom-laden walls remain standing.

Although the present building was used as a prison and courthouse between 1780 and 1980, there had been a court on the site since at least 1375, with prison cells added in 1449. The building that visitors can explore today stretches over seven floors and includes original prison cells, two impressive court rooms, sinister man-made caves beneath and a prison yard in which you can see the graffiti of 19th-century inmates.

The museum positively brims with ghostly activity, and there is hardly a section of the old and, in parts, very creepy building that does not play host to strange happenings on a regular basis. In the medieval dungeons, for example, visitors have been stroked, touched, even attacked by unseen entities. People have reported becoming nauseous when entering the dungeons, and foul smells are known to come and go with alarming rapidity. Elsewhere, there have been mysterious loud knockings, while in the Court Room dark figures have been seen on the balcony and anguished groans have been heard. The ghosts of a Victorian gentleman, a lady and a soldier have been encountered in the entrance hall to the Galleries of Justice, and keys have been heard jangling in the corridor that leads to the cells. Meanwhile, the door of the Laundry Room has been known suddenly to slam open with a loud bang, apparently of its own volition.

The Galleries of Justice is also a popular venue with paranormal investigation groups, and overnight ghost hunts are held on a regular basis. Rarely do participants leave without experiencing some decidedly otherworldly activity. When seances have been held during these investigations, stones have been thrown at some of the participants, while others have been tugged and pulled at by unseen hands. On one occasion, a medium advised a woman to leave the room she was in immediately for her own safety. She refused, whereupon 'something' took hold of her and began jerking her around in a violent frenzy. On leaving the room, she found that she had three bleeding marks on her body. On another occasion, during a Murder Mystery session, several of the participants were astonished when a black mist appeared among them and promptly formed itself into the figure of a man in a top hat.

There is little doubt that the Galleries of Justice is one of the most haunted places you could possibly imagine. It is also a fascinating venue with a great deal of history to offer the intrepid explorer in search of all things mysterious. Should you happen to encounter the wraith of a former resident or feel yourself grabbed by some unseen entity, you will feel a strange pride that the ghosts of ages past have decided to honour you with their own special welcome to what is certainly Nottingham's most haunted location.

Galleries of Justice Museum

The Lace Market,
Nottingham NG1 1HN

www.galleriesofjustice.org.uk

Haunted Rating

HARDWICK OLD HALL

DERBYSHIRE

The Ghost of the Man who Didn't Believe in Ghosts

There is a delicious irony about the spectral figure that haunts Hardwick Old Hall – in life, he was a man who didn't actually believe in ghosts. Indeed, Thomas Hobbes, the 17th-century philosopher and author of Leviathan *and* Behemoth, *believed that ghosts were nothing more than 'the imaginary inhabitants of man's brain'.*

The superstitious, he opined, 'possessed with fearful tales, and alone in the dark… believe they see spirits and dead men's ghosts walking in churchyards; whereas it is either their fancy only, or else the knavery of such persons as make use of such superstitious fear to pass disguised in the night to places they would not be known to haunt.' Furthermore, he

BELOW: *The stark grandeur of Hardwick Old Hall is still visible, although parts of the building are ruined*
RIGHT: *A grim view of the west staircase*

found it preposterous that ghosts always appeared fully clothed since he simply could not bring himself to believe that a dead man's old clothes could be resurrected. Strange, then, by some quirk of fate, that his fully clothed ghost has been seen wandering through the grounds and along the path that runs beneath the walls of Hardwick Old Hall.

Hardwick was the birthplace of one of the most remarkable women of the Elizabethan period: Elizabeth, Countess of Shrewsbury, or Bess of Hardwick, as she is more commonly known. Bess's start in life wasn't a particularly promising one. Her father, John Hardwick, an impoverished Derbyshire nobleman, died before she was one year old. However, Bess proved extremely ambitious and, via a sequence of four advantageous marriages, each to a husband wealthier than the previous one, she elevated herself from her humble origins to become one of the richest and most powerful women in England, her net worth second only to that of Elizabeth I.

Her second husband was the extremely wealthy Sir William Cavendish, with whom she acquired the estate at Chatsworth in 1559. Here she built one of her greatest legacies, Chatsworth House – the magnificent seat of the Cavendish family, the Earls of Devonshire. Bess's fourth husband was George Talbot, the Earl of Shrewsbury, from whom she separated in 1580 amid public accusations, mostly from Bess, that he was having an affair with Mary, Queen of Scots – he was her jailer from 1569 to 1584. The split was particularly acrimonious and Talbot refused to allow Bess to live at her beloved Chatsworth House. She, therefore, consoled herself by returning to her family home at Hardwick, where she began a rebuilding project to create a suitably splendid residence for the Cavendish dynasty, of which she was very much the matriarch.

When George Talbot died in 1590, Bess nevertheless inherited his vast fortune and decided to build an even grander house at Hardwick. Thus what is now Hardwick Old Hall was abandoned and work commenced on the magnificent Hardwick Hall in the grounds of which the Old Hall stands. In contrast to its elaborate neighbour, the Old Hall is a partial ruin, although it is possible to ascend four floors and to view surviving decorative plasterwork, as well as the kitchen and service rooms.

Thomas Hobbes, who was destined to become the resident ghost at Hardwick Old Hall, began his involvement with the Cavendish family in the year of Bess's death, 1608, when he became tutor to Bess's eldest grandson, William Cavendish. He remained connected to the Cavendish family for the rest of his life and would live at Hardwick Hall on and off over many years, dying there in December 1679 with the reputed last words 'a great leap in the dark'.

Hardwick Old Hall

Near Chesterfield,
Derbyshire S44 5QJ

Haunted Rating 🔑🔑⭕⭕⭕

TATTON OLD HALL

CHESHIRE

Tatton Old Hall

Tatton Park, Knutsford,
Cheshire
WA16 6QN

www.tattonpark.org.uk

Haunted Rating 👻👻👻👻👻

A Sylvan Retreat Where Time Stands Still

Nestling amid 2,000 glorious acres of stunning parkland, the rustic red-brick walls of Tatton Old Hall blend harmoniously into their surroundings. No one who seeks out this hidden gem of bygone Cheshire can deny that it lies in a time warp. From the moment you begin your tour in the building's Great Hall, you find yourself pitched back in time. The dull glow of tallow candles lights your way as the flickering flames from the fire cast long shadows into dark recesses. You can sense the eyes of former residents watching your every move from them.

It isn't known for certain who was responsible for the original building, which was constructed around 1490 as a single-storey structure. Some say it was the Stanley family, whose switch of allegiance on the battlefield at Bosworth in 1495 cost Richard III his life and established the Tudor dynasty on the throne of England. Others claim it was built by Sir Richard Brereton, who was related by marriage to the Stanley family. In 1598, the property came to be owned by Sir Thomas Egerton, Lord Chancellor of England, who created a more comfortable dwelling by adding a two-storey wing. The building was very much the hub of the large, thriving Tatton estate until the early 1700s, when a new house was built on the site of the current mansion house elsewhere in Tatton Park. The old hall was then used as a substantial farmhouse for the next hundred years, after which it was converted into three cottages for workers on the estate.

During World War II, the surrounding estate played a pivotal role in the training of allied paratroops and, between 1940 and 1946, around 60,000 trainees made their first training drops from cages suspended beneath barrage balloons over the park.

The Egerton family gave up ownership of Tatton Old Hall in 1958. Since the 1960s, it has been run by the local council as a museum,

where visitors can visit rooms furnished in the style of the various ages through which the hall has stood – from Tudor times, through the Victorian era and up to the 1950s.

Many of the visitors who have explored the hall's atmospheric interior have encountered ghosts. One of the more persistent phantoms is that of the weeping lady who, although she has been seen from time to time inside the house, is more often heard sobbing to herself in the darkness outside. Another spectral visitor is a ghostly matriarch. Mediums attending the overnight ghost hunts frequently held at Tatton Old Hall have named her Eleanor. She is followed about the property by the shade of a young girl. A far more sinister phantom figure is that of the misogynist who is sensed rather than seen. The psychically inclined who have been unfortunate enough to encounter his energy say that he is the ghost of a drunk who was a woman beater in life and who continues to harbour an intense hatred for women in death.

There is no doubt that Tatton Old Hall is a genuinely haunted property. Indeed, according to Phil Whyman of deadhaunted.com, who regularly hosts overnight ghost hunts at this fascinating building, 'Tatton Old Hall is one of those places which exudes the kind of spine-tingling atmosphere one would hope to find at a haunted location; you almost accept that you are going to see a ghost!'

Mary, Queen of Scots
Britain's Busiest Ghost

On 16 May 1568, Mary, the deposed Queen of Scots, arrived in England and sought the protection of her English cousin, Elizabeth I. Mary's arrival was both unexpected and unwanted. Not only was she next in line to the throne of England but she was also a Catholic, and there were many both at home and in Europe who believed her to be the rightful Queen of England rather than the Protestant Elizabeth. Furthermore, there were those who saw in Mary a chance to restore England to the Catholic faith and who would be only too happy to assassinate Elizabeth to achieve it.

Thus, for the next 19 years, Queen Elizabeth's personal supporters and those in authority in the English court did their best to ensure that Mary was kept well away from those who might try to further her claim to the throne. This resulted in poor Mary being imprisoned in various houses and castles scattered across the English heartland. However, her mere presence in the country proved a catalyst for numerous plots aimed at deposing or murdering Elizabeth and replacing her with Mary. It was largely thanks to the endeavours of the able and wily Sir Francis Walsingham, Elizabeth's trusted 'spymaster', that none of these plots succeeded.

LEFT: The unlucky Mary, Queen of Scots

RIGHT: Elizabeth I finally signed her cousin Mary's death warrant on 1 February 1587. Just seven days later, Mary was executed

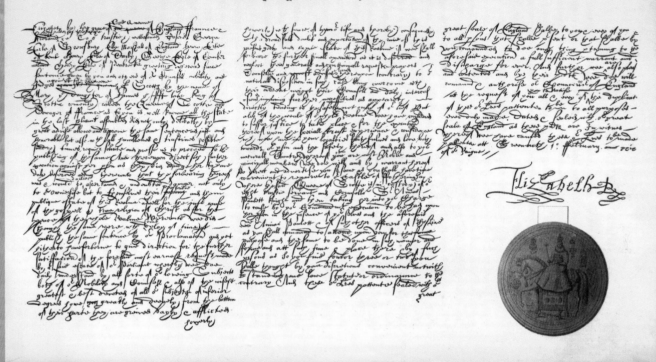

Warrant to Execute Mary Stuart, Queen of Scots, A.D. 1587.

However, by the mid-1580s, it had become obvious to Elizabeth's advisers that as long as Mary was alive, Elizabeth would be in danger. They urged the Queen to consider trying and executing her cousin for treason. Elizabeth, though, balked at the prospect of executing a fellow royal and so Walsingham began looking for a solution that would remove the threat once and for all.

By December 1585, Mary and her household had been moved to Chartley Hall near Stafford. Mary had found a new champion, Anthony Babington, a wealthy Catholic. An ingenious method of exchanging messages was devised, whereby coded letters were placed in watertight pouches and hidden in the bungholes of Mary's beer casks. Thus, in June 1586, Babington was able to furnish Mary with the details of his plot. Addressing her as 'My dread Sovereign Lady and

Queen', he wrote that 'six noble gentlemen, all my private friends' would 'despatch the usurper' Elizabeth. He himself would free Mary from Chartley and then, aided by a Spanish invasion, place her upon the throne of England. On 17 July, Mary sent her approval of the plan and, in so doing, sealed her death warrant. 'The affair being thus prepared,' she replied, 'and the forces in readiness both inside and outside the realm, then shall it be time to set the six gentlemen to work.' Unknown to Mary and Babington, their letters were intercepted by Walsingham's underlings, then copied and decoded by his clerks, before being sent on to their intended recipients. On 11 August 1586, Mary was arrested. Babington and his fellow conspirators were already in custody and, under torture, confessed everything. A search of Mary's rooms turned up hundreds of incriminating documents.

Trial and Punishment

Mary was moved to Fotheringhay Castle in Northamptonshire. Here, on 14 October 1586, her trial began in the castle's Great Hall. Mary conducted her own defence, denying all knowledge of the Babington plot and insisting that she had not endorsed harming her cousin. But the eloquence of her defence was far outweighed by the evidence against her and, on 29 October 1586, Mary Stuart was found guilty. Elizabeth, however, was still unwilling to contemplate executing her cousin and it was a further three months before she finally agreed to sign Mary's death warrant on 1 February 1587.

At 8am on Wednesday, 8 February 1587, Mary was brought into the Great Hall of Fotheringhay Castle, where she climbed the steps onto a black-draped scaffold before a crowd that numbered some 300 people. Blindfolded, she placed her head on the block and remained so still that she totally unnerved the executioner. As a result, his first blow, although cutting deep into the back of her head, failed to sever it. 'Sweet Jesus,' she cried softly, before a second stroke came down and ended her life. Stooping to pick up her head by its auburn ringlets and intending to hold it aloft with the cry 'God Save the Queen', the executioner discovered that she had been wearing a wig. The onlookers stared in horror as the grey stubbly head fell to the ground and rolled across the floor.

Mary was interred at Peterborough Cathedral and remained there until 1612 when her son – who had succeeded Elizabeth as James I, thus uniting the crowns of Scotland and England around 25 years after his mother's death – ordered her exhumation and afforded her a royal resting place in Westminster Abbey, just a short distance from the resting place of Elizabeth I.

Mary, Queen of Scots has since become one of the busiest ghosts in Britain. There is hardly a house that she visited, not to mention many she never went anywhere near, that she does not haunt. Nothing, however, survives of Fotheringhay Castle, save for a melancholic mound overlooking a pretty and tranquil stretch of the River Nene. In summer, the dense tangle of clinging vegetation that carpets its slopes is punctuated by a profusion of thistles, the national emblem of Scotland. Poignantly, they are known locally as Queen Mary's tears.

TOP LEFT: *Mary, Queen of Scots is seen praying at Fotheringhay prior to her execution*
BOTTOM LEFT: *The executioner, unnerved by Mary's composure, failed to execute her with one clean blow*
ABOVE: *Only a grassy mound remains of Fotheringhay Castle, which was razed in 1627. Mary, Queen of Scots was beheaded here in 1587*

WALES AND THE WEST

5

And travellers now, within that valley
Through the red-litten windows see
Vast forms, that move fantastically
To a discordant melody,
While, like a ghastly rapid river,
Through the pale door
A hideous throng rush out forever
And laugh – but smile no more.

From *The Haunted Palace*
by Edgar Allan Poe (1809–1849)

WALES AND THE WEST

5

①	HANBURY HALL – WORCESTERSHIRE	152
②	THE COMMANDERY – WORCESTERSHIRE	154
③	BERRINGTON HALL – HEREFORDSHIRE	156
④	ST MARY, AVENBURY – HEREFORDSHIRE	158
⑤	THE SWANSEA DEVIL – GLAMORGAN	160
⑥	COSMESTON MEDIEVAL VILLAGE – GLAMORGAN	162
⑦	TRETOWER COURT AND CASTLE – POWYS	164

⑧	SOUTH STACK LIGHTHOUSE – ISLE OF ANGLESEY	166
⑨	PLAS YN RHIW – GWYNEDD	168
⑩	BODELWYDDAN CASTLE – DENBIGHSHIRE	170
⑪	HOPTON CASTLE – SHROPSHIRE	172
⑫	RAF MUSEUM COSFORD – SHROPSHIRE	174

FEATURE – THE RED DRAGON
OF WALES 176

INTRODUCTION

The haunted locations featured in this chapter are as varied as the landscape through which our journey passes. We begin in Worcestershire with a visit to the truly stunning Hanbury Hall, to learn of an 18th-century scandal and the ghost that has been condemned to roam the property as a result. From here, we move on to the Commandery, a lovely old property dating back nearly a thousand years, which is haunted by the spectre of an illustrious figure who died from injuries received during the dark days of the Civil War. Crossing into Herefordshire, we pay a visit to Berrington Hall, which may not be one of the most haunted buildings on our journey but it certainly possesses the most breathtakingly ornate interior. However, our next stop, the church of St Mary, Avenbury, a melancholic ruin situated in the depths of rural Herefordshire, is most definitely haunted – few visitors leave without having experienced some form of ghostly activity. Heading over the border into Wales, we stop off at a shopping centre to encounter the sinister form of the Swansea Devil. Our journey then takes us to the Cosmeston Medieval Village, where spirits of a bygone age have been known to materialize in modern times. Paranormal activity is particularly rife in the next few Welsh properties. There is the forlorn phantom lady who seeks her dead husband at the wonderful Tretower Court and Castle; the ghost of a tragic lighthouse keeper who lost his life during one of the worst storms ever to sweep across Britain; the drunken old sot whose spectral footsteps have chilled the marrow of many a visitor to the lovely Plas yn Rhiw; and a plethora of phantoms known to roam Bodelwyddan Castle. Returning to England, we journey to Shropshire. We learn of the supernatural repercussions that resulted from an act of infamy long ago at Hopton Castle, before ending our journey with a Lincoln Bomber haunted by the wraith of a former pilot.

HANBURY HALL

WORCESTERSHIRE

The Society Beauty and the Curate

In 1580, the Reverend Richard Vernon arrived in the village of Hanbury to take up his post as the local vicar. Over the next 50 years, he and his family purchased land in the area and, by 1630, his eldest son Edward had bought the manor house. Thus began the Vernon family's association with Hanbury Hall, which, apart from an absence of some 15 or so years in the late 18th and early 19th centuries, lasted until 1962, when the house was taken over by the National Trust.

The man responsible for the present William and Mary-style house, which was completed in 1706, was the immensely wealthy lawyer Thomas Vernon, Richard's great grandson. However, the ghost of Hanbury Hall belongs to a later generation of the family. The story of the events behind the haunting is almost Shakespearean in the twists and turns of its plot, featuring as it does unrequited love, betrayal and a fair smattering of tragedy.

Emma Vernon (1754–1818) spent her childhood at Hanbury Hall. She grew up to become a renowned society beauty, and her good looks, coupled with fact that she was heiress to the Hanbury estate, made her extremely desirable as a wife. It was Henry Cecil, the future Earl of Exeter, who married Emma in 1776, and the couple set about remodelling parts of the house to turn it into a suitable family abode. Unfortunately, a combination of factors intervened to ensure that the course of their love did not run smoothly. First, they got into heavy debt and, second, they had several children but none survived infancy. As a consequence, the couple began to grow apart.

In 1785, the local vicar, William Burslem, took on a new curate by the name of William Sneyd. Soon, Sneyd was a regular guest at the Hanbury Hall dinner table at which, unbeknown to her husband, he had caught Emma's eye. By 1789, the lady of the house and the parish curate were conducting an illicit liaison, with Emma stealing away from her husband as often as she could to spend time with her lover. The couple were desperate to be together and hatched a cunning plan that they hoped would make that possible.

On 12 June 1789, the Cecils went to Birmingham on business. Emma sent word of their plans to Sneyd and, with her husband away at a meeting, the two lovers met at an inn, then eloped. Over the next few months, they travelled together as man and wife, staying at inns and hotels around the country. The crestfallen Henry, unable to bear the thought of remaining at Hanbury Hall, retreated to a farmhouse in Shropshire. He lodged with one Thomas Goggins and his family, adopting the nom de plume of John Jones to keep his true identity and social status secret from his hosts. It wasn't long before he had fallen in love with Goggins's beautiful 16-year-old daughter Sarah, also known as Sally. On 10 June 1791, he divorced Emma and, in the October of that year, he and Sally were married. The divorce left Emma free to marry Sneyd, which she did that same year, although their happiness was short-lived, as he died in 1793. Following the divorce, Cecil refused to allow Emma to return to her beloved Hanbury Hall, and he sold off all the contents. It remained empty until his death in 1804, after which Emma was able to move back in. She lived there for the remainder of her days with her third husband, John Philips, until her death in 1818.

Emotional vestiges of those long-ago events have, apparently, lingered on at Hanbury Hall. There have been a number of sightings of Emma's ghost, dressed in black, drifting serenely around the grounds. She is especially fond of the route between the house and the church, which her living self used to take on her way to illicit trysts with her lover, William Sneyd, the amorous curate.

Hanbury Hall

School Road, Droitwich,
Worcestershire
WR9 7EA

Haunted Rating

ABOVE: *The governess's day room at Hanbury Hall. Emma and her husband Henry had several children but, sadly, none survived past infancy*

THE COMMANDERY

WORCESTERSHIRE

The Commandery

Sidbury, Worcester,
Worcestershire
WR1 2HU

Haunted Rating ⚀⚀⚀⚀⚀

RIGHT: The Commandery building has seen a wide variety of uses since it was first founded as a hospital in around 1085

The Duke's Final Throes

Very little is known of the early history of the Commandery, although tradition maintains that it was founded as a hospital in around 1085 by St Wulfstan, Bishop of Worcester. Run as a monastic institution to serve the needs of travellers, the building continued to be used for this purpose until 1540, when it was closed during Henry VIII's Dissolution of the Monasteries. From then to the present day, the Commandery has seen a wide variety of uses, from family home, printers shop, factory, school, and even, for a short time, military headquarters – or Commandery. During the Battle of Worcester in 1651, the final battle of the Civil War, it was the home of William Hamilton, 2nd Duke of Hamilton.

In 1651, Hamilton raised a regiment of horses from his Scottish estates and accompanied the Scottish royalist force that invaded England, which was then under Parliamentarian control. Arriving in Worcester, Hamilton took up residence at the Commandery and, on 3 September 1651, the royalists and Parliamentarians came face to face at the Battle of Worcester. Hamilton led a courageous attack on a Roundhead position at Perry Wood. Although initially successful, the royalists were eventually driven off by the Roundheads and retreated towards Worcester. The retreat turned into a rout, with fierce hand-to-hand skirmishing at the gates of the city. In the melee, Hamilton was hit in the leg by a musket ball.

The injured duke was carried back to the Commandery to be treated but the wound became infected and, on 12 September, he died. Tradition maintains that his body was buried under the floorboards for a time before being exhumed and reinterred at Worcester Cathedral.

The Battle of Worcester was the final crushing defeat for the royalist forces and it brought the Civil War to an end. Charles II managed to escape from the battlefield and evade capture by the Parliamentarians for 45 days, after which he sailed to exile in France. There is, however, an intriguing postscript. Before the battle, Charles II had commissioned the Worcestershire Clothiers to provide uniforms for his army but, having lost the battle, paying them for their labours was the last thing on his mind. Their bill for £453 and 3 shillings remained outstanding for 357 years until, in June 2008, Charles, Prince of Wales finally settled the debt!

The Commandery has seen its fair share of death and tragedy, and it is considered to be a very haunted building. Over the 500 years that it was used as a hospital, hundreds of people would have passed through, and a large proportion of them may well have never left. Some years ago, a man arrived early for a meeting in the building's Solar Room. He was left there alone but, after a few minutes, came charging out, absolutely terrified. He refused to say what he had seen that had scared him so much but he refused point-blank ever to go into that room again. More recently, several visitors to that same room have experienced a cold, clammy sensation and have become aware of an overwhelming presence. Some believe it is the spirit of the Duke of Hamilton in his final death throes.

In another part of the Commandery now used as a museum, there have also been ghostly occurrences: an old lady who appears for a few fleeting moments only to vanish into thin air, and the apparition of a man who bears a striking resemblance to William, 2nd Duke of Hamilton. In addition, staff have been physically pushed from rooms, while locked doors have been rattled furiously by some unseen but chilling entity.

BERRINGTON HALL

HEREFORDSHIRE

ABOVE: A glamorous lady's dressing table. The ghosts that haunt Berrington Hall live in the lap of luxury

Ghosts in the Lap of Luxury

The austere exterior of Berrington Hall belies a stunningly ornate interior, resplendent with wonderful painted ceilings, sumptuous plasterwork and exquisite furnishings. The house dates back to 1778, when Thomas Harley, who had made a fortune as a supplier to the British Army, decided that his family needed a new home that would reflect the high esteem in which they held themselves. He, therefore, commissioned his son-in-law, the fashionable architect Henry Holland, to design a house in which generations of Harleys could live in palatial splendour. Determined to have the best that money could buy, Harley also commissioned the leading landscape architect of the day, 'Capability' Brown, to design the splendid grounds that surround the property and which afford sweeping views of the Black Mountains.

Today, Berrington Hall provides visitors with a glimpse of how the other half once lived, but as well as gazing in open-mouthed wonder at its dazzling interior, you can also see what life was like below stairs with visits to the Laundry, Butler's Pantry and Dairy.

An intriguing aspect of the gardens is the Drying Ground. This lawned section was where washing was aired out of sight of the family, who didn't want the elegance of their lifestyle and enjoyment of the surroundings to be spoiled by such commonplace items as sheets and towels.

Berrington Hall

Near Leominster,
Herefordshire
HR6 0DW

www.nationaltrust.org.uk/
berringtonhall

Haunted Rating

Thomas Harley's daughter Anne married the son of the naval commander Admiral Rodney. Since Harley didn't have a son, the hall passed to the Rodney family, who lived there for 95 years before George, 7th Lord Rodney, gambled away the family fortune. In 1901, he was forced to sell the hall to Frederick Cawley, who had made his fortune from cotton. In 1957, mounting death duties led to the Cawley family handing the house over to the National Trust, which now runs it and opens it to the public.

There were reports of a ghostly figure in the south wing of the house in the 1980s, although who it was, nobody was able to ascertain for certain. More recently, spectral activity appears to have confined itself to the outbuildings, where a ghostly figure has been seen unlocking the door of the stables, even though the key has been missing for years. Phantom horses have also been seen inside the stables, although it has been a very long time since any horses were stabled in them.

ST MARY, AVENBURY

HEREFORDSHIRE

St Mary, Avenbury

Avenbury,
Herefordshire
HR7 4LA

Haunted Rating 👻👻👻👻👻

Ask Not for Whom the Bell Tolls

Hidden away from the outside world by dense woodland, the ruined church of St Mary, Avenbury is both lovely and creepy. Come here on a bright spring or summer's day, or even on a crisp winter's morning, and you can honestly believe you've discovered a little slice of rural heaven in Herefordshire. But visit the church in the closing light of day or when the night's shadows have wrapped themselves around its toppled walls and solitary tower, and feelings of trepidation will take hold the moment you lay eyes on it. Indeed, this picturesque ruin, which stands in a woodland clearing close to the banks of the River Frome, has long held the reputation for being one of the most haunted churches in the county, if not the country, and visitors have frequently experienced varying degrees of paranormal activity.

A ghostly white mist flooded the viewfinder when the author took this photograph, even though it was a very clear day

The church dates from the 12th century. For nigh on 700 years, it served the now-disappeared village of Avenbury but, but by the late 19th century, it had fallen into a state of decay. Despite several attempts to repair it, the situation worsened until, in 1931, St Mary's was closed. By this time, though, reports that the old church was haunted were rife. On 8 September 1896, several people, including Mrs Wilson, the wife of the then vicar, heard ghostly organ music sounding from inside the church when it was known to be empty. The phantom organist was a frequently reported phenomenon throughout the late 19th and early 20th centuries. One couple even reported hearing the sound of a joyous celebration coming from inside the empty and dark church at midnight one Christmas night.

Strange White Mist

The church had three bells, the largest of which, 'Andrew', was said to ring out of its own accord whenever danger threatened the parish. It was reputed to have been heard in 1931 on the night that the last vicar of the church, The Reverend E.H. Archer Shepherd, died. Apparently, his death was unexpected and the bell had started tolling before it occurred. His daughter Marion later said that they should have known he was dying because 'everyone knows that bell never tolls for nothing'. She also recalled how one of the parishioners, Sarah Walton, had been kept awake by the tolling of the bell on the night of her father's death and told how her mother, who was entitled to stay on at the vicarage for three months after his death, had to '… hurry her departure because she continually complained of sleepless nights on account of 'that bell'. Following the church's closure, the bells were moved to the church of St Andrew-by-the-Wardrobe in London. True to form, it was heard ringing out shortly after its arrival when a vicar of that parish died.

Bell-ringing is traditionally used to herald momentous events such as births, marriages or deaths

In recent years, the forlorn ruin of St Mary, Avenbury has become something of a mecca for local ghost hunters, and many strange things continue to happen. Indeed, in the course of researching this book, I paid a visit to the site on a snowy January day in 2010. I was photographing one section of the church when, just before I clicked the shutter, the camera's viewfinder suddenly filled with mist. I looked at the picture and, sure enough, there was a white mist over one of the trees to the right, but there was no sign of mist on the photos I took immediately before or after. I was at a loss to explain it, although it dawned on me that I may have breathed out as I took some of the pictures, and my breath against the cold air may have caused the mist. So I took another photo and deliberately breathed out as I did so. This time there was no mist. In all, the mist appeared on five of my photos, and two of those were taken when I made sure I didn't breathe out. Consequently I'm still at a loss to explain what happened.

THE SWANSEA DEVIL

GLAMORGAN

The Swansea Devil

Old Nick,
Quadrant Shopping Centre,
Swansea,
Glamorgan SA1

Haunted Rating

The Hex of Old Nick

A modern and popular shopping complex might not be the sort of place you'd expect to encounter the Devil. Yet visitors to the Quadrant Shopping Centre in Swansea can spy Old Nick looking down on them whenever they step through the east entrance. Indeed, his bulging eyes and demonic expression are very much an integral part of Swansea folklore.

In 1896, Dean Allan Smith decided to flatten and rebuild St Mary's church in the centre of the city. The tender for the design was put out to various architectural practices and a short list of two was drawn up. One was a local architect, the other was Arthur (later Sir Arthur) Blomfield, who had an impressive list of church and civic building to his credit. At the time, he was also Vice President of the Royal Institute of British Architects. Needless to say, the committee charged with selection opted for Blomfield, and St Mary's was duly built.

The local architect didn't take the committee's decision well and saw it as a slight on his professional ability. So he set about devising a cunning plan to wreak devilish revenge on the church. A few years later, a row of cottages came up for sale opposite the church. The local man purchased them, tore them down and replaced them with an ugly red-brick building to house the offices of the local brewery. He then commissioned a wooden carving of a particularly sinister-looking devil and placed it on top of the new building so that it leered over at the church. He also prophesized that, 'My devil will be able to leer and laugh, for at some time in the future he will see St Mary's burn to the ground.'

In February 1941, the centre of Swansea was razed by German bombing and one of the casualties was St Mary's. The next morning, as the people of Swansea surveyed the devastation, it was noted that one of the few survivors was the building on which Old Nick, the Swansea Devil, was perched. Old Nick himself had also escaped harm, and there he squatted, leering across at the bombed remains of St Mary's, just as the architect had predicted.

Nick Gets a New Perch

Throughout the 1960s, the rebuilding of war-torn Swansea was well underway, and Old Nick watched from his lofty perch as the subject of his hex, St Mary's, rose from the ashes. Then, in 1962, the building from which Old Nick had looked down for nigh on 80 years was earmarked for demolition and the Swansea Devil was removed. After that, he wasn't seen for a good many years.

However, thanks to the determined efforts of a local historian, he was traced to a Gloucestershire garage and returned to his home town of Swansea. Unfortunately, Old Nick's building had by that time been replaced by the Quadrant Shopping Centre. After some negotiation, it was agreed to give him a new perch atop the shopping centre from where he could resume his watch over St Mary's. And there he resides to this day, a controversial figure who is loved and loathed by the people of Swansea in equal measure.

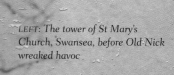

LEFT: The tower of St Mary's Church, Swansea, before Old Nick wreaked havoc

COSMESTON MEDIEVAL VILLAGE

GLAMORGAN

Living in the Past

Many of us today, overwhelmed by the relentless pace of the modern age, often find ourselves yearning for a less pressurized lifestyle. We long to throw off the yoke of our high-tech society, along with the frustrations that come with it, and dream of escaping to a bygone age when life was simple and your friends were people you actually knew rather than an endless list of cyber buddies. At Cosmeston Medieval Village, you really can step back in time, and experience what it was like to live in the distant past – albeit without the plague, grinding poverty, premature death, famine, despotic landowners, perpetual body odour and myriad other ailments that were the daily lot of your average medieval village dweller.

In 1978, during work to develop Cosmeston Lakes Country Park, the remnants of a 600-year-old village were uncovered. The Vale of Glamorgan Council quickly realized that these relics provided an opportunity to present history in an entertaining and informative manner. Thus, in conjunction with a team of local archaeologists, they set about reconstructing the village in a way that would bring to life the fascinating and diverse history of Wales.

Cosmeston Medieval Village is a unique attraction that transports visitors back to the year 1350, a lively and fascinating time in history, when Britain was recovering from the devastation wreaked by the Black Death of 1348. Edward III sat upon the throne of England, and the Hundred Years War with France was in its early stages, while relations between the English and the Welsh were, to say the least, strained.

As you wander through the huts and cottages, you can meet the villagers and learn about their various roles in the village, listen to

their stories and have the past brought vividly to life before you. There's Eleanor, the village Ale Wife and Wise Woman. In addition to quenching the thirsts of the villagers, she dabbles in herbs and spices to treat their ailments. This brings her into regular conflict with Father Edwin, the village priest, who, while acknowledging that Eleanor has cured many, suspects that her powers of healing may be the Devil's work. This concern, however, doesn't stop him imbibing at her house, which doubles up as the village tavern!

Then there's Henry Hogg, the village swineherd. His wife is Henrietta, who, so the local gossips maintain, married Henry for his fat, or to be more precise, the fat of his pigs – Henrietta is a candle-maker of sorts, and the candles used by poorer villagers to light their hovels were made from either sheep or pig fat.

In addition to encountering the day-time populace at this unique place, visitors also have the opportunity to encounter the village's 'other' residents on candlelit ghost tours. Indeed, it seems that some of the original villagers remain earthbound and are happy to mix and mingle with their modern counterparts who spend their days living in the past. During the medieval re-enactments frequently staged at the site, visitors have turned to speak to the person they can sense standing next to them only to find that there is nobody there. Two members of staff were locking up one night when they spotted two people walking across the field towards the spot where the village manor house once stood. Turning to look at each other to wonder who these people were and where they had come from, they looked back to find that the mysterious visitors had vanished into thin air.

Cosmeston Medieval Village

Lavernock Road,
Penarth, Glamorgan
CF64 5UY

Haunted Rating

LEFT: A pig stands outside a traditional beehive pigsty at Cosmeston Medieval Village

TRETOWER COURT AND CASTLE

POWYS

BELOW: Tretower Castle's position has been recognized as strategically important since Roman times, and many former residents return to the site in spectral form

The White Lady's Long Wait

First there was the castle, an imposing bulk of solid grey stone looming over the surrounding countryside and set against the hauntingly beautiful backdrop of the Black Mountains. Tretower Castle was originally a timber motte and bailey construction, built by Roger Picard in the wake of the Norman invasion of 1066 as the forces of William the Conqueror swept across the land to secure his new domain. Subsequent generations of the Picard family would strengthen and expand the fortification, rebuilding it in stone in the mid-12th century and adding the great round keep, the castle's most striking feature, in the 13th century.

The castle's location had been recognized as strategically important since Roman times. As the English and the Welsh battled for control of the surrounding area during the 13th, 14th and 15th centuries, it became a fought-over stronghold, its ownership changing frequently between the two countries, depending on which side had the upper hand at any particular time.

By the 14th century, ownership had passed to the Vaughan family, who moved into a fine new house, Tretower Court, which had been constructed close to the castle. For the next 350 years, this would be the Vaughans' spectacular residence and, since money was no object, they added to it and modified it constantly to reflect the changing domestic fashions of subsequent ages.

A House Full of Mysteries

The house was greatly extended in the mid-15th century by Roger Vaughan, the most prominent commoner in Wales. Tradition maintains that he was the man who led Owen Tudor, grandfather of Henry VII and father of the Tudor dynasty, to his execution in Hereford in 1461. Owen Tudor's death would be avenged in 1471 by his son Jasper Tudor, who summarily beheaded Vaughan at Chepstow and, in so doing, gave Tretower Castle and Court their most persistent phantom. The ghostly figure of a white lady is sometimes seen peering down from one of the battlemented walks overlooking Tretower Court's inner courtyard, as well as from the walls of Tretower Castle. She is thought by some to be Roger Vaughan's wife anxiously awaiting her husband's return, apparently unaware of his fate, even though 500 years have passed since his head was severed from his body.

The Vaughans' tenure at Tretower came to an end in 1783, when it was sold to the Parry family. After that, the house became a farm, with its once-grand rooms used as outhouses, barns and storage areas. By the early 20th century, it was in a sorry state and in danger of falling down. But, in the 1930s, a restoration project was begun and the building was eventually opened to the public.

Today, visitors can not only gain a unique insight into what life would have been like for the wealthier members of society in the Middle Ages, they may also catch fleeting glimpses of several other former residents known to return to the property in spectral form. In addition to the aforementioned White Lady, there is the apparition of a woman seen sitting by a window in the main bedchamber. Many visitors find this particular room somewhat overwhelming and some even stop abruptly at its threshold, refusing to enter. Some visitors have encountered the wraith of a small boy, sitting on the step of the house's courtroom. Who he is and why he sits gazing nonchalantly ahead, apparently unaware of those who see him, is unknown. His identity is just one of the many mysteries that a house of this age inevitably holds within its ancient fabric.

Tretower Court and Castle

Tretower,
Crickhowell,
Powys NP8 1RD

Haunted Rating 🔑🔑🔑🔑🔑

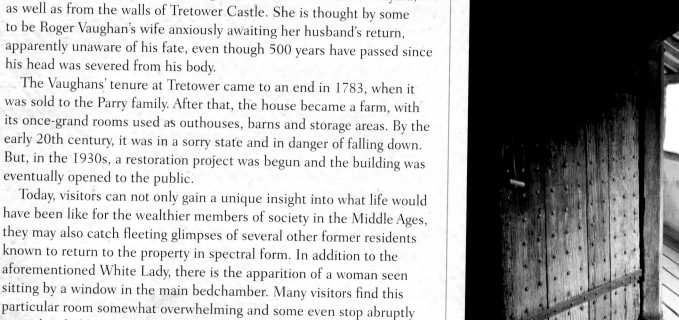

SOUTH STACK LIGHTHOUSE

ISLE OF ANGLESEY

South Stack Lighthouse

South Stack, Holyhead,
Isle of Anglesey LL65 1YH

http://southstack.co.uk

Haunted Rating 👻👻👻👻👻

The Storm-Tossed Phantom

Even approaching the South Stack Lighthouse is a dramatic experience. First, you must descend a precipitous flight of 400 steps hacked out of the 60-m (200-ft) high vertical cliffs that loom over the rocky crag on which the lighthouse stands. Having done so, you must then edge across a short suspension bridge that swings precariously over the foaming sea below and onto the small craggy islet of Ynys Lawd (South Stack). Once on the other side, you draw breath as the gleaming white lighthouse looms over you, not so much standing on as draped over the grey lump of jagged rock. The whole aspect of the place is wildly beautiful and genuinely awe-inspiring as you contemplate the ceaseless battle against the forces of nature that the South Stack Lighthouse has waged for over 200 years.

The original oil lamps of the lighthouse, which cost £12,000 to build, were first lit on 9 February 1809. You can only marvel at the tenacity of those long-ago workers, who transported the required building materials across to the island – it must have been an enormous, not to mention dangerous, undertaking. The original lighthouse keepers must have been a hardy bunch, too, as life on the islet would have been harsh. The early keepers often brought their families to live with them, and many children were born and raised here.

The first keeper was James Deans, who was replaced by his assistant Hugh Griffiths after a short time. In 1810, John Jones became his assistant, and the two remained at the lighthouse until Jones's death in 1828. His wife, Anne Jones, was then made assistant keeper on account of the fact that she had helped her husband for the previous 15 years and was, therefore, *au fait* with the workings of the lighthouse. She was succeeded by her son Jack Jones in the mid-1840s. It has been suggested that it is Jack's ghost that today haunts the South Stack Lighthouse – he died there under tragic circumstances a little over a decade later.

On 25 October 1853, one of the worst storms in Britain's history
battered its coasts. Before the tempest abated, it had wrecked over 200
ships and cost the lives of over 800 men and women. The greatest loss
of life during the storm occurred off the coast of Anglesey. The *Royal
Charter*, a steam clipper nearing the end of a voyage from Melbourne
to Liverpool, was hurled against the rocks at Moelfre on the east side of
the island, with the loss of over 450 lives. Such was the impact of this
tragedy that the storm became known as the Royal Charter Storm.

With the tempest raging around the South Stack Lighthouse, Jack
Jones began making his way over the iron bridge that then led to the
island so that he could assist the Principal Keeper, Henry Bowen, who
was on duty that night. Suddenly, a huge gust of wind smashed into the
sheer cliff face above him and dislodged a rock, which came crashing
down and struck Jones on the head. Almost senseless with concussion,
and with blood streaming from the resultant wound, Jones dragged
himself up the gale-lashed path, calling for help. But his cries were
drowned out by the storm. He wasn't discovered until the next morning,
when Henry Bowen found him lying on the ground just outside the
lighthouse door, barely conscious and covered in blood. Jack Jones died
of his injuries three weeks later.

It has been suggested that the spectral footsteps heard inside the
lighthouse are those of Jack Jones. He may also be responsible for the
tapping sometimes heard on the windows of the building. In addition,
the lighthouse door has been known to rattle furiously as though
someone is trying to get in. According to mediums who have visited
the property, this is Jack's ghost making a desperate attempt to find the
shelter that his living self was, tragically, denied.

ABOVE: *The dramatic position of South Stack
Lighthouse on its small craggy islet*

PLAS YN RHIW

GWYNEDD

Plas yn Rhiw

Rhiw, Pwllheli,
Gwynedd LL53 8AB

Haunted Rating

BELOW: *Spirits from a number of different historical eras haunt the cosy-looking interior of Plas yn Rhiw*

The Weeping White Lady and the Drunken Sot

Standing on foundations reputedly over a thousand years old, Plas yn Rhiw is a small manor house with stunning views over Cardigan Bay. The current building, however, dates from the 16th century and was extended in the 17th and 18th centuries. For much of its existence, the house was owned by the Lewis family before eventually passing to the Roberts family. The last Roberts family member to reside there moved out in 1922, after which the property became derelict.

Three Sisters

Three remarkable sisters – Eileen, Lorna and Honora Keating – came to its rescue. They had first visited the area on holiday as small children with their mother in 1904. They returned regularly over the next 30 years before settling in Rhiw permanently in the mid-1930s. In 1939, they bought the dilapidated Plas yn Rhiw and proceeded to restore it to its former glory. Having made the house habitable, the three sisters and their mother moved in and turned their attention to teasing out the original garden from beneath the thick carpet of bracken and bramble and bringing it back to life. Their goal achieved, the sisters presented the house to the National Trust in 1949, dedicating it to the memory of their parents (their father had died when they were infants). A slate plaque to the Keating parents bears the epitaph, 'There is no death while memory lives.' The Keating sisters remained in residence until the death of the last sister in 1981.

Several ghosts are known to roam the old house. Chief among them is that of an 18th-century servant, who is said to have died from excessive drinking. Her heavy, slow phantom footsteps have been heard ascending and descending the stairs in the dead of night. Another spectral resident is that of a girl who, tradition maintains, was a member of the Williams family, owners of the house in the mid-19th century. She is said to have fallen in love with a tinker, much to the disgust of her father who forbade her to have anything more to do with her Romany Romeo. But the girl paid scant heed to her father's wishes, and one morning she failed to appear at the breakfast table. A quick search revealed that her belongings had gone – she had eloped with her tinker lover in the dead of night. Eventually, so the story goes, the tinker abandoned her, leaving her destitute. Although in life she never returned to the family home, in death her spirit returns to wander Plas yn Rhiw as a forlorn white lady whose ghostly sobs have been heard emanating from dark corners of the house in the dead of night.

BODELWYDDAN CASTLE

DENBIGHSHIRE

A Plethora of Phantoms

Ghosts aplenty drift through the corridors and rooms of Bodelwyddan Castle, one of the most atmospheric locations you could wish to encounter. The building itself broods amid 260 acres of parkland, its picturesque walls and turrets more fairytale than fortress-like in appearance. This is because the present castle – which incorporates parts of an older manor house that had stood on the site since at least the 1400s – was not constructed for defensive or military purposes. Rather, it was built in the 19th century by Sir John Hay Williams, whose family had owned the estate since the 1690s, to provide a magnificent home that would stand as a testimony to the wealth and status of his family.

As work began on the conversion in 1829, a strange and gruesome find was made. According to Sir John's diary, human bones were discovered during the demolition of a wall by a fireplace. Whose bones they were, how they came to be there or even how old they were was never established. Since Sir John also recorded in his diary that he built the bones back into the wall, the person's identity is unlikely to be revealed as long as the castle walls remain standing. It will remain one of the many secrets that a building of this age inevitably keeps, hidden, in this case, literally within its ancient fabric.

Unfortunately, by the time the castle was finished in the 1850s, the Williams family fortune had begun to dwindle. By World War I, the size of the estate had been greatly reduced. The castle, although still owned by the family, was given over for use as a recuperation hospital for soldiers, while the grounds were pressed into service to prepare soldiers for fighting in the trenches. Indeed, the training trenches are one of the curiosities that visitors can wonder at today. In the 1920s, the Williams family sold the property to Lowther College, a private boarding school for girls. According to some of the former pupils, their sleep would often be interrupted by dragging noises heard in their dormitory. The school remained here until the 1980s, when it closed, owing to financial difficulties. The local council then took over the castle and opened it to the public as an attraction, art gallery and museum.

Today, not only is Bodelwyddan Castle a great place to visit for its artworks and sculptures but it's also a must for anyone interested in exploring a haunted building first-hand. The castle conducts frequent overnight paranormal investigations, which the general public can attend. Few who do so leave disappointed.

In the Watts Hall, where you can view paintings by the Victorian artist G.F. Watts, on loan from the National Portrait Gallery with which the castle is partnered, the figure of a lady dressed in white has been known to disappear into one of the walls. A member of staff on security patrol one night opened the gallery door, shone his torch along the corridor and noticed a pair of legs wearing white stockings and buckled shoes at the far end. After jumping back in shock, he recovered his composure and shone his torch back down the corridor only to find it completely empty.

Other ghosts that linger at Bodelwyddan Castle include the wispy wraith of a woman drifting through the Sculpture Gallery; the shadowy figure of a soldier, no doubt from the time when the castle was used as a hospital in World War I; and a blue lady who has been seen several times in the Tea Room.

All in all, Bodelwyddan Castle is a truly haunted and atmospheric place, and the opportunity to explore it when night has fallen and its many phantoms stir within its historic walls should not be missed.

Bodelwyddan Castle

Bodelwyddan, Rhyl,
Denbighshire LL18 5YA

www.bodelwyddan-castle.co.uk

Haunted Rating 🁢🁢🁢🁢🁢

HOPTON CASTLE

SHROPSHIRE

A Bloody Double Cross

The romantic ruin of Hopton Castle sits atop a grassy knoll, its mighty walls appearing to sag with the weight of the infamy they have witnessed. The ruined stone keep probably dates from the 13th century and, although standing on private land, it can be clearly seen from the road. It is therefore possible to witness the haunting at this melancholic ruin, which is connected to one of the most shameful and bloody episodes to take place in this tranquil landscape.

By the time of the English Civil War, Hopton Castle was owned by the Wallop family, who were Puritans and staunch Parliamentarians. To ensure that the castle was kept out of the hands of the royalists, its protection was entrusted to a garrison of around 30 men commanded by Colonel Samuel Moore.

In early 1644, the castle was besieged by a royalist force that numbered some 500 troops under the command of Sir Michael Woodhouse. Despite heavily outnumbering the defenders, the royalists found it almost impossible to take the castle. Attempts to bring down the walls by tunnelling under them, or to topple them by pummelling them with heavy artillery, proved futile. The defenders even managed to kill 200 royalist soldiers as they held their attackers at bay for almost a month. However, the pressure of enduring the siege for such a long period began to deflate morale. Concerned that his men wouldn't be able to take much more, Colonel Moore sent word to his counterpart, proposing a deal whereby they would surrender the castle in exchange for their lives. With these terms accepted, the motley crew of exhausted defenders began filing out, relieved that their ordeal was over. But no sooner had the last man walked out of the castle than the royalists – furious that the garrison had managed to defend such a hopeless cause for so long and determined to avenge their fallen comrades – went back on their word. They proceeded to herd the garrison together and hack them to death, cutting off limbs and slitting throats. The most shameful act, on a day that brimmed with shameful acts, was the stripping and attacking of two of the castle maidservants. One of them was killed, the other wounded and then sent to Brampton Bryan Castle in Herefordshire to inform the garrison there what had happened at Hopton and to warn them that they would face a similar fate if they didn't surrender forthwith. Colonel Moore was then taken to Ludlow Castle where he was imprisoned, and the royalists set about ensuring that Hopton Castle could never be used again by tearing down its walls and setting fire to it.

The reverberations of the slaughter continued throughout the Civil War years, with 'Hopton quarter' (mercy) becoming a byword for treachery. Later in the Civil War, after royalist fortunes had turned, Woodhouse was forced to surrender Ludlow Castle to the Parliamentarian forces, doing so on condition that it wasn't Samuel Moore who accepted his surrender.

The melancholic remnants of Hopton Castle still resonate with the emotions and the memories of that distant bloodbath. It is said that should you happen to be in the vicinity on 14 March, the anniversary of the slaughter, you will see a ragged band of spectral troops file from the castle, reliving those final moments before their relief gave way to the horror that they were about to be double-crossed.

Hopton Castle

Craven Arms,
Shropshire SY7 0QF

www.hoptoncastle.org.uk

Haunted Rating 👤👤👤

RAF MUSEUM COSFORD

SHROPSHIRE

The Ghost in the Machine

The spectral landscape of Britain is littered with an abundance of haunted houses, castles and inns. But the RAF Museum Cosford, where hundreds of aircraft are on show, must surely possess one of the country's most unusual paranormal locations – a haunted Lincoln Bomber.

The Lincoln Bomber was built by the A.V. Roe Aircraft Co. and was intended to be the successor to the Lancaster Bomber. Introduced in 1945, it was too late to see active service in World War II, and the coming of the jet engine soon after rendered piston engines obsolete and its usefulness proved relatively short-lived.

Stories of strange occurrences experienced around Avro Lincoln RF398 have been circulating since the early 1980s. The bomber, then in a sorry state of repair, was moved to the museum in 1977 and RAF volunteers, together with retired servicemen, devoted a great deal of their spare time to renovating it. One night, shortly after the work began, a member of the museum staff switched off the lights in the hangar and was locking the doors when he caught a glimpse of someone moving inside the plane. Switching the lights back on, he went to investigate but, after searching every corner of the bomber, he found no one. Not long afterwards, a volunteer was working alone inside the plane when he heard the rear door open and footsteps walking along the fuselage towards him. Thinking it was one of his workmates, he asked for a spanner, and one was duly thrust into his hand. But when he turned to thank the person, he was astonished to find that he was alone.

The secretary to the museum was once preparing an information board about the bomber when she heard a voice calling her name. Thinking it was a colleague, she turned to see what they wanted but no one else was there. Such was the effect of the ordeal that she point-blank refused to enter the hangar alone again.

Nobody knows for certain whose ghost it is that haunts the plane, although one contender is a Major Hiller, the pilot who flew the plane on its last flight on 30 April 1963. He is said to have been very fond of the plane and reputedly promised that he would 'haunt his baby'. Shortly after that last flight, he was killed in a plane crash near Cosford.

One of the strangest stories is that of an electrician who was working on the plane 4.6m (15ft) above the ground when he suddenly slipped and fell. Bracing himself for what he was convinced would be a fatal impact, he suddenly floated to a stop and hovered above the floor. He later recalled it was as though an invisible force had saved his life.

RAF Museum Cosford

Shifnal, Shropshire
TF11 8UP

www.rafmuseum.org.uk

Haunted Rating ☠☠☠☠☠

LEFT AND ABOVE: Front and side aspect of the haunted Lincoln Bomber, on display in the Warplanes Hangar at RAF Cosford

The Red Dragon of Wales

Although the dragon has been the symbol of Wales for centuries, it was only in 1959 that the Red Dragon (Y Ddraig Goch) on a green-and-white background became the official Welsh flag. Quite why the dragon became synonymous with Wales in the first place is uncertain. But although history remains mute on the subject, legend has been only too willing to imbue the instantly recognizable emblem with supernatural origins and to link it to one of the most significant figures ever to stride across Britain's mythical landscape – Myrddin, or Merlin, the name by which the Welsh wizard is better known today.

LEFT: *An ornate Welsh dragon guards the gates and the entrance to Powis Castle*

RIGHT: *Dinas Emrys, Snowdonia*

In the wilds of Snowdonia National Park, an exhausting, though exhilarating, climb to a remote rocky, wooded hilltop brings the intrepid rambler to the remnants of an ancient fortress known as Dinas Emrys. It is among these ragged vestiges that the youthful Myrddin made his first appearance as a precocious boy wizard, spouting wise saws and prophetic utterances.

The story begins with the tyrannical usurper Vortigern. Having lost his kingdom to the Saxons, he took the advice of his magicians and headed for Wales in search of a location where he could establish a citadel and be safe from his enemies. It was atop this remote summit that his wise men told him to construct a fortress.

His masons duly set to work but each night, when the workers had downed tools, their construction would mysteriously disappear. Sensing evil afoot, Vortigern summoned his magicians and demanded an explanation. They were mystified but informed him that the solution would be to sacrifice a boy who had been born without a human father, and sprinkle his blood about the foundations of the building.

Messengers were duly sent to find such a boy and, in the streets of Carmarthen, they came across a youth being taunted by another because he had never had a father. The boy's name was Myrddin Emrys, the future Merlin of King Arthur's Court. When he and

his mother appeared before Vortigern, she said that she knew of no man who was the boy's father. All she could tell him was that something had appeared to her in the shape of a handsome young man, embraced her, then suddenly vanished. Later, she said, she bore a child. Vortigern was at first sceptical of the claim but when he sought the opinion of his druids, they informed him that she had probably been the victim of an incubus – a male demon, which, it was believed, could ravish sleeping women.

Then Myrddin stepped forward and demanded to know why he and his mother had been brought before Vortigern. When told the reason, the boy denounced the magicians, claiming that the towers had collapsed because two dragons, one white, the other red, lived in a pool beneath the hill and each night they would awake and fight so ferociously that they caused the walls of the citadel to collapse into the ground. The masons dug deep into the hill and, just as Myrddin had predicted, discovered a pool in the depths of which lay two sleeping dragons. The red dragon, Myrddin told the court, represented the Britons, and the white one the Saxons. They would continue to fight for many generations until eventually the red dragon would be victorious and drive the white one away.

Enduring Emblem

Over the centuries, the dragon became the symbol of the legendary leaders of the Britons, such as Uther Pendragon and his son King Arthur. Later, it would be used as the emblem of several famous figures from Welsh history, including Owen Glyndwr (1354–1417), the Welsh nationalist hero. But it was the adoption of a dragon crest by Edmund and Jasper Tudor – father and uncle respectively of Henry VII – that laid the foundations for the red dragon becoming the enduring emblem of Wales.

When Henry Tudor met Richard III at the Battle of Bosworth in 1485, he had three battle standards: the Cross of St George, the arms of the Beauforts (the family of Henry's mother, Margaret Beaufort) and the Red Dragon, representing Henry Tudor's claim to being the true representative of the ancient kings of Britain. For the Welsh, Henry's victory was their victory – for the first time in centuries, theirs was no longer a conquered land but the country of the king.

Thus did the Red Dragon of Wales become victorious, albeit not quite as Myrddin had prophesized – the Saxons were long gone by the time Henry defeated Richard at the Battle of Bosworth. The red dragon formed part of the royal coat of arms from 1485 to 1603, when it was replaced with a unicorn by order of James I. In 1807, it was readopted as the royal badge of Wales and thereafter it was frequently used in the regalia of Welsh patriotic societies until its official recognition as the Welsh national flag by Queen Elizabeth II in 1959.

LEFT: *A carved wooden heraldic bed-end featuring a dragon in Cardiff Castle*

RIGHT: *A dragon-shaped cloud formation fills the skies over Brecon in Wales*

THE NORTH

O 'tis a fearful thing to be no more;
Or if to be, to wander after death;
To walk as Spirits do, in Brakes all day;
And when the darkness comes
to glide in paths
That lead to graves: and in the silent Vault,
Where lyes your own pale shrowd,
to hover o'er it,
Striving to enter your forbidden Corps;
And often, often, vainly breathe your Ghost
Into your lifeless lips.

From *Oedipus* by John Dryden (1631–1700)
and Nathaniel Lee (c.1653–1692)

THE NORTH

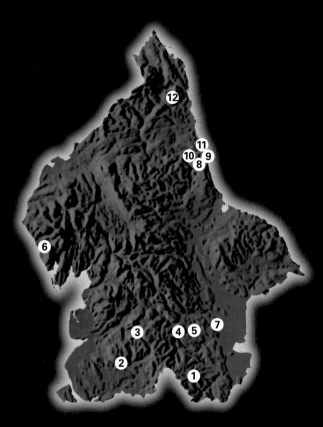

1	THE STOCKSBRIDGE BYPASS (A616) – SHEFFIELD	184
2	YE OLDE MAN AND SCYTHE – LANCASHIRE	188
3	TOWNELEY HALL ART GALLERY AND MUSEUM – LANCASHIRE	190
4	BOLLING HALL – BRADFORD	192
FEATURE – AWAY WITH THE FAIRIES		194
5	TEMPLE NEWSAM HOUSE – LEEDS	198
6	MUNCASTER CASTLE – CUMBRIA	200
7	TOWTON BATTLEFIELD – NORTH YORKSHIRE	202
8	THE NORTH EAST AIRCRAFT MUSEUM – SUNDERLAND	204
9	MARSDEN GROTTO – TYNE & WEAR	206
10	CASTLE KEEP – NEWCASTLE-UPON-TYNE	208
11	SOUTER LIGHTHOUSE – SUNDERLAND	210
12	EDLINGHAM CASTLE – NORTHUMBERLAND	212

INTRODUCTION

Our journey across the haunted landscape of the north of England begins with the phantom of a monk and a group of spectral children that have appeared to travellers on the Stocksbridge bypass. From here we travel to Bolton to visit an atmospheric old hostelry where the 7th Earl of Derby spent his last hours before being beheaded outside and which he now visits in ghostly form. Next, to Burnley. Here, we encounter the wraith of Sir John Towneley who has been condemned to return to his ancestral seat at Towneley Hall every seven years to lament an act of infamy he perpetrated against the poor of the area. Moving on to Bradford, we pay a visit to delightful Bolling Hall and discover one of the oldest accounts of a ghostly appearance in England. Then follows the poignant tale of an unfortunate girl driven to distraction and then death by the theft of her pearls in the 17th century. She still roams impressive Temple Newsam House in Leeds looking for them. Moving across to the Lake District we go to wonderful Muncaster Castle, where a distant murder has left its indelible stain on the ethereal fabric of the building. Via the Towton Battlefield, where the bloodiest battle of the War of the Roses took place, we make our way to the North East Aircraft Museum in Sunderland, where strange phenomena aplenty have been reported. On then to South Shields and the Marsden Grotto, Europe's only cave pub. Here, a thirsty revenant has been known to consume a tankard of ale obligingly left out for it overnight. Having learned of the spirits that haunt the Castle Keep in Newcastle, we make our way to the coast in search of the ghosts that roam the distinctive Souter Lighthouse. Our final destination is the picturesque, though chilling, ruin of Edlingham Castle where there is the opportunity to make the acquaintance of the Witch of Edlingham.

THE STOCKSBRIDGE BYPASS (A616)

SHEFFIELD

The Haunted Road

A long time ago – as with much local folklore, exact dates are difficult to come by – a monk from a nearby monastery became disillusioned with the monastic lifestyle and left the order. When he died, his body was buried for some unknown reason in unconsecrated ground. This didn't go down too well with the monk, and his ghost began to be sighted around the area where his remains were reputed to lie.

Centuries passed and, by the early 1980s, the High Street of Stocksbridge – a small town through which the main route from Sheffield to Manchester passed – was suffering severe traffic congestion. It was, therefore, decided to build a bypass. In 1987, work commenced on a new road that would take cars and lorries away from the narrow streets of the town centre. According to local tradition, the proposed road would pass straight over the land where the remains of the disenchanted monk had been buried. Unsurprisingly, he did not take too kindly to the prospect of heavy lorries thundering over his place of unrest at all times of the day and night.

Another local rumour connected to the area relates how, in the distant past, children had fallen down mine shafts nearby and their bodies had never been recovered.

So it was that, as work on the road began, something slightly unearthly began to stir beneath its foundations. Construction workers living in caravans on the site began complaining that their slumbers were being disturbed by the sound of children singing in the dead of night. Two security guards on patrol one night spotted a group of children dressed in old-fashioned clothing and dancing in a circle in a field alongside the construction site. On their way to investigate, they were somewhat taken aback when the children just faded away, and there were no footprints or signs of disturbance in the soft earth where they had been dancing.

Barely had the two guards recovered their composure than they saw a figure standing above them on the newly constructed Pearoyd Bridge. At the time, the bridge, which went over the bypass, could not be accessed from the road below. One of the guards kept watch, while his colleague drove their van around behind the figure and switched the headlights to full beam, directing them up at the bridge. What they saw terrified them. The figure was wearing a long cloak, and the beam of the headlights shone straight through it. But most frightening of all was the fact that the figure was headless. Within moments the apparition had disappeared and the security guards fled in terror.

Soon afterwards the men contacted the local police, who, noting their agitated state, decided to investigate. Around midnight on 11 September 1987, Police Constable Dick Ellis and Special Constable John Beet drove to the site. Parking close to the Pearoyd Bridge, PC Ellis wound down his driver's window as it was a pleasantly warm

The Stocksbridge Bypass (A616)

Stocksbridge, Sheffield

Haunted Rating 🎃🎃🎃🎃🎃

BELOW: The sight and sound of long-ago children singing and playing have haunted security guards and construction workers employed to build the Stocksbridge bypass

night. After about 20 minutes of waiting, he began to feel very cold and uneasy. Suddenly, Special Constable Beet let out an almighty scream and grabbed his colleague by the arm. Turning, Ellis saw a man's torso pressed up against the passenger window. As the two men looked on in horror, whatever or whoever it was moved quickly to PC Ellis's side of the car. Seconds later the figure had gone. The two officers searched the immediate vicinity, convinced they had been the victims of a practical joker. But, finding no trace of anyone, they got back into the car and drove towards the bridge, intending to radio for assistance. Suddenly, a series of bumps and jolts shook their patrol car violently. The officers, terrified by now, quickly fled the scene, and PC Ellis made an official report concerning inexplicable phenomena at the Stocksbridge bypass.

Given the strange events that had occurred while the road was being constructed, it was perhaps tempting fate that the date chosen for the official opening of the bypass was Friday, 13 May 1989. This fact, coupled with the continuing appearances of the ghostly monk and the

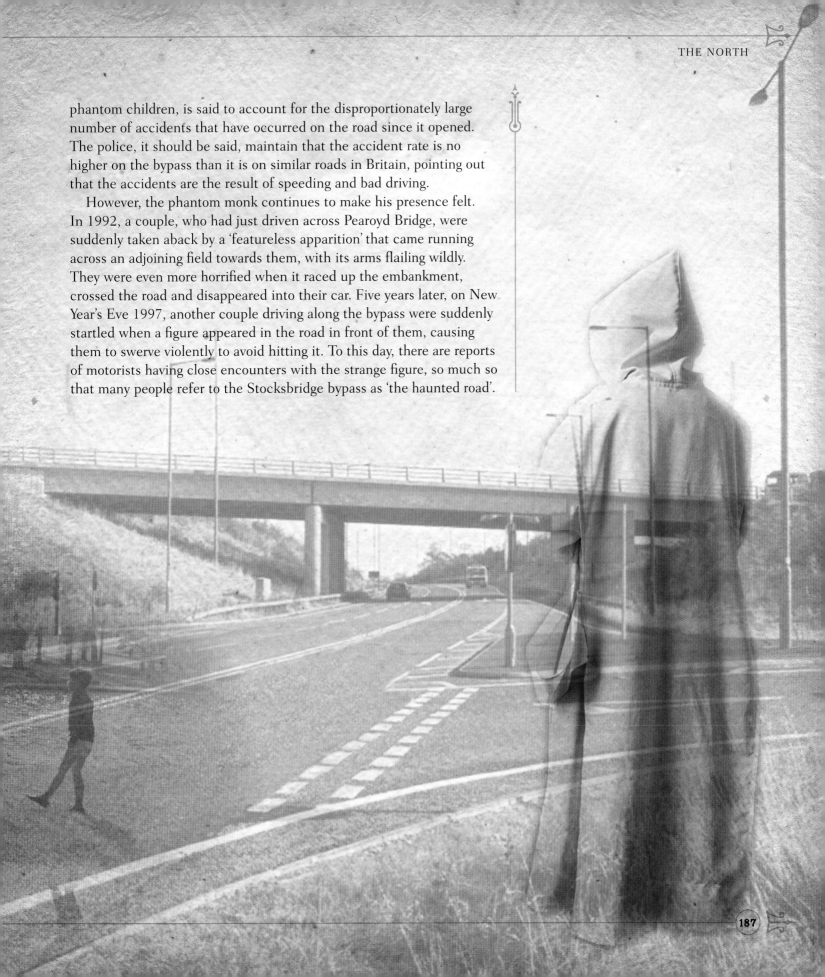

phantom children, is said to account for the disproportionately large number of accidents that have occurred on the road since it opened. The police, it should be said, maintain that the accident rate is no higher on the bypass than it is on similar roads in Britain, pointing out that the accidents are the result of speeding and bad driving.

However, the phantom monk continues to make his presence felt. In 1992, a couple, who had just driven across Pearoyd Bridge, were suddenly taken aback by a 'featureless apparition' that came running across an adjoining field towards them, with its arms flailing wildly. They were even more horrified when it raced up the embankment, crossed the road and disappeared into their car. Five years later, on New Year's Eve 1997, another couple driving along the bypass were suddenly startled when a figure appeared in the road in front of them, causing them to swerve violently to avoid hitting it. To this day, there are reports of motorists having close encounters with the strange figure, so much so that many people refer to the Stocksbridge bypass as 'the haunted road'.

YE OLDE MAN AND SCYTHE

LANCASHIRE

The Bloodstained Hands

Ye Olde Man and Scythe is certainly a very ancient hostelry – it's even mentioned in a charter of 1251. The current building, however, dates from only 1636 – which still makes it old – although the pub cellars of the original were reputedly incorporated into the design of the present building and are, therefore, much older.

It is one of those places that positively oozes history and atmosphere in equal measure. As befits such a historic location, it can also boast an illustrious ghost in the form of James Stanley, the 7th Earl of Derby.

The Portraicture of the Right Honorable IAMES Earle of DERBY Viscont KINTON Lord STANLEY. STRANGE of KNOKING. Lord MOHVN BVRNEL BASSETT and LACY Lord of MAN and the ISLES. Cap.t GENERAL of his MAIESTIES Forces within the Counties of CHESTER. LANCASTER. SALOP. STAFFORD. WORCESTER and NORTHWALES. Chamberlain of y.e County Palatine of CHESTER. and Knight of the Most Noble order of the GARTER.

ABOVE: *A portait of James Stanley, 7th Earl of Derby, who was beheaded outside the Old Man and Scythe during the English Civil War*

During the English Civil War, the town of Bolton had been a Puritan stronghold and was unsuccessfully attacked by royalists on several occasions. Finally, in May 1644, after a brief siege, the royalist forces, of whom the Earl of Derby was joint commander, successfully broke through the Parliamentarian defences. Once inside the town, they showed little mercy to the citizens. Estimates put the number of Puritans dead at around 1,000, with some of them innocent civilians. A further 700 were taken prisoner. It was one of the most shameful acts of the Civil War. Following the beheading of Charles I in 1649, his son Charles II made one last attempt to overthrow the Parliamentarians but was soundly beaten at the Battle of Worcester. The Earl of Derby was then captured and sentenced to death for his part in the Bolton massacre. His beheading took place in the centre of town, directly outside the Old Man and Scythe, at 3pm on 15 October 1651. Stanley's last hours were spent inside the pub. The chair in which he sat to take his last meal is still on display inside the pub's Museum Room, and his ghost is said to haunt the building, in particular this room.

Gruesome Occurrence

One customer appears to have had a particularly close and dramatic encounter with the Earl's wraith. As she was sitting enjoying a drink, she looked at her hands and found them to be covered in blood. Terrified, she fled the pub as fast as her legs would carry her. The barman, believing the blood must have come through the ceiling, raced upstairs to ensure that the landlord, who lived upstairs on the premises, hadn't been injured. He found the landlord was fine, and when they searched the area where the woman had been sitting, they could find no rational explanation for the gruesome occurrence.

Ye Olde Man and Scythe

6–8 Churchgate,
Bolton, Lancashire
BL1 1HL

http://yeoldemanandscythe.com

Haunted Rating

TOWNELEY HALL ART GALLERY AND MUSEUM

LANCASHIRE

The Seven Year Spectre

For over 500 years, Towneley Hall was home to the Towneley family until they sold it, along with 62 acres of surrounding parkland, to Burnley Corporation in 1901. Converted for use as a museum and an art gallery, the hall was opened to the public in 1903. Today, visitors can wander through evocatively furnished period rooms and enjoy a variety of displays that encompass a number of topics, including natural history, Egyptology, local history and the decorative arts, to name but a few.

There have long been stories of mysterious happenings at the hall and it is generally accepted in paranormal circles that Towneley Hall is every bit the haunted house of tradition. Reports exist of footsteps being

ABOVE: *The Long Gallery at Towneley Hall*

heard in upstairs rooms after all the visitors have left and the hall is
deserted. Attendants locking up at the end of the day have encountered
a 'strange uniformed figure' that disappears before their eyes.

The best known of Towneley Hall's phantoms belongs to the
16th century. Sir John Towneley decided to extend his estate and
commandeered 194 acres of common land at nearby Horelaw (Wholaw)
and Hollin Hey Clough, where the poor of the district had grazed
their cattle since time immemorial. Having done so, he then enclosed
it and evicted any locals who had lived on the land, denying them a
vital means of eking out their meagre existence. Since he was an all-
powerful local landowner, there was little that the poor could do other
than accept it and move elsewhere. However, fate was only too prepared
to wreak a fearful vengeance on behalf of the dispossessed poor. As
punishment for his greed, Sir John's spirit was condemned to return to
the grounds of his house every seven years. A very dramatic return it
was as well. His forlorn phantom was said to pace fitfully around the
grounds moaning a baleful warning to subsequent generations of the
Towneley family: 'Be warned! Lay out! Be warned! Lay out! Around
Horelaw and Hollin Hey. To her children give back the widow's cot.
For you and yours there is still enough.' To 'lay out' meant to open up
the land that had been enclosed, something that Sir John's descendants
were unwilling to do. Following an enquiry in 1556, the enclosure of
the land was, in fact, deemed illegal and it was seized by the Crown.
However, the land was not restored to the people. Indeed, James I
gave it to the Earl of Devon, who then sold it to Sir Richard Towneley
in 1612. And, since his family appeared to pay little heed to Sir John's
seven-yearly spectral rant, his ghost continued to appear, taking on
the added horror of presaging the death of a member of the family in
Towneley Hall.

**Towneley Hall Art Gallery
and Museum**

Towneley Park, Burnley,
Lancashire BB11 3RQ

Haunted Rating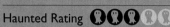

BOLLING HALL

BRADFORD

Bolling Hall
Bowling Hall Road, Bradford BD4 7LP
Haunted Rating 🟊🟊🟊🟊🟊

The Tempestuous Tempests

There is little doubt that Bolling Hall is haunted. Indeed, any lingering uncertainty is easily dispelled by the fact that one of the rooms is helpfully called The Ghost Room. The house occupies an unusual location, surrounded by a sprawling housing estate. Yet no amount of urban encroachment can detract from the air of antiquity that enshrouds it, and the moment you clap eyes on its rambling bulk, you just know that this is a house with secrets.

Bolling Hall wasn't so much built as gradually pieced together over several centuries. It consists of a cornucopia of differing architectural styles, each of which stands as testimony to different generations of the various families that have owned it.

The first owners were the de Laci family, who were awarded the manor shortly after the Norman Conquest of 1066. Quite how long they remained in residence is uncertain, but by 1316 it had passed to the Bolling family, after whom the hall is named. It was during their tenure that the earliest parts of the building were probably constructed.

In the Wars of the Roses, Robert Bolling fought on the Lancastrian side, a fact that didn't stand him in good stead when the Yorkist king, Edward IV, ascended the throne. Although Edward spared Robert's life, he confiscated his lands and property. For 11 years, Robert lived in impoverished circumstances with his wife and ten children, trying to dream up a way to return him to favour and reunite him with his lands. Finally, after much agonizing, he claimed that he had been forced to fight for the Lancastrians against his will. As excuses go it wasn't, perhaps, the greatest, but it did gain him the support of the Duke of Gloucester (later Richard III) and he was, therefore, able to win back his estates.

In 1497, his granddaughter Rosamund married Richard Tempest, and Bolling Hall passed to the Tempest family, during whose tenure life at the hall turned somewhat tempestuous. In 1536, Richard took part in the ill-fated Pilgrimage of Grace, the Yorkshire uprising to protest at

Henry VIII's break with Rome. He died in prison while awaiting trial, leaving Rosamund to run the estate until her death in 1553. The last Tempest to own the hall was Sir Richard Tempest. He inherited the property in 1639 and continued the family's venerable tradition of backing the wrong side by declaring himself for the royalist cause during the English Civil War. It was during this period that the Ghost Room acquired its ghost.

The people of Bradford were strongly Puritan and had, therefore, backed the Parliamentarian cause. In June 1643, a royalist army numbering some 10,000 men, commanded by William Cavendish, the Earl of Newcastle, arrived to lay siege to the town. Cavendish stayed at Bolling Hall, which then stood outside the town. Despite having no fortifications, the people of Bradford put up a strong resistance and the Duke was furious. One Sunday evening, as he looked down on the town from the heights of Bolling Hall, he told his men that the next day they would take Bradford, and he vowed that he would slaughter every man, woman and child as punishment for the resistance. So saying, he retired to bed. During the night he was awoken by the bedclothes being pulled off him. Opening his eyes, he found himself confronted by the dreadful apparition of an anguished woman in white who wailed at him to 'Pity poor Bradford!' The experience had a profound effect on Cavendish. The next morning, the visibly shaken Duke countermanded his order and gave instructions that only those who put up armed resistance were to be killed. Bradford was duly taken by the royalists and, thanks to the intercession of the spectral lady, there were indeed very few casualties, with some estimates putting the number of deaths at less than ten.

However, the ghosts of Bolling Hall are not confined to the dim and distant past. Reports of paranormal activity have continued since it was taken over by the council and opened as a museum in 1915. A foul smell has been known to permeate the air around the house's Georgian staircase, and a strange rattling noise has been heard there in the dead of night. The ghosts of a grey and a pink lady have been seen on this same staircase. In the house's Blue Room, people report the sensation of being watched, while a man in long coat-tails has been seen standing by the fireplace.

Bolling Hall is a truly atmospheric building. With a haunted heritage stretching back to at least 1643, it can also lay claim to being the proud possessor of one of Britain's oldest recorded ghost stories.

Bolling Hall has a history of haunting stretching back to the mid-17th century

Away with the Fairies

Every time you say you don't believe in fairies, a fairy dies.
(From *Peter Pan* by J.M. Barrie)

In December 1920, readers of the *Strand* magazine were confronted with the sensational headline 'Fairies Photographed'. The subsequent article informed them that two girls, Iris and Alice, who lived in the north of England and were the daughter and niece of a Mr Carpenter, had managed to take two photographs of fairies. The first, taken in July 1917, showed a group of fairies dancing around one of the girls. The second, taken in the September of the same year, showed a winged gnome tip-toeing in front of the other girl. The article caused uproar when it was published, not so much for its claim that fairies existed and had been photographed, but rather because its author was none other than Sir Arthur Conan Doyle, the famous creator of logical detective Sherlock Holmes.

ABOVE AND RIGHT: The sensational photographs that appeared in the Strand magazine convinced many people that fairies exist

By 1920, it must be said, Conan Doyle's beliefs, writings and lectures on spiritualism had severely discredited him in the eyes of the more hardened sceptics and cynics of the age. But this article, although cautious in tone, was the last straw, even for some of those who had being willing to accept his spiritualistic musings. One critic, responding to Conan Doyle's assertion that the photographs were '… a triumph for the children, who had been smiled at, as so many children are smiled at by an incredulous world for stating what their own senses have actually recorded', unsympathetically observed that '… knowing children, and knowing that Sir Arthur Conan Doyle has legs, I decide that the Miss Carpenters have pulled one of them…'

C. ALICE AND LEAPING FAIRY.
Copyright. Photograph taken August, 1920.

Meanwhile, the fact that Conan Doyle had admitted in the article that he had been compelled to give the girls and the family pseudonyms, and that he had withheld their exact address to prevent them being pestered, caused a veritable frenzy among journalists. The hunt was on to discover the identity of the two girls who had convinced the creator of the icily logical Sherlock Holmes that fairies existed.

It wasn't long before the *Westminster Gazette* had managed to discover the family's true identity. Mr Carpenter, it transpired, was in fact Mr Arthur Wright, an electrical engineer, who lived in the Yorkshire village of Cottingley. The two girls were his daughter, Elsie, who was 16 in 1920, and her cousin Frances Griffiths, who was three years younger.

The girls had taken the photographs in the glen behind their cottage, and Arthur Wright, an enthusiastic photographer who had built his own darkroom in the family home, had developed the plates on which his daughter and niece had captured the mysterious figures. At first, the images were just copied and shown to friends as a bit of a novelty but they were not otherwise taken particularly seriously.

But, in 1919, Mrs Wright became interested in the theosophical movement, a westernized version of Tibetan Buddhism, and at a meeting of the local Theosophical Society the subject of fairies came up. Mrs Wright happened to mention that her daughter had once taken a photograph of some fairies and brought copies along to the next meeting. Soon, word of the fairy photographs had reached Edward L. Gardner, president of the Society's London Lodge and a man who sincerely believed in the existence of fairies, pixies and goblins – beings that he considered were ancient links in the evolutionary chain. After writing to Mrs Wright asking if he might use the fairy photographs in his lectures, copies were duly dispatched to him.

Parisian Trends

By May 1920, news of the photographs had
reached Conan Doyle who, coincidentally, had been
commissioned by the *Strand* magazine to write an
article about fairies. He, therefore, arranged to have
lunch with Gardner and came away convinced that
there was something to the fairy photographs. As a
precaution, however, he showed the photographs to
some of his spiritualist friends and received mixed
responses. Some were enthusiastic about them,
others expressed incredulity, and pointed out that
the woodland sprites seemed exceedingly fashion-
conscious, their hairstyles and clothing apparently in
keeping with the latest Parisian trends.

Hoping to alleviate any doubt, Gardner showed the
plates to a photography expert by the name of Harold
Snelling, who declared them 'entirely genuine and un-
faked'. Conan Doyle, meanwhile, took the plates to
the offices of Kodak in London and was told by their
experts that there was no evidence of double exposure
or other camera tricks. However, the experts refused
to endorse the photographs since they could, they said,
undoubtedly produce similar photographs themselves.

Seeking further proof, Gardner took a camera to Elsie
and Frances in Yorkshire and asked them to take more
photographs of the fairies. In September 1920, the girls
duly obliged, producing three further images, which
Snelling again pronounced genuine. Conan Doyle, who
at the time was on a lecture tour of Australia, received
news of the most recent pictures with enthusiasm. He
wrote to Gardner, declaring himself 'proud to have
been associated with you in this epoch-making event'.
Thus, to the bemusement of the public at large, the
fairy article appeared in the *Strand* in December 1920
and, two years later, Conan Doyle further endorsed the
authenticity of the photographs in a book *The Coming
of the Fairies*. He continued to profess his belief that
they were genuine until his dying day.

Toward the ends of their lives – Frances died in July
1986 and Elsie in April 1988 – the girls finally confessed
to what many sceptics had been convinced of at the
time. They had indeed faked the photographs using
paper cut-out figures mounted on hat pins, and the
whole thing had been a schoolgirl game that had got
horribly out of hand when Sir Arthur Conan Doyle and
Edward L. Gardner became involved.

TEMPLE NEWSAM HOUSE

LEEDS

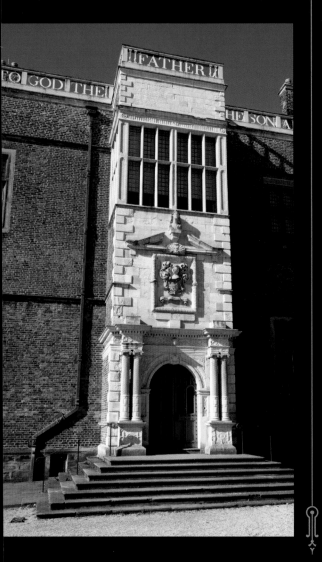

The Blue Lady of Temple Newsam House

At all times of the year, Temple Newsam House is an impressive property. Silhouetted against a stormy winter sky, its Tudor-Jacobean walls of warm red brick stand steadfast against the worst that nature can hurl at them. Approached on a bright summer's morning, those same walls take on an almost nonchalant air as they bask amid the 1,550 acres of glorious parkland that surround them.

The land hereabouts was originally owned by the Knights Templar, the monastic, military order that protected pilgrims on the road to Jerusalem. When they were suppressed in the 14th century, their lands here passed to the Darcy family. In 1520–22, Thomas Darcy, a powerful statesman, became the first person to build a house on the site. He was executed in 1537 for his part in the Pilgrimage of Grace, the Yorkshire uprising to protest at Henry VIII's break with Rome, and his property was forfeited to the Crown. Henry VIII then gave the house to Margaret, Countess of Lennox, and it was here that her son Lord Darnley, the future consort of Mary, Queen of Scots, was born. In 1622, after a period of neglect, the house was acquired by Sir Arthur Ingram, a wealthy financier. He remodelled the old Tudor building, and successive generations of his family would reside there until, in the 1920s, it was acquired by Leeds Council and opened to the public.

The house's best-known ghost is that of the Blue Lady, thought to be the shade of Sir Arthur Ingram's granddaughter Mary Ingram, whose portrait can be seen over the fireplace in the building's Green Damask Room. One night she and her governess were returning home from visiting friends when their carriage was held up by highway robbers. A pearl necklace that had been a christening present from her grandfather was ripped from her neck in the attack, and Mary fainted. The unconscious girl was brought home and put to bed. The next morning she had no recollection of the robbery, but kept murmuring over and over again, 'Where are my pearls? Where are my pearls?' Thereafter she kept searching for the missing valuables, unpicking the stitching on cushions to see if they were inside and trying to lift floorboards, believing they were underneath. Her condition deteriorated over the next few days and within a fortnight of the attack she died at the age of just 14. Her forlorn shade still roams the house, her appearances being presaged by a cold blast of air. A member of staff who recently encountered her coming towards him on the Gallery Passage was so unnerved that he hid and didn't dare come out until his colleagues came to his rescue.

Other phenomena experienced at the house include doors slamming, footsteps being heard pacing across empty rooms, and an unseen presence felt brushing past people on the stairs. Finally, a ghostly small boy has been known to climb out of a cupboard in the room where Lord Darnley was born. He doesn't do a great deal other than pace around the room for a few moments and then return to the cupboard.

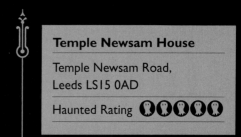

Temple Newsam House

Temple Newsam Road,
Leeds LS15 0AD

Haunted Rating 🟡🟡🟡🟡🟡

The seemingly impervious walls of Temple Newsam House

MUNCASTER CASTLE

CUMBRIA

Muncaster Castle

Muncaster, Ravenglass,
Cumbria CA18 IRQ

www.muncaster.co.uk

Haunted Rating

The Luck and the Fool

This stunning building of red sandstone was mostly constructed in the 1860s when the architect Anthony Salvin totally remodelled what had been the residence of the Pennington family since 1208. Among its many treasures is the 'Luck of Muncaster', a gift to the family from Henry VI. Following his defeat at the Battle of Hexham in 1464, the king was found wandering on Muncaster Fell and was brought to the castle where the owners, Sir John Pennington and his wife, sheltered him for nine days. In gratitude, the king presented his hosts with his gilded glass drinking cup, promising that as long as it remained unbroken, the Penningtons would remain at Muncaster. The cup, or luck, remains undamaged within, and the Pennington family has retained possession of the castle for over seven centuries.

Winding passages and long corridors inside haunted Muncaster Castle

Another castle treasure is the superb portrait of Thomas Skelton, the 16th-century fool, or jester, to the Penningtons, who gave the word 'tomfoolery' to the English language. His master, Sir Ferdinand Pennington, is said to have asked the spiteful and vicious Skelton for his assistance when his daughter Helwise fell in love with the village carpenter. Skelton lured the lad to the castle on the pretence that Helwise was anxious to see him. Having plied him with strong cider to render him senseless, he used the carpenter's own blunt chisel and heavy mallet to hack off his head. He then took the bloody trophy to Sir Ferdinand, as proof that he had perpetrated the foul deed. Today, the aftermath of the heinous crime still hangs heavy around the castle, and many is the time that the eerie stillness is broken by the sound of a dull thudding of a body being dragged down the stairs. Occasionally, this is accompanied by the mournful wailing of a woman, thought to be the grief-stricken Helwise, lamenting her lost love.

The Tapestry Room

The castle's Tapestry Room has a decidedly chilling atmosphere, and many guests who have spent the night there have reported bizarre occurrences. Some have heard the sound of rustling skirts, as an invisible entity brushes by them. Others have been woken by the disturbing sound of an unseen baby crying. There are reports of a three-dimensional but very dark figure gliding towards astonished witnesses and then vanishing right before their eyes. Staff have long grown used to visitors approaching the door to the Tapestry Room and hesitating on the threshold as if fearful of venturing inside.

Muncaster Castle appears to have a veritable host of lost souls constantly prowling its rooms and corridors. Perhaps John Ruskin's description of it as 'the gateway to Paradise' refers to more than just the beauty of the surroundings.

Spooky figures adorn this grand Elizabethan fireplace in the haunted Tapestry Room

TOWTON BATTLEFIELD

NORTH YORKSHIRE

Towton Battlefield

Near Wetherby,
North Yorkshire

Haunted Rating

Revenants from the Bloodiest Battle Ever Fought on English Soil

The Battle of Towton was fought on Palm Sunday, 29 March 1461. As well as being a decisive engagement in the Wars of the Roses, it was also one of the largest battles in English history, with estimates putting the number of participants at anywhere between 50,000 and 80,000 men. These included 28 lords, the majority of them fighting on the Lancastrian side. The clash is often referred to as the bloodiest battle ever fought on English soil, costing the lives of at least 15,000 men, although some estimates put the number of dead at closer to 30,000. The horrendous carnage was a result of an understanding between the two sides – the Yorkists and Lancastrians – that no quarter (mercy) would be given.

Atrocious Weather Conditions

It is generally agreed that the Lancastrians had the numerically superior force. In addition, they also occupied a strong position on a plateau of high ground, thus forcing the Yorkist army to attack uphill. But the weather conditions on the day of the battle were atrocious, with heavy winds whipping the snow and freezing rain into a frenzy. The foul weather proved disastrous for the Lancastrian soldiers. With the wind blowing against them, they were not only blinded by the driving snow but also at a disadvantage to the Yorkist archers who had the wind behind them. They were able to inflict heavy losses on their opponents whose arrows were falling short of their intended targets, blown back by the strong winds.

Unwilling to endure the constant shower of arrows, the Lancastrian men-at-arms moved forward to engage their adversaries in hand-to-hand combat. The fighting swayed back and forth between the two sides for several hours. It proved so intense that the opponents had to pause from time to time in order to clear the bodies of fallen comrades out of the way before resuming. By the afternoon, neither side had gained an advantage. But then Yorkist reinforcements arrived and the Battle began turning against the Lancastrians, who finally broke and ran.

Their retreat turned into a rout as their opponents came after them and cut them down in their thousands. Cock Beck, the little stream that runs close to the site of the battle, is said to have run red with blood, and elsewhere the surviving Lancastrians are said to have crossed the nearby River Cock by walking on the bodies of their fallen. The fields between Towton and Tadcaster were piled high with the bodies of dead Lancastrians, many of whom had dropped their weapons and thrown off their armour and helmets to be able to run faster and breathe easier. However, this meant they were able to put up little resistance against their pursuers.

Memories of the carnage and dreadful loss of life appear to linger on in the peaceful countryside that surrounds the battlefield. There have been reports of ghostly soldiers and their phantom horses being seen on the lanes and fields round about. A group of two men and two women, along with a rider mounted on a large brown horse, all wearing 15th-century garb, were seen by a motorist driving along the B1217 one evening in December 1997. Presuming that they were some form of re-enactment group, he slowed his car down so as not to startle their horse, whereupon all the figures melted away into thin air.

The Battle Monument, left, marks the site in Towton where the Yorkists defeated the Lancastrians during the Wars of the Roses

THE NORTH EAST AIRCRAFT MUSEUM

SUNDERLAND

The North East Aircraft Museum

Old Washington Road,
Sunderland, Tyne & Wear
SR5 3HZ

www.neam.org.uk

Haunted Rating

The Bouncing Czech

The North East Aircraft Museum began life in 1916 as RAF Usworth and was the base for 36 Squadron, which was charged with defending the northeast coast of England between Whitby and Newcastle during World War I. The squadron achieved a notable success on 27 November 1916, when Lieutenant I.V. Pyrott brought down a LZ34 zeppelin, which crashed into the mouth of the Tees. The sight of the downed airship caused other zeppelins accompanying it to turn back, sparing northeast England from a bombing raid.

At the end of the war, the squadron was disbanded. The airfield remained derelict for over ten years until, in March 1930, it became the base for 607 Squadron. On 15 August 1940, the Luftwaffe planned a bombing raid on the base, but their planes were spotted as they approached the east coast. The Hurricanes of 607 Squadron, along with planes from several other bases, were scrambled and intercepted them, bringing down many enemy aircraft over the coast before they could reach their intended target. In 1962, the former base became Sunderland Airport. This closed in 1984 and the site was divided between the North East Aircraft Museum and a Nissan car factory. The museum has the reputation of being one of the region's most paranormally active sites, and several spirits of those who served here have lingered on.

The Treacherous Preucil

One of them is the wraith of one of the most treacherous airmen to pass through the base during the war years. Augustin Preucil was a Czech reconnaissance pilot. When the Germans invaded Czechoslovakia in 1939, he volunteered to join the Luftwaffe but was turned down because he wasn't a German national. He was then recruited by the Gestapo and sent to Poland to report on Czech airmen who had fled there. At the outbreak of war, he joined the French Armée de L'Air and then, with the fall of France in 1940, he escaped by ship to England, where he joined the RAF Volunteer Reserve. In the summer of 1941, he was transferred to RAF Usworth. On 18 September 1941, he took off in a Hurricane plane to practise dogfighting with a trainee Polish pilot over the North Sea. During the mock battle, the Polish flier watched in horror as Preucil's plane plummeted towards the sea trailing smoke. Convinced his comrade had crashed, he returned to the base where he reported the accident. But unknown to him, Preucil had pulled out of the dive just before hitting the water and had flown to Europe, where he landed at Ortho in Ardennes, Belgium. Here, he was sheltered by members of the Belgian Resistance, who took him for a downed RAF pilot. The next day he repaid his rescuers by informing on them to the Germans. They were later shot by the Gestapo. The Hurricane that Preucil had successfully stolen from right under the noses of the RAF was put on display in Berlin's National Aviation Museum, only to be destroyed later by an allied bombing raid.

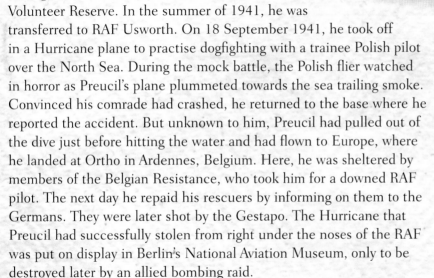

Heading back to Prague, Preucil joined the Gestapo, on whose behalf he interrogated captured Czech pilots, many of whom he had served with in the RAF. His final treachery came when he was sent to infiltrate Czechoslovakian political prisoners at the Theresienstadt concentration camp, where he won their trust and then betrayed them, costing many of them their lives. However, some of the prisoners he had befriended began to have their suspicions about him and, in May 1945, shortly after liberation, he was arrested. Brought before a military court, he was found guilty of treason and hanged on 14 April 1947. It is at the place where he performed his audacious theft, however, that his ghost is said to linger. Mediums visiting the museum on night-time ghost hunts have picked up on the spirit of a Czech airman, and several, who have no knowledge of his fate, have reported feeling an uncomfortable, choking tightness around their throats.

Bootless Ghost

Another World War II ghost is connected with the wreckage of a Hurricane displayed at the museum. On 12 March 1942, Sergeant Edward Grenville Shaw was killed in a training accident when he and another pilot were flying their Hurricanes towards each other. The intention was to roll aside at the last moment and fly safely past each other. Unfortunately, their wings clipped and Shaw's plane crashed. He was thrown from the aircraft but the impact killed him instantly. He was found lying in marshy ground and, when his body was recovered, his boots were left in the bog. His ghost has been heard calling out for help at the museum, and some people who have stooped to look under the aircraft displayed in the main hangar have seen a pair of legs wearing black trousers but no boots walking past on the other side.

MARSDEN GROTTO

TYNE & WEAR

The Thirsty Revenant

In 1782, Jack Bates, a miner, found himself both unemployed and homeless. Determined to remedy his situation, he and his wife Jesse made their way to South Shields, where Jack found gainful employment as a quarryman. Looking for a suitable place to live, Jack hit upon the novel idea of using some explosives from the quarry and blasting a hole out of the cliff face at Marsden Bay, acquiring the nickname of Jack the Blaster in the process. He then hacked a flight of steps out of the rock to provide access to their new abode. Their cave house soon became a local curiosity, and people flocked to see it. Jack and Jesse began providing their visitors with light refreshments and thus the foundations were laid for one of Britain's most curious hostelries – the Marsden Grotto.

After Jack died in 1792, his curious cave abode lay empty for over 30 years until, in 1826, Peter Allan, son of a local gamekeeper, saw the money-making potential offered by this Marsden Bay curiosity. He moved into Jack Bates's one-roomed cave and began excavating further into the cliff, eventually hacking numerous separate chambers out of the rock. In doing so, he is said to have uncovered 18 skeletons, reputedly the remains of smugglers who had died going about their illicit business.

Using the rock from his burrowing, Peter created a raised promenade on the beach in front of the cave and on it he constructed two whitewashed cottages that backed onto the cliffs. Here, he and his wife raised eight children and continued the Bates tradition of providing light refreshments and alcoholic beverages to summer visitors to Marsden Bay. Business was thriving when, in 1848, John Clay bought the Leas – the area of land now owned by the National Trust that stretches for 2 miles (3.2km) along the local coastline – and claimed that this entitled him to ownership of the Marsden Grotto. Peter's response was that he would never give it up 'so long as he could wag a leg'. A two-year legal battle ensued, the outcome of which was that Peter was told that he could keep the Grotto for 20 years at an annual rent of £10 a year. He was also ordered to pay the court costs of £50. The stress of losing the case sent him spiralling into a deep depression, and he took to his bed, where he died on 31 August 1850.

As it transpired, the Allan family stayed on at the inn for another 35 years after Peter's death, and his children extended the property further. Since they gave up running it in the late 19th century, the inn's fortunes have been mixed. Ownership has passed through a succession of different companies, with some doing better than others. There have also been long periods of closure, most recently from September 2007 to March 2008, when the local council, which maintains the stairs that lead to it, deemed one of the steps unsafe and closed them off. Since the stairs were the only means of evacuation from the Grotto, the council ordered the pub to close while their workmen spent six months labouring to fix one step.

In addition to its colourful history, the Marsden Grotto also has many ghostly tales associated with it. The best-known relates to a member of a smuggling gang who was coerced into betraying his colleagues to the local customs officers. Those members who managed to evade capture reputedly suspended him in chains from the roof of a nearby cave and left him there to starve to death. Long after he was dead, his piteous moans and groans were still said to echo from the shaft.

One day, a former landlord was drawing off a mug of ale when he heard a curious noise. Setting the full tankard down on the bar, he went to investigate. On his return he was puzzled to find that the tankard was empty, even though there was no one else in the bar. Wishing to placate the beer-swilling phantom, the landlord began leaving a full tankard of ale on the bar every night before retiring to bed. Many times he would come down in the morning to find the tankard had been emptied over night. When he moved on, successive landlords continued the tradition with similar results. Evidently, this true curiosity of a place, the only cave pub in Europe, is home to a revenant with a raging thirst.

Marsden Grotto

Coast Road, South Shields,
Tyne & Wear NE34 7BS

Haunted Rating 🎃🎃🎃🎃🎃

Marsden Grotto located in Marsden Bay is the only restaurant and bar in a cave to be found in Europe

CASTLE KEEP

NEWCASTLE-UPON-TYNE

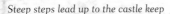
Steep steps lead up to the castle keep

The Fragrant Flower Seller

Standing on the site of a Roman fort, the current castle was begun in 1080 as a motte and bailey construction by Robert Curthose, son of William the Conqueror. It was called Novum Castellum, meaning 'New Castle'. Henry II ordered it to be rebuilt in stone between 1168 and 1178, while in 1174 it received an illustrious prisoner in the robust form of William 'the Lion', King of Scotland, who had invaded England. He was later taken to Northampton, from where he was sent to Falaise in Normandy. There he agreed to swear allegiance to England in the Treaty of Falaise and was allowed to return home. On his way back to Scotland, he stopped off at Newcastle, where the mob welcomed him by attacking him. Other famous visitors that passed through the castle over the next 200 years included the Scottish patriot Sir William Wallace, en route to his trial and execution in London in 1305.

By the early 15th century, Castle Garth's strategic importance had declined and so the keep was pressed into service as the county jail for Northumberland. Newcastle had become a town and county in its own right in 1400, but Castle Garth and its land were, in fact, part of Northumberland. This led to a peculiar anomaly. All that anyone wanted for a crime in Newcastle had to do to avoid justice was to walk the few feet over the boundary into the castle area. Since they were now technically in Northumberland, the Newcastle authorities couldn't touch them! This situation remained until 1589, when Elizabeth I gave the Newcastle authorities the right to enter the castle grounds and arrest felons taking refuge there.

Today, the Castle Keep is open to the public and, with such a history of violence and misery, is widely considered to be one of Newcastle's most haunted buildings. In his book Ghostly Tyne and Wear, Rob Kirkup tells of several apparitions encountered inside the Castle

Keep. One is the ghost of a 17th-century flower seller who, tradition maintains, was named Briony. Aged just 15, she was thrown into a cell deep beneath the Castle Keep with a group of hardened male prisoners who had been sentenced to death. Since these men had nothing to lose, you can imagine the horrors that Briony was forced to endure before, after eight days of torment, death finally released her. However, her ghostly sobs and agonized screams have been known to chill the blood of more than one visitor to the Garrison Room, while others have smelt the delicate fragrance of flowers following them around.

Other phenomena experienced inside the Castle Keep include a spectral chanting heard coming from the chapel; a white light seen moving around the Mezzanine Chamber; and a tall man in a cloak and top hat seen striding across the Great Hall.

Castle Keep

Castle Garth,
Newcastle-upon-Tyne
NE1 1RQ

Haunted Rating 👻👻👻👻👻

The ghost of a 17th-century flower seller, imprisoned in a cell beneath the castle, still haunts it to this day

SOUTER LIGHTHOUSE

SUNDERLAND

Ghostly Keepers and Sleepless Nights

When it first opened in 1871, the Souter Lighthouse was the most technologically advanced lighthouse of its day and the first to make use of alternating electric current. It was built to provide protection for shipping on an extremely precarious section of rocky coastline, where dozens of ships had been wrecked over the years, 20 of them in 1860 alone. Indeed, this stretch of coast was considered one of the most dangerous in the country and had, so it is said, claimed an average of 44 wrecks for every mile of coastline. Initially, the lighthouse was going to be sited at Souter Point but it was, in fact, built a mile (1.6km) to the north at Lizard Point, where the cliff top was considerably higher. The lighthouse retained its original name, however, since there was already a lighthouse at The Lizard in Cornwall – two Lizard lighthouses would have been confusing.

The Souter Lighthouse's carbon arcs gave off an impressive 800,000 candle power beam that was visible for some 26 miles (42km). In addition, the lighthouse possessed what was reputed to be the loudest foghorn in the country. Such was its volume that keepers were paid an extra 2d per shift in foggy weather to compensate them for the deafening noise they had to endure. For the local populace, however, there was little choice but to grin and bear it whenever a blanket of fog descended. They would be subjected to a five-second blast from the foghorn that sounded out every 30 seconds to alert shipping to the hazardous coastline. Many of them must have breathed a sigh of relief when, in 1988, it was announced that the Souter Lighthouse was to close. In 1989, it was taken over by the National Trust and is now open to the general public.

Visitors can look forward to learning about life at the lighthouse over its 117-year working history. In addition to touring the various rooms inside the striking red-hooped and gleaming white walls, there is also the possibility of meeting the ghosts of some of the former inhabitants. In the kitchen and living areas, there have been reports of objects levitating in front of astonished witnesses. Parts of the lighthouse are prone to sudden drops in temperature, while strong tobacco smoke has been smelt in the kitchen corridor. It has been suggested that this may be connected to the mysterious figure of a man once seen at the end of this corridor. The figure wore an old-fashioned uniform but disappeared the moment he was noticed.

Souter Lighthouse

Coast Road, Whitburn,
Sunderland, Tyne & Wear
SR6 7NH

Haunted Rating

EDLINGHAM CASTLE

NORTHUMBERLAND

The haunted ruin of Edlingham Castle

The Witch of Edlingham

The picturesque ruin of Edlingham Castle is but a shadow of what it must once have been. Its origins go back to the mid-13th century, when John de Edlingham built himself a house near to the picturesque little burn that still babbles close to the castle today. In 1294, it was sold to William de Felton, who reinforced it with sturdy ramparts and a gatehouse. The fortifications were further strengthened at various times between 1300 and 1600, a period that saw frequent skirmishing between the English and the Scots. Thereafter, Edlingham Castle gradually fell into decay, with its buildings being pulled down and used in the construction of nearby farmhouses.

In 1683, the Castle featured in the trial of Margaret Stothard, the so-called 'Witch of Edlingham'. John Mills, who gave his address as Edlingham Castle, testified that one night, as he was lying in his bed in the castle, he heard a strong blast of wind go past his window, whereupon 'something fell with a great weight upon his heart and gave a cry like a cat'. There then appeared a light at the foot of his bed and at the centre of the light was 'Margaret Stothard or her vision'. He related how he saw this unearthly vision several times and it so terrified him that 'the very hairs of his head would stand upward'.

His brother Jacob, who also gave his address as Edlingham Castle, told an even more sinister and – for Margaret Stothard – incriminating tale. According to his testimony, Margaret had approached a local couple for alms and, on being turned away, had waved a 'white thing' at them three times. The next morning, their daughter became unwell and cried out that 'the woman was pressing her like to break her back and press out her heart'. A short while later, the girl died. It would appear that Margaret Stothard was probably a local wise woman or healer who had incurred the wrath of some of her clients. Indeed, another witness testified that Margaret had actually cured another sick child by transferring its illness into a calf, which then died. Certainly, the magistrate, Henry Ogle, considered the allegations against her unfounded as he threw the case out.

Today, the castle is a peaceful place and the public can visit it free of charge. However, people have been known to have their clothes tugged by unseen hands, and strange lights have been seen floating around the ruins at night. There are also reports of footsteps being heard walking across floorboards above the heads of visitors, even though there are no floorboards in the ruin.

Edlingham Castle

Edlingham, Northumberland
NE66 2BL

Haunted Rating 👤👤👤👤👤

SCOTLAND

7

Unhinged, the iron gates half-open hung,
Jarred by the gusty gales of many winters,
That from its crumbled pedestal had flung
One marble globe in splinters.

O'er all there hung the shadow of a fear;
A sense of mystery the spirit daunted;
And said, as plain as whisper in the ear,
The place is haunted.

From *The Haunted House*
by Thomas Hood (1799–1845)

SCOTLAND

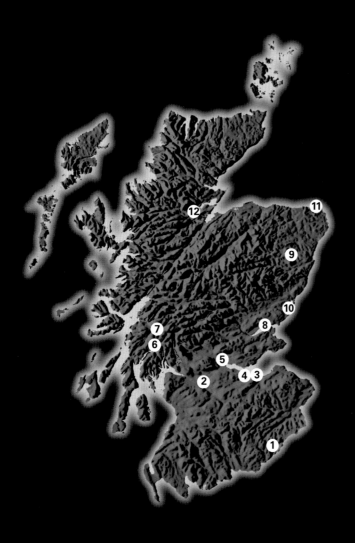

1	HERMITAGE CASTLE – SCOTTISH BORDERS	218
2	PROVAN HALL – GLASGOW	222
3	THE MACKENZIE MAUSOLEUM – EDINBURGH	224
4	THE CORSTORPHINE SYCAMORE – EDINBURGH	226
5	ALLOA TOWER – CLACKMANNANSHIRE	228
6	INVERARAY JAIL – ARGYLL	230
7	KILCHURN CASTLE – ARGYLL	232
8	RRS *DISCOVERY* – DUNDEE	234
9	CASTLE FRASER – ABERDEENSHIRE	236
10	LUNAN LODGE – ANGUS	238
11	KINNAIRD HEAD CASTLE – FRASERBURGH	240
12	TULLOCH CASTLE – DINGWALL	242
	FEATURE – THE LOCH NESS MONSTER	244

INTRODUCTION

The final leg of our journey around the haunted locations of Britain takes us across Scotland, where we encounter some absolutely stunning scenery. We begin at Hermitage Castle, a truly creepy location that stands close to what was, for centuries, the disputed and fought-over border between England and Scotland. Having learned of the castle's legends and hauntings, we move on to visit Glasgow's oldest house, Provan Hall, where you may experience the ghosts said to roam this ancient property. Crossing to Edinburgh, we step through the gates of Greyfriars Kirkyard to pay a visit to the Mackenzie Mausoleum, close to which the notorious Mackenzie Poltergeist has made numerous attacks on passers-by in the last few years. A tale of murder and betrayal follows as we make our way to the village of Corstorphine. Now indistinguishable from the rest of Edinburgh, this was once an isolated hamlet where a murder in the distant past has resulted in the nocturnal roamings of the ghostly white lady. We then head north to Alloa Tower, where we hear about a curse long ago that was placed upon the family that owned it. A spell in prison awaits us next in the grim interior of Inveraray Jail, where an aggressive jailer is just one of several ghosts lurking in the darker recesses. On then to the picturesque banks of Loch Awe and the magnificent ruin of Kilchurn Castle, where the poignant pleadings of a ghostly child have chilled the blood of many a visitor. Heading across to Dundee, we visit RRS *Discovery*, to learn about life on board this splendid vessel and hear of the ghosts of former crew members that have lingered on. Having stopped off to hunt for the green lady of Castle Fraser and paused to rest at Lunan Lodge, Scotland's most haunted bed and breakfast, we pay a visit to Kinnaird Head Castle. This was converted into a lighthouse in the 18th century and is haunted by a distraught phantom who seeks her drowned lover. Our journey through haunted Britain ends within the sturdy walls of Tulloch Castle, where you just may become acquainted with the ghost of a 19th-century daughter of the house.

HERMITAGE CASTLE

SCOTTISH BORDERS

A Truly Creepy Castle

Sir Walter Scott, recording local feeling towards Hermitage Castle, wrote that this solid, impregnable fortress '... unable to support the load of iniquity which had long been accumulating within its walls, is supposed to have partly sunk beneath the ground; and its ruins are still regarded by the peasants with peculiar aversion and horror'.

The castle was built around 1300. It stood as a brooding guardian over the wind-rattled moorland of the surrounding countryside that made up what was the disputed and much fought-over border between England and Scotland. As a result of the frequent conflicts, ownership of the castle switched regularly between the two countries, depending on which of them had the upper hand at any particular time.

One of the earliest owners of Hermitage Castle was Sir William de Soulis, who held it during the reign of Robert the Bruce (1274–1329).

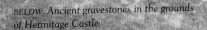

BELOW: Ancient gravestones in the grounds of Hermitage Castle

According to legend, de Soulis dabbled in the black arts. Apparently, he would kidnap local children, murder them and use their blood in despicable rituals, conjuring up a devilish familiar by the name of Robin Redcap, who would wreak all manner of evil upon those who dwelt in the surrounding district. Finally, the local people had enough of the wicked lord and stormed the castle. They seized de Soulis, wrapped him in lead and plunged him head first into a cauldron of boiling water. In reality, de Soulis was imprisoned and died at Dunbarton Castle in 1320 for his involvement in a conspiracy against Robert the Bruce, but that should not be allowed to detract from the far more colourful end that legend has bestowed upon him! Furthermore, his actual death, although rather mundane in comparison to the mythical version, hasn't prevented his enraged wraith from wandering Hermitage Castle. His nebulous flitting is frequently said to be accompanied by the heart-rending sobs of children echoing along the crumbling corridors.

The next haunting of Hermitage Castle dates from the tenure of Sir William Douglas, who had wrested the castle from the clutches of the Englishman Sir Ralph de Neville in 1338. Douglas was much respected throughout Scotland on account of his victories against the English. However, when David II made Sir Alexander Ramsay Sheriff of Teviotdale, the ruthless and envious Douglas lured the unfortunate Ramsay to Hermitage and imprisoned him in a 'frightful pit or Dungeon, apparently airless and devoid of sanitation'. Here, Ramsay slowly starved to death, and his ghostly groans of agony have echoed down the centuries ever since.

Hermitage Castle

Hermitage, near Newcastleton,
Scottish Borders
TD9 0LU

Haunted Rating

Menacing Ambience

Hermitage Castle is without doubt one of the creepiest places you could ever wish to discover, and its malevolent ambience can send cold shivers racing down the spine. Its indefinable aura was perfectly captured by the pioneering journalist and leading spiritualist W.T. Stead (1849–1912), who visited it as a teenager and later wrote of the experience in his book *Real Ghost Stories*.

Having obtained the key from the caretaker, who lived some distance away, Stead walked to the castle and unlocked the heavy door. 'As it creaked on its hinges,' he wrote, 'and I felt the chill air of the ruin, I was almost afraid to enter. Mustering my courage, however, I went in and explored the castle… suddenly, while the blood seemed to freeze down my back, I was startled by a loud prolonged screech, over my head, followed by a noise which I could only compare to the trampling of a multitude of iron-shod feet through the stone-paved doorway. This was alarming enough, but it was nothing to the horror which filled me when I heard the heavy gate swing on its hinges with a clang which for the moment seemed like the closing of a vault in which I was entombed alive.' He was relieved to find that he could open the gate and recalled the profound relief he felt when he '… stepped across the threshold and felt that I was free once more'. He then wondered if the door might have been simply blown shut and if the screech had been '… a gust of wind whistling through the crannies'. So he returned and spent another hour inside the castle, during which time, he noted, there was absolutely no wind.

Stead's experience, whether real or imagined, typifies similar experiences had by many who have visited the old castle. Hermitage Castle is a truly eerie place, and as you explore its creepy corridors and cold stone staircases that meander between the moss-clad walls of its ruinous interior, its very fabric seems imbued with a genuinely menacing ambience.

RIGHT: *The eerie shell of 14th-century Hermitage Castle stands on a hillock overlooking Hermitage water*

PROVAN HALL

GLASGOW

Ghosts and History

Provan Hall has been described as 'probably the most perfect pre-Reformation house in Scotland'. Dating from the 15th century, it is one of the oldest buildings in the Glasgow area. Somewhat on the compact side, the interior boasts some impressive and intriguing features. These include a kitchen fireplace that is large enough to roast an entire ox in, while the kitchen itself possesses one of the finest examples of a Roman-styled, barrel-vaulted ceiling in Scotland.

It's possible that Mary, Queen of Scots stayed at the house in the 1500s, while her consort, Lord Darnley, was being treated in St Nicholas's Hospital in Glasgow. By this time, the house was in the hands of the Baillie family, successive generations of which held it until, in 1562, it passed to William Baillie, who was President of the College of Justice. He died in 1593, and the property went to his daughter, Elizabeth, and through her to the Hamiltons, the family that she married into.

The last of the Hamiltons to reside at the property was Sir Robert Hamilton, who held it at the time of the Civil War. An ardent royalist, he was obliged to build the outer wall of the courtyard in 1647 as a defensive measure against the staunchly Covenanter locals. The Civil War crippled Sir Robert financially and he sold the property in 1667. Several owners later, the house passed into the hands of Dr John Buchanan, a former ship's surgeon, who made radical alterations to it in the 18th century. The house then passed through marriage to the Mather family, who ran it as a working farm. The descendents of this family, William and Reston Mather, were the house's last occupants, both dying at the property in 1934 at the ages of 80 and 78 respectively.

The house is now open to the public. As well as appreciating the superb interior and fascinating history, visitors can keep their eyes peeled for the numerous ghosts that are known to roam the property. These include the wraiths of a mother and child, who are said to have been murdered in the master bedroom. Staff members have reported being touched by unseen hands and also sensing that they are being followed as they make their way around the premises.

Provan Hall

Trenear Wendron,
45 Conisborough Road,
Glasgow G34 9QN

www.eastglasgow.co.uk/provanhall

Haunted Rating 👻👻👻👻👻

Provan Hall has been described as perhaps the most perfect example of a pre-Reformation house in Scotland, but within its walls there lurks a ghostly atmosphere

THE MACKENZIE MAUSOLEUM

EDINBURGH

The Mackenzie Mausoleum

Greyfriars Kirkyard,
Greyfriars Place,
Edinburgh EH1 2QQ

Haunted Rating

Bluidy Mackenzie

Sir George Mackenzie (1636–1691) generated respect and loathing in equal measure. He wrote learned essays on a wide variety of subjects such as history and philosophy. He was also the author of a pioneering legal work, An Institute of the Law of Scotland, *and even penned one of Scotland's earliest novels* Aretina; or the Serious Romance, *which was published in 1660. As an advocate, Sir George showed himself to be an enlightened thinker, challenging the ignorance that had seen so many people persecuted as witches in the Edinburgh of his day.*

In 1677, Sir George became Lord Advocate, in which capacity he was charged with prosecuting the Covenanters. These Scottish Presbyterians had protested against Charles I's attempts to bring the churches of England and Scotland together by introducing a new *Book of Canons* and a modified *Book of Common Prayer* into Scotland. During the Civil War, the Covenanters had sided with Parliament and

so were ruthlessly persecuted after Charles II regained the throne in 1660. Following their eventual defeat in 1679, 1,200 Covenanters were taken prisoner, with 400 of them herded into an area of Greyfriars Kirkyard that became known as the Covenanters Prison. They were kept in appalling conditions with little shelter for five harsh winter months, and were given only the minimum of food and water. Many of them died and were buried in the Kirkyard, in the area traditionally reserved for felons.

Mackenzie was tasked with meting out the king's retribution on the Covenanters. He did this with such ruthless inhumanity that the people of Edinburgh came to regard him as a 'species of ogre' and bestowed on him the sobriquet of Bluidy Mackenzie. It is said that because of the cruelty that he inflicted in life, his spirit has been unable to find rest and has been condemned to haunt the domed Black Mausoleum in Greyfriars Kirkyard, where his mortal remains were placed following his death in 1691.

There was a time when local schoolchildren would sneak into the Kirkyard after dark. They would creep up to the door of the mausoleum, stoop down and shout through its keyhole, 'Lift the sneck and draw the bar: Bluidy Mackenzie, come out if ye daur!' They would then run in the opposite direction for all they were worth, lest Mackenzie obliged them with an appearance!

In 1998, a homeless man broke into the Mackenzie vault to seek shelter from the rain. He promptly fell through the floor onto what has been described as 'a bed of corpses'. He fled the mausoleum in terror. His actions appeared to have roused a malevolent spectre from the depths of the tomb. Since then, there have been hundreds of reported attacks by what has become known as the Mackenzie Poltergeist. The raging revenant's temperament was not exactly improved by the nefarious antics of two teenagers who, in 2004, broke into the mausoleum and removed a skull, which they then subjected to various acts of abuse, including kicking it about like a football!

Sir George Mackenzie is buried just a short distance from the alleged site of the Covenanters Prison. Although some of the poltergeist attacks have taken place in the Black Mausoleum, the majority have occurred in the gated-off area of the prison featured on 'The City of the Dead' night-time ghost tours. Indeed, many taking these tours complain of being touched, pulled, slapped and even scratched by whatever malicious force is loose in one of Edinburgh's creepiest locations.

ABOVE: *The domed Black Mausoleum in Edinburgh's Greyfriars Kirkyard*
BELOW: *Monuments and tombs in Greyfriars Kirkyard, which is sometimes called 'Edinburgh's Westminster Abbey' due to the number of famous citizens buried there*

The White Lady's Return

Very little survives of the Corstorphine Sycamore, which was a local landmark for between 400 and 600 years, until it was blown down by severe winds at 8.10pm on 26 December 1998. Its few splintered remnants can be seen in a garden at the end of Dovecot Road in the village of Corstorphine, just a short distance from the centre of Edinburgh. Legend holds that the tree grew from a sapling brought here from the East by a monk in the early 15th century. It was once part of an avenue of magnificent trees lining the approach to Corstorphine Castle. Nothing now remains of the castle, save a fine 16th-century dovecote. Standing a few feet away from the remains of the tree, it contains 1,060 nest boxes. In the past, these would have provided fresh meat for the castle during winter and a goodly amount of fertilizer for a variety of crops at other times of the year.

Corstorphine Castle was dismantled in the 18th century and now lies in ruins. The only surviving remnant is its 16th-century 'doo'cot', (dovecot), standing near to the sycamore

Corstorphine Castle was home to the Baillie family, the Forrester Lairds, from the 14th to the 18th century, and several ghostly tales and legends are associated with their tenure. One of them is said to have buried his money and his jewels beneath the tree, where they were watched over by a secret guardian to ensure that they didn't fall into unworthy hands. One night a villager arrived at the tree with a pick and shovel and began digging up the ground around it, hoping to uncover the Forrester treasure. But no sooner had he turned the first sod than a booming voice from deep beneath the ground roared at him to desist immediately. The man promptly complied and scurried away terrified into the night.

However, the Corstorphine Sycamore's most famous ghost is that of the white lady, whose nocturnal wanderings hark back to a notorious murder that occurred by the tree. James Baillie, the Second Lord Forrester, was an ardent royalist who, at the end of the Civil War, was heavily fined by Oliver Cromwell's Commonwealth. Thereafter, he sought solace in alcohol and began drinking heavily. He also embarked upon a tempestuous affair with an attractive woman by the name of Christian Nimmo, the wife of a wealthy Edinburgh merchant. However, when it transpired that Christian was the niece of his wife, Joanna, the laird thought it best to end their relationship. Enraged, Christian came to Corstorphine on the night of 26 August 1679. Learning that Forrester was drinking at his favourite watering hole, the Black Bull, which then stood at the end of the High Street, she sent her maid to ask him to meet her beneath the branches of the sycamore. According to her later testimony, Forrester arrived at the tree very drunk. After calling her a whore, he drew his sword and lunged at her. In self-defence, Christian grabbed the weapon in both her hands, whereupon the laird fell onto its point and was killed instantly.

Christian then hid at Corstorphine Castle, but was soon found and taken to Edinburgh, where she was charged with murder. She pleaded that she was pregnant but doctors found no evidence of this. A month later, she managed to escape but was captured and sentenced to death. On 12 November 1679, Christian Nimmo, dressed in a 'whyte taffetie hood and dress' was beheaded in Edinburgh. Her ghost, though, wearing the attire in which she was executed, returns often to the scene of her crime and has become known as the white lady. Indeed, a market gardener who worked for many years at an adjoining site was in the habit of referring to her as 'his' white lady, so often did he see her.

There were also several reports of her forlorn phantom drifting from the tree to the road in the 1980s.

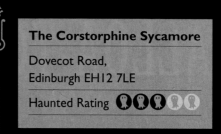

The Corstorphine Sycamore

Dovecot Road,
Edinburgh EH12 7LE

Haunted Rating 🗝🗝🗝🗝🗝

ALLOA TOWER

CLACKMANNANSHIRE

The Curse of the Erskines

Fourteenth-century Alloa Tower presents the visitor with the largest surviving keep in Scotland. Its 3-m (11-ft) thick walls, impressive medieval oak-beamed roof, not to mention its creepy medieval dungeons, all combine to make it not only an ideal historic location but also a perfectly haunted one.

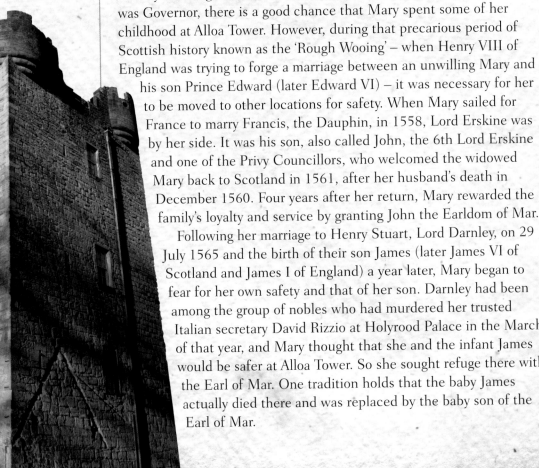

The impressive medieval keep of Alloa Tower

For centuries, the tower was owned by the Erskine family. John, the 5th Lord Erskine, was guardian to Mary, Queen of Scots in her infancy. Although her main residence was Stirling Castle, where John was Governor, there is a good chance that Mary spent some of her childhood at Alloa Tower. However, during that precarious period of Scottish history known as the 'Rough Wooing' – when Henry VIII of England was trying to forge a marriage between an unwilling Mary and his son Prince Edward (later Edward VI) – it was necessary for her to be moved to other locations for safety. When Mary sailed for France to marry Francis, the Dauphin, in 1558, Lord Erskine was by her side. It was his son, also called John, the 6th Lord Erskine and one of the Privy Councillors, who welcomed the widowed Mary back to Scotland in 1561, after her husband's death in December 1560. Four years after her return, Mary rewarded the family's loyalty and service by granting John the Earldom of Mar. Following her marriage to Henry Stuart, Lord Darnley, on 29 July 1565 and the birth of their son James (later James VI of Scotland and James I of England) a year later, Mary began to fear for her own safety and that of her son. Darnley had been among the group of nobles who had murdered her trusted Italian secretary David Rizzio at Holyrood Palace in the March of that year, and Mary thought that she and the infant James would be safer at Alloa Tower. So she sought refuge there with the Earl of Mar. One tradition holds that the baby James actually died there and was replaced by the baby son of the Earl of Mar.

A Sapling Grows From the Tower

The Erskines continued to prosper, and the 6th Earl of Mar became Secretary of State for Scotland during the reign of Queen Anne. In 1700, they extended the tower by tacking a grand house onto it, which effectively created a manor house, with the tower becoming a wing of the enlarged building. But then things began to go wrong for the family. Its members could have been forgiven for thinking the change in their fortunes might owe something to a curse placed upon them at the time of the Reformation. Following the Dissolution of the Monasteries, the Erskines had purchased Cambuskenneth Abbey and had sold off its stone to local builders. The former Abbot didn't take too kindly to the destruction, and he placed a curse upon the Erskines, promising that strangers would take over their lands one day. Furthermore, he prophesized that a future Erskine would see his home consumed by fire. The curse, he said, would not be lifted until Alloa Tower was used as a stable, a weaver sat in the laird's chamber, and a sapling grew from the top of the tower.

In 1715, the 6th Earl led the ill-fated Jacobite uprising and was forced to flee to France. Thereafter, the Erskines were stripped of their title and their estates and, for a time, strangers did indeed take over their lands. The situation was remedied in 1724, when Sir John's brother, Lord Grange, bought the estate and held it in trust for the family. On 28 August 1800, the mansion was destroyed by fire, although the local people managed to save the tower by placing turf cut from the lawn around its walls. The family then resided at their other properties, and dragoons took over the tower, using it to stable their horses. In 1815, a homeless weaver took shelter in what had been the laird's chamber. Then, in 1814, an ash sapling was noticed sprouting from the roof of the tower. By 1824, the Erskines were able to put the curse behind them, as their titles were reinstated.

Alloa Tower, however, continued to fall into decay, and by the 1980s it was little more than a forlorn ruin. But then the tower was restored to its former glory. Now, visitors can marvel at its magnificent interior and, it is said, also smell the spectral smoke that supposedly wafts around the tower on the anniversary of the fire.

Alloa Tower

Alloa, Clackmannanshire
FK10 1PP

Haunted Rating

INVERARAY JAIL

ARGYLL & BUTE

The Jailer Can See You Now

There can be no doubt about it, Inveraray Jail is a truly marrow-chilling location. Many of those who visit it – either during the day, when it is open as a living museum, or by night, when you are allowed to explore its cells and corridors on ghost hunts – have encountered the desolate phantoms of those who were either prisoners or jailers.

The building was constructed in two phases during the 19th century – in 1820, when the Old Prison and Courthouse were completed, and in 1848, when the New Prison was added. It served as the courthouse and jail for the whole of Argyll. Until its closure in 1889, thousands of men, women and children had spent time in its dank, dismal cells. Most prisoners were kept in solitary confinement, forbidden to communicate or have any contact with fellow prisoners – it was believed that this

ABOVE AND RIGHT: *Statues of prison guards and former inmates add to the sinister atmosphere at the Jail Museum in Inveraray*

would encourage them to devote their days to prayer, simple work and be influenced to reform by 'the ministrations of sober, upright, God fearing attendants'. In reality, their time here must have been hell on earth, and the spirits of several former inmates appear to have been condemned to remain earthbound – eternal prisoners at a place where their living selves endured unimaginable horrors and torment.

The most fearsome spectre to roam the prison is that of the jailer. This menacing revenant terrifies visitors with his threatening and aggressive manner, then simply dissipates into thin air. Dark figures have been seen scurrying along corridors or cowering in corners, and many people find themselves unable to enter Cell 10. Instead, they pause on its threshold because of an indefinable something that they can sense inside. Children who visit the prison are often seen chatting to somebody, although whoever it is remains invisible to adults looking on. Dogs will suddenly stop in corridors, again apparently able to see something or someone that remains invisible to humans.

All in all, Inveraray Jail is an intriguing and fascinating location, which provides an insightful glimpse of the darker, more sinister side of Scottish history. The fact that you have a good chance of encountering some of those who passed through when it was a place of incarceration and reform only serves to make your visit even more memorable and spine-tingling.

Inveraray Jail

Main Street, Inveraray,
Argyll & Bute PA32 8TX

www.inverarayjail.co.uk

Haunted Rating

KILCHURN CASTLE

ARGYLL & BUTE

The Sobbing Spectre

Kilchurn Castle dates from the late 1440s, and was built by Sir Colin Campbell on what was then a tiny rocky island in Loch Awe. Legend holds that it was Sir Colin's wife, Margaret, who oversaw the construction of the castle, as he was away on his travels during the seven or so years it took to build it. Although Sir Colin wrote to his wife regularly throughout his absence, she never actually received his letters, as they were intercepted by an Argyllshire chieftain by the name of M'Corquodale, who had designs on Margaret. As time passed, the treacherous chieftain managed to convince Margaret that, since she hadn't heard from her husband for so long, he must be dead.

Believing his lies, the grief-stricken Margaret accepted M'Corquodale's proposal of marriage, and arrangements were made for their wedding. Fortunately, Sir Colin arrived back from his travels just in the nick of time and was able to prevent the marriage and reclaim his wife. M'Corquodale was allowed to depart and the reunited couple were then able to settle down in their island fortress, which remained the residence of subsequent generations of the family until it was abandoned completely in the early 18th century.

A romantic view of Kilchurn Castle

Struck By Lightning

During the Campbells' tenure, Kilchurn Castle was extended and modified, the last major alterations made by Sir John Campbell, Earl of Breadalbane, towards the end of the 17th century. In addition to heightening the castle walls, he also added a large barrack block, the first purpose-built barracks in Scotland. The castle was subsequently garrisoned by government troops during the Jacobite uprisings of 1715 and 1745. However, the Campbells were spending less and less time at their island fortress and when, in 1769, the castle was struck by lightning, they abandoned it altogether, leaving it to fall into decay. Weed and bracken crept over its once proud walls, and the local populace carted away some of its slates and timbers to incorporate into buildings elsewhere. In the 19th century, the water level of Loch Awe was lowered and, as a result, Kilchurn Castle was for the first time in its history accessible by land. Even so, its descent into ruin continued. At one stage, a homeless woman nicknamed the Witch of Kilchurn took refuge in the castle and became something of a local character, often making her way to Loch Awe Stores to purchase her pipe tobacco.

Thankfully, the decay was halted by Historic Scotland, which restored it in the 1950s. Today, visitors can approach the castle either over land or, in the summer months, via a little steamer that takes them over the loch on what is a truly picturesque approach.

Many visitors to the castle have heard a pitiful ghostly voice crying out for help as they explore the stunning site. Tradition holds that the cries are those of a child who was locked away in a room high in the castle at some stage in its long history. Quite why, or what fate befell the unfortunate child to cause its ghostly pleadings to echo down the centuries, is not recorded.

Kilchurn Castle

Near Dalmally,
Argyll & Bute PA33

www.kilchurncastle.com

Haunted Rating

RRS DISCOVERY

DUNDEE

RRS *Discovery*

Discovery Point,
Discovery Quay,
Dundee DD1 4XA

www.rrsdiscovery.com

Haunted Rating 🯄🯄🯄🯄🯄

BELOW: *The crew's sleeping quarters aboard the RRS Discovery at Discovery Point*
ABOVE RIGHT: *An officer's cabin*

Ghosts Below Deck

The Royal Research Ship Discovery was built in Dundee in 1900–1 and was launched on 21 March 1901. She was the last wooden three-masted ship to be constructed in Britain, and was built specifically for Antarctic research. The massive flat, shallow hull was specially constructed to be able to withstand being frozen into ice. As an extra precaution against the harsh conditions the ship would encounter, the propeller and rudder were designed so that they could be hoisted out of harm's way to avoid them being damaged by ice.

On 6 August 1901, she set out on her first voyage, taking the British National Antarctic Expedition, which included Robert Falcon Scott and Ernest Shackleton, on its first successful journey to the Antarctic. It wasn't long before it was discovered that the flat hull, specifically designed for icy conditions, provided minimal stability, and the ship rolled badly on open seas. After five months at sea, the crew spotted the coast of Antarctica on 8 January 1902 and set about their task of charting the coastline. After the first month, with winter closing in, Scott dropped anchor in McMurdo Sound, from where he intended to continue the voyage in the spring. Unfortunately, they remained there ice-locked for the next two years until, on 16 February 1904, they literally blasted their way out using controlled explosives. The expedition did, however, make some important discoveries, such as establishing that Antarctica was indeed a continent, and relocating the South Magnetic Pole before sailing for home, arriving in late September 1904.

Following a career that saw her used as a troop carrier in World War I and later as a cargo ship, *Discovery* was presented to the Boy Scouts Association in 1936 and berthed on the River Thames in London, to be used as a training ship for Sea Scouts. By 1955, the cost of maintaining her was requiring too many bob-a-jobs, and ownership was transferred to the Admiralty, which put her into service as a drill ship for the Royal Navy Auxiliary Reserve. Over the next 30 years, her condition

deteriorated and, in 1985, ownership was transferred to the Dundee Heritage Trust. She was then transported from London to Dundee, where she received a tumultuous welcome on her arrival in the River Tay on 3 April 1986. RRS *Discovery* is now displayed in a purpose-built dock facility. The public can climb aboard the ship and view, among other exhibits, Captain Scott's rifle and pipe, as well as examples of the games played by the crew to while away the time during the Antarctic expedition.

Visitors can perhaps also look forward to encountering some of the former crew members who show a marked reluctance to disembark. The ship has an undoubtedly distinctive atmosphere, and there are some rooms that visitors regularly refuse point-blank to enter. Ghostly footsteps are frequently heard and, on one occasion, a guest at a dinner function held on board spent the evening talking to a man whom she swore she could see but who remained invisible to other guests.

CASTLE FRASER

ABERDEENSHIRE

The Green Lady

More chateau-like than castle-like in appearance, Castle Fraser is an atmospheric building that was begun in 1575 by Michael Fraser, 6th Laird Fraser, and completed in 1636. Its towering grey walls are surrounded by 300 acres of woodland and farmland, and there is a good chance that you have seen it before, even if you've never actually visited it – it was featured as a backdrop in some of the scenes in the award-winning film The Queen, *starring Helen Mirren in the title role. So it is, perhaps, rather apt that the castle's best-known roaming revenant is, reputedly, that of a princess.*

RIGHT: The elegant chateau-like exterior of Castle Fraser is home to a phantom princess and some ghostly children

According to legend – and it should be pointed out that unconfirmed folklore as opposed to recorded history is how the story has been passed down through the generations – a princess sleeping in the Green Room of the castle was brutally murdered. The poor girl's body was then dragged unceremoniously down a flight of stone stairs, leaving behind a trail of blood as it bumped from stair to stair. Once the body had been disposed of, the perpetrators attempted to clean up the bloodstains but, try as they might, they could not scrub them away. Eventually, all they could do was hide the indelible evidence of their infamous act by covering the stone stairs with wooden panelling, which remains in place to this day. However, this hasn't prevented the princess's phantom from roaming the castle's rooms and corridors, chilling the blood and sending shivers down the spines of those who encounter her.

Over the years, there have been reports of much paranormal activity at Castle Fraser. Piano music has been heard echoing from empty rooms, and ghostly whispering has been heard at sundry locations around the property. People working in the kitchen have reported the sound of children laughing and singing, only to be told that there were no children present in the castle at the time.

Castle Fraser is a true gem of a location, and to wander its corridors and rooms is to walk through history. The chance of an encounter with the phantom princess or the ghostly children, whose presences are as much a part of the castle's appeal as any of the exhibits on display, is reason enough to pay it a visit.

Castle Fraser

Inverurie,
Aberdeenshire AB51 7LD

Haunted Rating

LUNAN LODGE

ANGUS

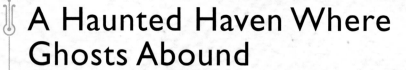

A Haunted Haven Where Ghosts Abound

Lunan Lodge has just about everything a seeker of the mystical and the ghostly could wish to experience. A cosy, family-run bed and breakfast, it offers guests a secluded haven in a region renowned for its stone circles, haunted castles and ancient energy lines. It also brims with so many revenants – 47 in total – that its owners, Jules and Samantha, positively encourage visitors to seek them out on regular ghost safaris.

The oldest part of the house dates from the 18th century, and many of the original features have been retained. It was built as a manse for the local minister and, over the years, its walls have, apparently, absorbed many of the energies and the personalities of those who have dwelt within them. Indeed, many former residents are so attached to the property that a little thing like death isn't going to cause them to move out, and their ghosts linger on long after their living selves have departed.

Some of the ghosts have, over the years, proved very useful. For example, there is the apparition of the maidservant who vanishes into walls or walks around invisible obstructions on her ethereal meanderings around the building. Jules and Samantha have knocked down sections of wall at the sites of her disappearances and have uncovered long-forgotten doorways. They've also lifted floorboards and dug up flowerbeds, and discovered the remains of walls and other objects. Another ghost has provided snippets of what proved to be surprisingly accurate information about the house, which was invaluable in helping Jules and Samantha piece together its history and that of its residents over the past 250 years.

But, as Jules and Samantha point out, most of their ghosts 'just get on with their afterlives without bothering anybody'. Indeed, they suspect that many of the spirits don't even realize they are dead, and the fact that the two pet cats like to chase after them probably re-enforces the ghosts' belief that they are still very much alive and in residence.

Lunan Lodge is, without doubt, one of the most haunted locations in Scotland, and its ghosts are extremely active. Visitors frequently encounter some form of paranormal activity, including cold spots, ghostly singing coming from rooms that are known to be empty, and even full-blown manifestations. Ghost hunters who have conducted paranormal investigations at the house have achieved impressive results. There is even a standing challenge that if a guest can spend the night in the 'shouty man room' without 'running away like a chicken', they will be given a certificate to mark their achievement.

But there is another side to Lunan Lodge. It is also a very spiritual place. Its location at the convergence of several ancient energy lines, coupled with the stunning views over Lunan Bay, are sufficient to recharge the batteries of even the most jaded city dweller. Once you have attuned yourself to the enchantment of your surroundings, you can then begin to make the acquaintance of the ghosts, their presence so perfectly in keeping with the overall ambience of a house where the past and present merge so completely and so comfortably.

Lunan Lodge

Lunan, by Montrose,
Angus DD10 9TG

www.lunanlodge.co.uk

Haunted Rating 👤👤👤👤👤

KINNAIRD HEAD CASTLE

FRASERBURGH

Kinnaird Head Castle

Kinnaird Head,
Stevenson Road,
Fraserburgh AB43 9DU

Haunted Rating 👻👻👻👻👻

The Phantom Piper and the Love He Lost

Two of the creepiest types of haunted location are possibly castles and lighthouses. Over the centuries, castles have experienced tragedy, betrayal, intrigue and bloodshed, which have been virtually seared into their stonework. Lighthouses, too, have seen their fair share of drama, with their keepers enduring isolated existences in days gone by. Picturing what it must have been like to live and work in them on dark nights when storms lashed their walls and rattled their windows can send cold shivers racing down the spine. It stands to reason that a location that's both a castle and a lighthouse must surely be right up there on the list of 'must visit' for anyone seeking the most atmospheric haunted locations in Britain.

The Museum of Scottish Lighthouses, formerly the Kinnaird Head Castle Lighthouse, is not just haunted but also fascinating. The castle was built around 1570 as an occasional residence by Sir Alexander Fraser of Philorth. A later Alexander Fraser, the 8th Laird, took a close interest in the affairs of the Northern Lighthouse Board when it was established in 1786. A year later, concerned at the danger to shipping off the headland on which the fortress stood, he gifted the castle to the Board so that it could be converted into a lighthouse. It became operational at the end of 1787, then was reconstructed in 1824 by Robert Stevenson, grandfather of the author Robert Louis Stevenson. The lighthouse was decommissioned in 1991 and the site now holds the finest collection of lighthouse exhibits in the whole of the UK.

Piper's Cave

The castle's ghost story concerns Isobel, a daughter of Sir Alexander Fraser, who was forbidden by her father to mix with the local riffraff. However, when he was away one day, she offered shelter to a piper during a snowstorm. As often happens when a daughter of the house takes a storm-drenched piper in from the cold, the two of them got talking, found they had a lot in common – musical tastes, dress sense, love of animals, that sort of thing – and, before the first rays of the new day had risen over the surrounding headland, the two of them had fallen madly in love. Thereafter, they met in secret or whenever Sir Alexander's absences permitted it, and their relationship blossomed. Inevitably, Sir Alexander found out about their involvement and told them, in no uncertain terms, that they were never to see each other again. This they were unable to do and arranged another tryst, which Sir Alexander also found out about. Enraged, he locked Isobel in her room and had the piper seized and put in chains in a cave beneath the castle's wine tower. He wanted to break the piper's spirit so that when he took his daughter to her lover the following day, he would no longer wish to marry her.

What Sir Alexander hadn't banked on, though, was that a ferocious storm broke out in the middle of the night, causing the sea to flood into the cave. The next day, when he took Isobel to the cave, they were confronted with the sight of her drowned lover still locked in his chains. The distressed girl let out a scream of despair, ran to the top of the tower and flung herself to her death on the rocks below. From then on the cave became known as the Piper's Cave, and it is said that the sound of ghostly pipe music sometimes drifts from it as the phantom piper plays a lament for his lost love. And, whenever a fierce storm breaks across the headland, the sorry spectre of a sobbing Isobel is said to drift around the castle, desperately seeking her piper lover.

TULLOCH CASTLE

DINGWALL

The Ghost In Room 8

The origins of Tulloch Castle date back to the mid-12th century, although little now remains of the original structure. The word 'Tulloch' derives from the Gaelic 'Tuich', meaning hillock, and the castle was first known by this name in the early 16th century, when it was owned by the Bayne clan. They remained in residence until 1762, when the castle was sold to the Davidson family, which owned it until the early 20th century. It then passed to the Vicars family, before becoming a hospital during World War II. After several other incarnations, it became the delightful hotel that it is today.

The castle acquired its resident ghost during the tenure of the Davidson clan. Duncan Davidson, the 4th Laird of Tulloch, one of the more colourful family members, was born in 1800. He took his Highland heritage very seriously indeed and was one of the few lairds of his age always to wear Highland dress. He was a great favourite of Queen Victoria, although whether she would have been amused by his amorous antics is doubtful. He was nicknamed The Stag, and during a long and lust-filled life, he managed to get through five wives, fathering 18 legitimate children. Then there were the 30 illegitimate children that he fathered with a veritable assortment of local totty.

According to tradition, one of his daughters, Elizabeth Davidson, entered a castle bedroom at a particularly inopportune moment, catching her father in flagrante with a woman he had no business being in flagrante with. The shock sent her scurrying off along a corridor, at the end of which she tripped and fell down the stairs, sustaining injuries from which she died.

Her ghost has returned to the castle ever since and is such a regular feature that the bar has been named The Green Lady Lounge after her. However, she appears to have a particular fondness for Room 8 at the castle. A guest spending the night in this room was once woken by the

feeling of somebody, or something, pinning him to the bed. During a very troubled night, he dreamt of a lady and two young girls wearing Victorian dresses. The next morning, he was astonished when, in the Great Hall of the castle, he saw a portrait of Elizabeth Davidson and other members of the Davidson family. He instantly recognized them as the women he had dreamt about.

Indeed, Room 8 has quite a reputation for things going bump in the dead of night, and it's a very popular venue with ghost hunters who specifically request it to see if they, too, can make the acquaintance of its spectral occupant. In a newspaper article published in February 2008, The *Highland News* quoted Anne MacDonald, the manager of the hotel, as saying, 'I'm not a coward and I don't scare easily but I wouldn't sleep in Room 8 for love nor money. The room has quite a reputation and we have people coming from all over to stay in it… It doesn't matter how much heating you have on, but when you go along that corridor there is always a chill, summer or winter. People frequently say that someone had been knocking at their door but when they looked there was nobody there.'

On 28 May 2008, the *Sun* newspaper reported that a 14-year-old boy named Connor Bond, who was attending a wedding at Tulloch Castle, obtained a photograph of what appeared to be a ghostly hand gripping a banister with an apparition floating behind it. Although professing scepticism about ghosts, Connor's father Mike admitted that he just couldn't see '… what else it could be – it's a digital camera so you can't accidentally double-expose the shot, and Connor swears there was no one around at the time. It's a mystery.'

<table>
<tr><td colspan="2">**Tulloch Castle**</td></tr>
<tr><td colspan="2">Tulloch Castle Drive, Dingwall, Highlands IV15 9ND</td></tr>
<tr><td>Haunted Rating</td><td>🂠🂠🂠🂠🂠</td></tr>
</table>

ABOVE: *Tulloch Castle, now a hotel, is popular with ghost hunters keen to stay the night in the infamous Room 8*

The Loch Ness Monster

Loch Ness lies at the northern end of the Great Glen, a geological fault that slashes across the Scottish Highlands. Its 24 miles (39km) of dark rippling water present the wayfarer with an ever-changing panorama of hill, water and woodland. No one knows for certain exactly how deep this mysterious loch is, but its deepest and most sinister portion is that which ripples before the hollow shell of Urquhart Castle. Legend holds that beneath the castle there exist underwater caves, which are home to a colony of monsters. And, of course, Loch Ness, despite its stunning scenery, is best known for the enigmatic creature said to lurk beneath its peat-blackened waters, and whose forays to the surface have made it one of the world's most famous legendary beasts.

Whatever dwells in the chilly depths of Loch Ness is neither a newcomer nor an idle legend to be derided out of hand. Indeed, the very first recorded encounter with either 'Nessie' or, more probably, one of her ancient ancestors, occurred in AD 565, when a disciple of the Irish missionary St Columba was swimming across the River Ness to fetch a boat for his master. Suddenly, a fearful beast appeared and, 'with a great roar and open mouth', rushed upon the swimmer. St Columba immediately made the sign of the cross and bellowed at the beast, 'Think not to go further, nor touch thou that man! Go back....' The monster obeyed and, despite making regular appearances in the 1,400 years since, it has never harmed anyone nor, for that matter, emitted even the slightest roar.

It was with the opening of a main road along the north shore of the loch in 1933 that modern-day interest in Nessie began. In the December of that year, the Daily Mail sponsored the first endeavour to find the monster, engaging the services of big game hunter Marmaduke Wetherell and photographer Gustav Pauli. An immense amount of excitement was generated when, deep in the undergrowth by the side of the loch, the pair discovered a large footprint, apparently left by a massive creature. Unfortunately, this was soon revealed to be a hoax, perpetrated with a dried hippopotamus foot, otherwise used as an umbrella stand!

Then, on 19 April 1934, Harley Street consultant Robert Kenneth Wilson took the famous 'surgeon's photograph' (opposite) of a seemingly long-necked creature swimming across Loch Ness, and gave the world its most enduring image of the fabled beast. Although his picture has been proved a fake, there have since been over 1,000 reported sightings. Disregarding proven hoaxes, mistaken identifications of natural objects, optical illusions or wishful thinking – and it must be said that these certainly account for a large proportion of the sightings – there still remains sufficient evidence from sober, honest and publicity-shy witnesses to suggest that something mysterious does indeed reside in Loch Ness.

Debate still rages over the nature of the beast. Those who claim to have seen the monster close-up say that it is slug- or eel-like, with a head resembling that of a sheep or a seal. Its length has been estimated at anywhere between 7.6 and 23 metres (25 and 75 feet), and its skin texture is warty and slimy. Some say that it is an unknown species of fish, others that it is a survivor from prehistoric times, possibly a plesiosaurus.

Fact or Fiction?

Reported sightings of 'Nessie' have been dismissed by sceptics as a mass of rotting vegetation, a group of frolicking water otters, a swimming deer, even a sunken World War I zeppelin that periodically rises to the surface. Numerous scientific expeditions have failed to provide conclusive proof, one way or the other, of her existence, and the many photographers who come here in the hope of catching Nessie on film have long grown used to her coquettish and annoying habit of only appearing when they are sans camera.

One of the more recent Nessie sightings was on 26 May 2007, when Gordon Holmes, a 55-year-old lab technician, filmed the loch and captured footage of a black object, which was about 14m (45ft) long and moving at great speed through the water. The footage was later screened on several news programmes throughout Scotland. As per usual, there was considerable debate as to whether it was the fabled Loch Ness Monster or merely an otter, a seal or a water bird.

Whatever may or may not live beneath the waters of Britain's greatest volume of fresh water, the legend of the Loch Ness Monster refuses to die, and visitors continue to flock from all over the globe in the hope of catching a glimpse of this elusive creature.

Perhaps the final word should go to naturalist Dr David Bellamy, who said of the monster, 'I hope it's there. But I hope they don't find it – because if they do, they'll do something nasty to it.'

Index

A

Abbeys: Dorchester Abbey, Oxfordshire 120–1
  Torre Abbey, Devon 20–1
Abingdon, Earls of 119
Agnes, Sister 63
aircraft: North East Aircraft Museum 204–5
  RAF Museum Cosford 174–5
airships 72–3, 204
Albert, Prince Consort 94
Allan, Peter 206–7
Alloa Tower 228–9
Alsop, Jane 66
Anglesey, Isle of 166–7
Archer Shepherd, Rev. E.H. 159
Arthur, King 178
Avenbury 158–9

B

Babington, Anthony 145
Baddesley Clinton 126–7
Baillie, James 226–7
Baillie family 223
Baskerville, Harry 104
Bates, Jack 206
battlefields: Bosworth Battlefield Heritage Centre 134–5
  Tewkesbury Battlefield 36–9
  Towton Battlefield 202–3
Beard, Police Sergeant Samuel 43
Beet, Special Constable John 185–6
Bellamy, Dr David 246
Berkeley Square, London 50–1
Berrington Hall, Leominster 156–7
Bess of Hardwick 141
Black Shuck 102–3
Blackburn, William 42
Blomfield, Arthur 160

Blythburgh 102
Bodelwyddan Castle 170–1
Bodmin Jail 18–19
Boleyn, Anne 118
Bolling, Robert 192
Bolling Hall, Bradford 192–3
Bolton 188–9
Bond, Connor 243
Bosworth, Battle of 178
Bosworth Battlefield Heritage Centre 134–5
Bradford 192–3
Brankner, Sir Sefton 73
Breamore House, Fordingbridge 78–9
Brereton, Sir Richard 142
Bristol 32–3
Brome, John 127
Brome, Nicholas 127
Brooksby, Eleanor 127
Brown, 'Capability' 156
Brunel, Isambard Kingdom 32
Buchanan, Dr John 223
Buckstone, John Baldwin 57
Bulkeley, John 78
Bungay 102

C

Cabinet War Rooms, London 52–5
Campbell, Sir Colin 232
Campbell, Sir John 233
Campbell, Lady Margaret 232
Canewdon 86–7
Cardington Hangars 72–3
Cary, Lady 21
castles: Alloa Tower 228–9
  Castle Fraser, Inverurie 236–7
  Castle Keep, Newcastle-upon-Tyne 208–9
  Coalhouse Fort, East Tilbury 84–5
  Edlingham Castle 212–13

Fotheringham Castle 146–7
Guildford Castle 68–9
Hastings Castle 60–1
Hermitage Castle 218–21
Hopton Castle, Craven Arms 172–3
Kilchurn Castle 232–3
Kinnaird Head Castle 240–1
Landguard Fort, Felixstowe 92–3
Muncaster Castle 200–1
St Briavels Castle 40–1
Tretower Castle 164–5
Tulloch Castle, Dingwall 242–3
Cavendish family 141
caves: Chislehurst Caves 58–9
  Hell Fire Caves, West Wycombe 76–7
  Kents Cavern 22–5
  Marsden Grotto, South Shields 206–7
Cawley, Frederick 157
Charles I, King 88, 109, 119, 188, 224
Charles II, King 94, 154–5, 188, 225
Chislehurst Caves 58–9
Christchurch Mansion, Ipswich 94–5
churches: Knowlton Church, Dorset 26–7
  Rycote Chapel, Thame 118–19
  St Mary, Avenbury 158–9
  St Mary, Bungay 102
  St Mary, Swansea 160–1
  St Nicholas Church, Canewdon 86–7
Churchill, Winston 52–4, 99
Churchill Museum, London 52–5
Civil War 35, 109, 119, 154, 172–3, 188–9, 193, 223, 224–5, 226
Clay, John 206–7
Clibbon, Walter 70–1
Clibbon's Post, Hertfordshire 70–1
Clinton family 127
Coalhouse Fort, East Tilbury 84–5
Cobbold, Felix 94
Coke, Thomas and Charlotte 90
Cole, Thomas 75

Columba, St 245
The Commandery, Worcester 154–5
Constable, John 94
Coombe Abbey Hotel, Coventry 128–9
Cornish pasties 44–5
Corstorphine Sycamore, Edinburgh 226–7
Cosford 174–5
Cosmeston Medieval Village 162–3
Covenanters 223, 224–5
Coventry 128–9
Cowan, Sir John 66
Craven family 128–9
Crispin, Milo 74
Cromwell, Oliver 88–9, 226
The Crooked House, Himley 136–7

D

Darcy, Thomas 198
Darell, Captain Nathaniel 92
Darnley, Lord 198, 199, 223, 228
Dartmoor 104
Dashwood, Sir Francis 76
Davidson, Duncan 242
Davidson, Elizabeth 242–3
Deloney, Thomas 74
Derby, James Stanley, 7th Earl of 188–9
Dickens, Charles 57
Dinas Emrys, Snowdonia 177
Discovery, RRS 234–5
Dodington, Christian 78–9
Dodington, Sir Henry 78
Dodington, William 78
Dodington, Sir William 78–9
dogs, Black Shuck 102–4
Dorchester Abbey, Oxfordshire 120–1
Doughty, Vivienne 88
Douglas, Sir William 219
Doyle, Sir Arthur Conan 73, 104, 194–7
dragons 176–8
Drake, Sir Francis 21
Dymond, Charlotte 18–19

E

Edinburgh 224–7
Edlingham Castle 212–13
Edward, Prince of Wales 36, 38, 39
Edward III, King 162
Edward IV, King 36–9, 127, 192

Edward VI, King 228
Egerton, Sir Thomas 142
Elizabeth I, Queen 94, 118–19, 127, 144–7, 208
Elizabeth II, Queen 178
Ellis, Police Constable Dick 185–6
Ely 88–9
English Heritage 92
Erskine family 228–9
Everett, Nigel 56
Exeter, Henry Cecil, Earl of 153

F

fairies 194–7
Felbrigg Hall, Norfolk 96–7
Felixstowe 92–3
Ferrers, Henry 127
Ferrers, Rebecca 127
Ferrers, Major Thomas 127
Fitzwilliam, 3rd Earl 90
Fletcher, Sarah 120–1
The Folklore Society 7
forts: Coalhouse Fort, East Tilbury 84–5
    Landguard Fort, Felixstowe 92–3
Fotheringham Castle 146–7
Fraser, Sir Alexander 241
Fraser, Isobel 241
Freda 108
Fullerton, Fiona 57

G

Gainsborough, Thomas 94
Galleries of Justice Museum, Nottingham 138–9
Gardner, Edward L. 196–7
Garrett, Eileen 73
Geoffrey, Abbot 129
Ghost Club 85
ghost-hunting 125
gibbets 30–1
Glasgow 222–3
Glynne, Sir Stephen 137
Graham, Winston 16
Gray, Captain John 33
Great Britain, SS 32–3
Great Yarmouth 103
Griffiths, Frances 196–7
Guildford Castle, Surrey 68–9

Gunby Hall, Lincolnshire 106–7
Guy of Warwick 122–4
Guy's Cliffe House, Warwick 122–4

H

Hamilton, Sir Robert 223
Hamilton, William, 2nd Duke of 154–5
Hanbury Hall, Droitwich 152–3
Hardwick Old Hall, Derbyshire 7, 140–1
Hare, Augustus 97
Harley, Thomas 156–7
Harper, Charles 51
Harrington, Sir John 128
Hastings Castle 60–1
Hay-Williams, Sir John 170–1
Haynes, Margaret 88
Hell Fire Caves, West Wycombe 76–7
Henry II, King 208
Henry III, King 60
Henry V, King 86
Henry VI, King 36, 127, 200
Henry VII, King 39, 134–5, 178, 198
Henry VIII, King 61, 92, 118, 128, 154, 193, 228
Hereford, Milo Fitz Walter, Earl of 40
Hermitage Castle 218–21
Herthill, John 127
Hiller, Major 175
Hobbes, Thomas 7, 140–1
Holbein, Hans the Younger 111
Holland, Henry 156
Holmes, Gordon 246
Holmpton 112–13
Hopton Castle, Craven Arms 172–3
hotels: Coombe Abbey Hotel, Coventry 128–9
    Tulloch Castle, Dingwall 242–3
    The Vine Hotel, Seacroft 100–1
Hotham, Sir John 109
houses: Baddesley Clinton, Warwickshire 126–7
    Berrington Hall, Leominster 156–7
    Bodelwyddan Castle 170–1
    Bolling Hall, Bradford 192–3
    Breamore House, Fordingbridge 78–9
    Christchurch Mansion, Ipswich 94–5
    Felbrigg Hall, Norfolk 96–7

Gunby Hall, Lincolnshire 106–7
Guy's Cliffe House, Warwick 122–4
Hanbury Hall, Droitwich 152–3
Hardwick Old Hall, Derbyshire 140–1
Lunan Lodge, Angus 238–9
Lydiard House and Park, Wiltshire 34–5
Lyveden New Bield, Oundle 130–1
Oliver Cromwell's House, Ely 88–9
Plas yn Rhiw, Pwllheli 168–9
Preston Manor, East Sussex 62–3
Provan Hall, Glasgow 222–3
Tatton Old Hall, Cheshire 142–3
Temple Newsam House, Leeds 198–9
Tretower Court, Powys 164–5
Howard, Simon 22, 25
Hull 108–9
Hull, James 25
Hulse, Sir Edward 79
Hulse, Sir William 79
Hunter, Thomas 91
Hutchinson, Philip 69

I

Ingram, Sir Arthur 198
Ingram, Mary 198–9
Inverary Jail 230–1
Ipswich 94–5
Irwin, Flight Lieutenant H. Carmichael 73

J

James I, King 78, 147, 178, 191, 228
Jarman (pub landlord) 74–5
John, King 40, 60
Johnson, Dr Samuel 96
Jones, Andy and Nicola 42, 43
Jones, Jack 166–7

K

Keating sisters 169
Kents Cavern, Devon 22–5
Kilchurn Castle 232–3
Kinnaird Head Castle 240–1
Kitton, John 97
knockers 45
Knowlton Church and earthworks, Dorset 26–7

L

Landguard Fort, Felixstowe 92–3
Leeds 198–9
Leicester Guildhall 132–3
lighthouses: Kinnaird Head Castle, Fraserburgh 240–1
   Souter Lighthouse, Whitburn 210–11
   South Stack Lighthouse, Anglesey 166–7
Littledean Jail, Gloucestershire 42–3
Loch Ness Monster 244–7
London 50–7, 64–7
Lunan Lodge, Angus 238–9
Lydiard House and Park, Wiltshire 34–5
Lynn, Dr 97
Lyveden New Bield, Oundle 130–1

M

McCartney, Paul 72
MacDonald, Anne 243
Macdonald, Lily 63
McKellen, Sir Ian 56
Mackenzie, Sir George 224–5
Mackenzie Mausoleum, Edinburgh 224–5
Mar, Earls of 228–9
Margaret of Anjou, Queen 36
Marsden Grotto, South Shields 206–7
Mary, Queen of Scots 141, 144–7, 198, 223, 228
Massingberd, Algernon 106
Massingberd, Sir Hugh 106
Mather family 223
Mills, John and Jacob 212
mines 44–5
   Chislehurst Caves, Kent 58–9
   Poldark Mine, Cornwall 16–17
Montgomery-Massingberd, Sir Archibald 107
Moore, Colonel Samuel 172–3
Mostghosts 17
Muckleburgh Collection, Weybourne 98–9
Muffon, David 96
Muncaster Castle, Cumbria 200–1
Murray, Dr Margaret 7
museums: Galleries of Justice Museum, Nottingham 138–9
   Inverary Jail 230–1
Muckleburgh Collection, Weybourne 98–9
Museum of Scottish Lighthouses 241
North East Aircraft Museum, Sunderland 204–5
Peterborough Museum 90–1
RAF Museum Cosford 174–5
Tatton Old Hall, Cheshire 142–3
Towneley Hall Gallery and Museum 190–1
Myrrdin (Merlin) 176–8

N

National Laboratory of Psychical Research 73
National Trust 96, 107, 131, 152, 157, 169, 206, 211
Newcastle, William Cavendish, Earl of 193
Nimmo, Christian 227
Norreys, Henry 118–19
Norreys, Marjorie 118–19
North, Fletcher 104
North, Frederick 96–7
North, Shock 70–1
North East Aircraft Museum, Sunderland 204–5
Nottingham 138–9

O

Ye Olde Man and Scythe, Bolton 188–9
Ye Olde White Harte, Hull 108–9
The Ostrich, Colnbrook 74–5
Owen Tudor 165

P

Palmerston, Lord 84
pasties, Cornish 44–5
Paul, Sir George Onesiphorous 42
Pauli, Gustav 245
Peach, Charles Stanley 62
Pengally, William 22
Pennington, Sir Ferdinand 201
Pennington, Helwise 201
Pennington, Sir John 200
'Penny Dreadfuls' 67
Peterborough Museum 90–1
Picard family 164
Pickingill, George 87
Plas yn Rhiw, Pwllheli 168–9
Poldark Mine, Cornwall 16–17
Preston Manor, East Sussex 62–3

Preucil, Augustin 205
prisons: Bodmin Jail 18–19
    Inverary Jail 230–1
    Littledean Jail 42–3
Provan Hall, Glasgow 222–3
pubs: The Crooked House, Himley 136–7
    Marsden Grotto, South Shields 206–7
    Ye Olde Man and Scythe, Bolton 188–9
    Ye Olde White Harte, Hull 108–9
    The Ostrich, Colnbrook 74–5
Pye, Rose 86

Q

Quatremayne, Richard 118

R

R101 airship 72–3
RAF Holmpton 112–13
RAF Museum Cosford 174–5
RAF Unsworth 204–5
Ramsay, Sir Alexander 219
Red Dragon of Wales 176–8
Richard III, King 39, 134–5, 142, 178, 192
Richardson, Ralph 57
roads: Stocksbridge bypass 184–7
Robert the Bruce 218–19
Robert Curthose 208
Rodney family 157
Rycote Chapel, Thame 118–19

S

St Briavels Castle, Gloucestershire 40–1
St John, Edward 34
St John, Sir John 34, 35
St Mary, Bungay 102
St Mary, Avenbury 158–9
St Mary, Swansea 160–1
St Nicholas Church, Canewdon 86–7
Salvin, Anthony 200
Savory, Berry and Michael 99
Scales, Lucy and Margaret 66
Scott, Major G.H. 73
Scott, Robert Falcon 234, 235
Scott, Sir Walter 218
Shackleton, Ernest 234
Shakespeare, William 111
Shaw, Sergeant Edward Grenville 205

Sheringham 103
ships: RRS *Discovery* 234–5
    SS *Great Britain*, Bristol 32–3
Shrewsbury, George Talbot, Earl of 141
Simon, Sir John 73
Sinden, Sir Donald 57
Skelton, Thomas 201
skulls 108–9, 111
Snelling, Harold 197
Sneyd, William 153
Snowdonia National Park 177
Somerset, Duke of 36–9
Soulis, Sir William de 218–19
Souter Lighthouse, Whitburn 210–11
South Shields 206–7
South Stack Lighthouse 166–7
Spring-heeled Jack 64–7
Stanley family 134–5, 142
Stanton Drew Stone Circle, Somerset 28–9
Stead, W.T. 220
Stevens, Mary 64
Stevenson, Robert 241
Stewart, Sir Patrick 56–7
Stewart, Rod 72
Stocksbridge bypass 184–7
Stone Circle, Stanton Drew 28–9
Stothard, Margaret 212–13
Sukie 76–7
Sunderland 204–5
The Swansea Devil 160–1

T

Tatton Old Hall, Cheshire 142–3
Tempest, Richard 192–3
Temple Newsam House, Leeds 198–9
Tennyson, Alfred, Lord 100, 101
Ternan, Ellen 57
Tewkesbury Battlefield, Gloucestershire 36–9
Theatre Royal, London 56–7
Theosophical Society 196
Thomas-Stanford, Ellen 62, 63
Thomson, Lord 72–3
tin mines, Cornwall 44–5
Torre Abbey, Devon 20–1
Towneley, Sir John 191
Towneley Hall Gallery and Museum 190–1
Towton Battlefield, Yorkshire 202–3

Tresham, Sir Francis 130
Tresham, Sir Thomas 130, 131
Tretower Court and Castle 164–5
Tudor, Edmund and Jasper 178
Tulloch Castle, Dingwall 242–3

V

Vaughan family 164–5
Vaux, Anne 127
Vernon, Emma 153
Vernon family 152–3
Victoria, Queen 94, 242
Villiers, Major Oliver 73
The Vine Hotel, Seacroft 100–1
Vortigern 177–8

W

Wallace's Cave 123
Wadge, Selina 19
Walford, Jane and John 30–1
Walford's Gibbet, Somerset 30–1
Wallace, Sir William 208
Walsingham, Sir Francis 144–5
Wars of Roses 36–9, 134–5, 192, 202–3
Warwick 122–4
Waterford, Henry Beresford, 3rd Marquess of 66
Weeks, Matthew 18–19
West Wycombe 76–7
Westwood, James 19
Wetherell, Marmaduke 245
Whittenbury, Benjamin 70
Whittenbury, William 70
Whyman, Phil 143
William the Conqueror 60, 164
William 'the Lion', King of Scotland 208
Williams, Sir John 118
Wilson, Robert Kenneth 245
Windham, William 96–7
Windham, William Frederic 97
Windsor Castle 75
Withypoll, Edmund 94
Woodhouse, Sir Michael 172–3
Woodward, Sara 113
World War I 124, 171
World War II 52–5, 58, 79, 92–3, 98–9, 107, 112, 124, 142, 204–5
Wright, Elsie 196–7

Further Reading

Adams, Norman. *Haunted Scotland*. Mainstream, 1998.

Alexander, Marc. *Phantom Britain*. Muller, 1975.

Baldwin, Gay. *Ghost Island. Books One to Five*. Gay Baldwin, 2004.

Brooks, J.A. *Ghosts and Witches of the Cotswolds*. Jarrold, 1981.

Brooks, J.A. *Ghosts and Legends of the Lake District*. Jarrold, 1988.

Clarke, David. *Ghosts and Legends of the Peak District*. Jarrold, 1991.

Coventry, Martin. *Haunted Places of Scotland*. Goblinshead, 1999.

Coxe, Anthony D. Hippisley. *Haunted Britain*. Pan, 1975.

Forman, Joan. *Haunted East Anglia*. Jarrold,1993.

Green, Andrew. *Our Haunted Kingdom*. Fontana/Collins,1973.

Hallam, Jack. *The Haunted Inns of England*. Wolfe,1972.

Harper, Charles. *Haunted Houses*. Bracken, (Reprint) 1993.

Jeffery, P.H. *Ghosts, Legends and Lore of Wales*. The Old Orchard Press.

Jones, Richard. *History and Mystery: London*. AA Publishing, 2008.

Jones, Richard. *History and Mystery: Edinburgh*. AA Publishing, 2009.

Jones, Richard. *Walking Haunted London*. New Holland, 1999.

Jones, Richard. *Haunted Britain and Ireland*. New Holland, 2001.

Jones, Richard. *Haunted Castles of Britain and Ireland*. New Holland, 2003.

Jones, Richard. *Haunted Inns of Britain and Ireland*. New Holland, 2004.

Jones, Richard. *Haunted London*. New Holland, 2004.

Jones, Richard. *Haunted Houses of Britain and Ireland*. New Holland, 2005.

Marsden, Simon. *The Haunted Realm*. Little, Brown, 1986.

Puttick, Betty. *Ghosts of Hertfordshire*. Countryside Books, 1994.

Puttick, Betty. *Ghosts of Essex*. Countryside Books, 1997.

Puttick, Betty. *Oxfordshire Stories of the Supernatural*. Countryside Books, 2003.

Seafield, Lily. *Scottish Ghosts*. Lomond, 1999.

Turner, Mark. *Folklore and Mysteries of the Cotswolds*. Hale, 1993.

Whyman, Phil. *Dead Haunted*. New Holland, 2007.

Author's Acknowledgements

So many people helped with the researching and writing of this book. There were the staff at the numerous historic properties who answer my questions and graciously furnished me with updates on their haunting. To all of you, and to those I haven't mentioned in the text, a very big thank you.

At AA Publishing I'd like to thank Donna Wood for her encouragement and Lesley Grayson for her patience. I'd also like to say a massive thank you to Andrew Milne for his evocative design and to Helen Ridge for her astute copy-editing.

I'd like to thank Mike Covell for his assistance on haunted Hull, Rob Kirkup for his advice on haunted Tyne & Wear, and the Australian folk/rock group Spiral Dance for their inspirational music.

I'd like to thank Sir Donald Sinden for telling me the full story of how he came to see the ghost at the Theatre Royal, Haymarket at the actual spot on which he saw it. My immense gratitude also goes to Tom Baker for agreeing to write the foreword for the book.

On a personal note I'd like to thank my sister Geraldine Hennigan for her assistance and for being ever willing to lend an ear and proffer useful opinions. I'd like to thank my wife Joanne for being there for me and for the support she has always given willingly and generously. A big thank you to my sons Thomas and William who were happy(ish) to listen to my stories and offer critical appraisal.

Finally, to those who have gone before and whose stories have made this book possible, as always, long may you wander but may it always be at peace.

Richard Jones

Acknowledgements

The Automobile Association would like to thank the following photographers, companies and picture libraries for their assistance in the preparation of this book.

Abbreviations for the picture credits are as follows: (t) top; (b) bottom; (l) left; (r) right; (AA) AA World Travel Library.

Trade Cover Photolibrary.com; spine © The Marsden Archive/Alamy; back cover © The Marsden Archive/Alamy; back flap Bec Wingrave Photography; SS Cover © The Marsden Archive/Alamy; spine © The Marsden Archive/Alamy; back cover © The Marsden Archive/Alamy; back flap Bec Wingrave Photography; 1 Mary Evans Picture Library; 4 Sue Jerrard; 5 Oliver McNeil; 6 6 Mary Evans Picture Library; 9 Mary Evans Picture Library/SPR; 13 © Barry Bateman/Alamy; 16 Hulton Archive/ Getty Images; 17 SSPL/Getty Images; 18 © Nick Gregory/Alamy; 19 © Barry Bateman/Alamy; 20 © andrew payne/Alamy; 21 © andrew payne/Alamy; 22 © Apex; 23 © Glyn Thomas/Alamy; 24/25 © Apex; 26 Photolibrary.com; 26/27 © Mark Bauer/Alamy; 28 Photolibrary.com; 29 AA/A Lawson; 30/31 Yale Center for British Art, Paul Mellon Collection, USA/The Bridgeman Art Library; 31b Mary Evans Picture Library; 32 © Peter Barritt/Alamy; 32/33 Photolibrary.com; 34 © Sean Bolton/Alamy; 35 © Sean Bolton/Alamy; 36/37 © Nick Turner/Alamy; 38 © Timewatch Images/Alamy; 39 © Paul Felix Photography/Alamy; 40 © architecture UK/ Alamy; 41t Photolibrary.com; 41b © Neil McAllister/Alamy; 42 b/g © Adrian Sherratt/Alamy; 42 bl © Adrian Sherratt/Alamy; 43 © Adrian Sherratt/Alamy; 44/45 AA/A Burton; 45 Photolibrary.com; 46 © Haunted Images inc/Alamy; 50t © PSL Images/Alamy; 50b © Michael Jenner/Alamy; 51 b/g © KIM/Alamy; 51 © KIM/ Alamy; 52 AA/J Tims; 53 AA/J Tims; 54/55 b/g AA/J Tims; 54 AA/J Tims; 55 AA/J Tims; 56 Terry Harris/Rex Features; 56 b/g AA/J Tims; 57 Getty Images; 58 Robert Harding; 59 Chislehurst Caves; 60/61 © Carolyn Clarke/Alamy; 61 © Martin Beddall/Alamy; 62/63 b/g © travelbild.com/Alamy; 62 Mary Evans Picture Library; 63 Mary Evans Picture Library; 64/65 b/g Hulton Archive/Getty Images; 64 Hulton Archive/Getty Images; 65 Hulton Archive/Getty Images; 66/67 b/g Hulton Archive/ Getty Images; 67 Mary Evans Picture Library; 68 AA/J Tims; 68/69 AA/J Tims; 70 Richard Jones; 71 b/g Richard Jones; 71 Mary Evans Picture Library/Grosvenor Prints; 72/73 b/g © Trinity Mirror/Mirrorpix/Alamy; 72 © James Jenkins - Travel Photography/Alamy; 74 AA/J Tims; 75 Mary Evans Picture Library; 76 © Robert Stainforth/Alamy; 77t © Michael Winters/Alamy; 77b © Robert Stainforth/Alamy; 78 AA/M Moody; 79t AA/M Moody; 79b Breamore House; 80 © Gothic Images inc/Alamy; 84 © Colin Palmer Photography/Alamy; 84/85 © UK21/Alamy; 85t © Gordon Scammell/Alamy; 86 John Whitworth; 87 John Whitworth; 88/89 AA/T Mackie; 89 AA/M Birkitt; 90 Mary Evans/Rue des Archives/Tallandier; 91 Mary Evans Picture Library; 92 © geogphotos/Alamy; 92/93 b/g © The Art Archive/Alamy; 93 © KIM/Alamy; 94 Mary Evans Picture Library/Lesley Bradshaw; 95 AA/R Surman; 96 © The National Trust Photolibrary/Alamy; 97 AA/S & O Mathews; 98 © David Chilvers/Alamy; 98/99 b/g © Ashley Cooper/Alamy; 99 © Ashley Cooper/Alamy; 100 Mary Evans Picture Library; 101 b/g Mary Evans/Rue des Archives/ Tallandier; 101 Mary Evans Picture Library/Grosvenor Prints; 102/103 Photodisc; 103 Ian Harvey; 104t Mary Evans Picture Library; 104b Mary Evans Picture Library; 105 Mary Evans Picture Library; 106 © The National Trust Photolibrary/Alamy; 107 b/g © The National Trust Photolibrary/Alamy; 107 © The National Trust Photolibrary/Alamy; 108 © David Gadsby/Alamy; 109 Mary Evans Picture Library; 110/111 AA/A Mockford & N Bonetti; 112/113 Defence Archive Unit at RAF Holmpton; 114 Imagestate; 118 Robert Estall photo agency/Alamy; 119t Robert Estall photo agency/Alamy; 119b AA; 120 Richard Donovan/Alamy; 120/121 b/g Julia Catt Photography/Alamy; 121 Rolf Richardson/Alamy; 122/123 The Marsden Archive/Alamy; 124 Colin Underhill/Alamy; 124/125 b/g Colin Underhill/ Alamy; 125r Mary Evans Picture Library; 126 The National Trust Photo Library/Alamy; 127t The National Trust Photo Library/Alamy; 127b The National Trust Photo Library/Alamy; 128/129 b/g Kurt Banks/Alamy; 128 Glyn Thomas/Alamy; 129 Stuart Crump/Alamy; 130 Photolibrary.com; 131 Photolibrary.com; 132 Nigel Stollery/ Alamy; 133 Nigel Stollery/Alamy; 133 b/g flab lstr/Alamy; 134 Alan King engraving/Alamy; 134/135 b/g AA/M Birkitt; 135 Mary Evans Picture Library/Alamy; 136 Jason Friend Photography Ltd/Alamy; 137 b/g Topical Press Agency/Getty Images; 137 Bob Caddick/Alamy; 138 Tracey Foster/Alamy; 139 Tracey Foster/Alamy; 140 Photolibrary.com; 140/141 b/g Ian Bottle/Alamy; 141 Photolibrary.com; 142 b/g Mary Evans Picture Library; 143t The National Trust Photo Library/Alamy; 143b Mary Evans Picture Library; 144 Mary Evans Picture Library; 144/145 b/g Mary Evans Picture Library; 145 Mary Evans Picture Library; 146t Mary Evans/ National Magazines; 146b Mary Evans Picture Library/Grosvenor Prints; 146/147 b/g Mary Evans Picture Library; 147 Mary Evans Picture Library; 148 Jeff Morgan 02/Alamy; 152l Mary Evans Picture Library; 152 Photolibrary.com; 153 The National Trust Photolibrary/Alamy; 154/155 b/g Interfoto/Alamy; 155 David Newham/ Alamy; 156 The National Trust Photolibrary/Alamy; 157t The National Trust Photolibrary/Alamy; 157b The National Trust Photolibrary/Alamy; 158 Richard Jones; 158/159 Sid Frisby/Alamy; 159 Alan King engraving/Alamy; 160 Chris Elphick; 161l Matt Botwood (CStock)/Alamy; 161r The Photolibrary Wales/Alamy; 162 Chris

Howes/Wild Places Photography/Alamy; 162/163 b/g Chris Howes/Wild Places Photography/Alamy; 163 graham bell/Alamy; 164 AA/D Santillo; 165t Jeff Morgan 14/Alamy; 165b Jeff Morgan 10/Alamy; 166 Nathaniel Whitley/Alamy; 167 Alan Novelli/Alamy; 168 The National Trust Photolibrary/Alamy; 169 wales Alan King/ Alamy; 169r Mary Evans Picture Library; 170t The Photolibrary Wales/Alamy; 170b Arcaid/Alamy; 171 imagebroker/Alamy; 172 John Snowdon/Alamy; 173 Mike Hayward/photoshropshire.com/Alamy; 174 Photolibrary.com; 174/175 david pearson/Alamy; 175 Peter Wheeler/Alamy; 176 Photolibrary.com; 176/177 b/g travelib prime/Alamy; 177 Tim Cann/Alamy; 178 Neil McAllister/Alamy; 179 Justin Leighton/Alamy; 180 Gothic Images inc/Alamy; 184 Mary Evans Picture Library; 185 Mary Evans Picture Library; 186 Mary Evans Picture Library; 186/187 b/g Ross Parry Syndication/Sheffield Star; 187 Mary Evans Picture Library; 188 Mary Evans Picture Library; 189 Mary Evans Picture Library; 190 worldthroughthelens/ Alamy; 191 Trinity Mirror/Mirrorpix/Alamy; 192/193 b/g Wild Life Ranger/Alamy; 193 Bill Wymar/Alamy; 194 Glenn Hill/Science & Society Picture Library; 195 Glenn Hill/Science & Society Picture Library; 196 Glenn Hill/Science & Society Picture Library; 197 Glenn Hill/Science & Society Picture Library; 198 steven gillis hd9 imaging/Alamy; 199 steven gillis hd9 imaging/Alamy; 200 Pat Behnke/Alamy; 200/201 b/g AA/T Mackie; 201 Photolibrary.com; 202 Timewatch Images/Alamy; 203 Mary Evans Picture Library; 203cr AA/D Clapp; 203br AA/D Clapp; 204t The Print Collector/Alamy; 204b mediablitzimages (uk) Limited/Alamy; 205 Mary Evans Picture Library; 206 Roger Coulam/Alamy; 207t Jason Friend Photography Ltd/Alamy; 207b Jason Friend Photography Ltd/Alamy; 208 Photolibrary.com; 209l Clearview/Alamy; 209r Mary Evans Picture Library; 210/211 AA/R Coulam; 212 Steve Allen Travel Photography/Alamy; 213 Photolibrary.com; 214 StockImages/Alamy; 218 AA/R Coulam; 218/219 AA/R Coulam; 220/221 The Marsden Archive/Alamy; 222 www.undiscoveredscotland.co.uk; 223 www. undiscoveredscotland.co.uk; 224 catherine lucas/Alamy; 225t Rebecca Beusmans/ Alamy; 225b AA/D Corrance; 226 Richard Jones; 227b Richard Jones; 227r Mary Evans Picture Library; 228 Gus Nicoll/Alamy; 229 Gus Nicoll/Alamy; 230 Joseph Gaul/Alamy; 231 TNT Magazine/Alamy; 231r AA/J Carney; 232/233 AA/J Carney; 234 AA/J Smith; 235l AA/J Smith; 235r AA/J Smith; 236 Mary Evans Picture Library/Alamy; 237 Mic Walker/Alamy; 238 Jules May; 238/239 David Robertson/Alamy; 240 Simon Price/Alamy; 241t doughoughton/Alamy; 241b Private Collection/The Bridgeman Art Library; 242 Adrian Muttitt/ Alamy; 243 david sanger photography/Alamy; 244 Mary Evans Picture Library; 244/245 AA/J Smith; 246/247 Mary Evans Picture Library; 253 Mary Evans/Alinari Archives; 255 AA/S & O Mathews.

Every effort has been made to trace the copyright holders, and we apologise in advance for any accidental errors. We would be happy to apply the corrections in the following edition of this publication.

When I am dead, my dearest,
Sing no sad song for me;
Plant thou no roses at my head,
Nor shady cypress tree:
Be the green grass above me
With showers and dewdrops wet;
And if thou wilt, remember,
And if thou wilt, forget.

I shall not see the shadows,
I shall not feel the rain;
I shall not hear the nightingale
Sing on, as if in pain;
And dreaming through the twilight
That doth not rise or set,
Haply I may remember,
And haply may forget.

Song by Christina Rossetti (1830–1894)